Higher Than Me

Scripture quotations marked (KJV) are taken from the Holy Bible, King James Version, Cambridge, 1769. All rights reserved.

Scripture quotations marked (NIV) are taken from the Holy Bible, New International Version®, NIV®, Copyright © 1973, 1978, 1984 by Biblica, Inc.™ All rights reserved.

Scripture quotations marked (Message) are taken from the Message. Copyright © 1993, 1994, 1995, 1996, 2000, 2001, 2002. All rights reserved.

Scripture quotations marked (GWT) are taken from the God's Word Translation. Copyright© 1995.

Scripture quotations marked (NKJV) are taken from the New King James Version. Copyright © 1982 by Thomas Nelson, Inc. All rights reserved.

Graphic artwork produced for Higher Than Me and used by permission of Joy Cole Spruill

Poetry: *Butterfly* written and use authorized by James Cole

Writing of this book is authorized by Voices of Glory and Michael, Felicia, Michael II, Avery and Nadia Cole.

Printed by Litho Printers & Bindery, Cassville, Missouri

Published by Invention Discovery Center
Branson, Missouri. 877-517-0001
www.inventiondiscoverycenter.com

Cover and interior designed by Heidi Lowe
Cover images by Heidi Lowe, www.heidilowephoto.com

ISBN: 9780985826680

Inquiries to Claudia@readtheirstory.com

HIGHER THAN ME

The Story of Voices of Glory

CLAUDIA STEWART FARRELL

From the end of the earth will I cry unto thee,

When my heart is overwhelmed:

Lead me to rock that is higher than I

—Psalm 61: 2-3 KJV

Dedication

THE MICHAEL COLE FAMILY wishes to dedicate this book to those who may be struggling with the issues of life. So many hardships are common to man: injury, illness, failure, hunger, prejudice, lack of stability in the home, mental health disturbances in the family, sexual abuse, alcohol and drug abuse, and many more.

"It's not what happens to us in life; it's how we react to what happens to us that makes the difference," quotes Mr. and Mrs. Michael Cole Sr. As people who can speak from a position of experience, they would like to encourage you. This is the position they took to meet the challenges they faced in their lives. You, too, can make it your motto.

May you glean from this story, hope for yourself, and mercy towards others, the goodness of God our Father and revelation of Jesus Christ.

"These things I have spoken to you, that in Me you might have peace. In the world you shall have tribulation; but be of good cheer, I have overcome the world." John 16:33 (KJV)

Contents

Preface

✦

IT WAS MOTHER'S DAY, 2010. The sanctuary of Faith Life Church in Branson, Missouri was buzzing with activity. After the Sunday service, the center aisles were blocked with people visiting, giving hugs and Happy Mother's Day wishes. My husband and I always exited our seats to our left, but since the crowd wasn't moving, we went to the right. I mention this because it was highly unusual for us to exit to the right and it "just happened" to put me in just the right place at just the right time. If we had waited and taken our usual route, our paths would not have crossed with the Cole family that day.

My husband stopped to visit with a man, and so, in order not to block traffic on the right side, too, I moved on up the aisle. I noticed a family I did not recognize and assumed they were visiting Branson for the weekend. The husband was standing up, looking around, his wife still seated and the children were talking to each other. I attempted to make eye contact with him to acknowledge them, but he seemed to be looking past me, so I went on. I don't know if you have ever had such an experience, but I distinctly heard deep inside, "go back." I have had such urgings before and hate to confess that I have ignored them later wishing I had not. I know it was a prompting from the Holy Spirit. The prompting was so strong, I was compelled to turn and walk back down the aisle. The scenario had not changed in those few seconds, so I stepped into the row of seating in front of them and said, "Welcome to Faith Life. Where are you from?" This is a common opener since Branson is a tourist destination bringing many visitors to our church.

Mike Cole introduced himself telling me they were from New York. "We are Voices of Glory," he stated confidently. I am sure the look on my face was a disappointment to him, as I had no idea what he was talking about. He went on to say they ranked fifth place on America's Got Talent in 2009. Still he saw no reaction from me.

"This is my wife, Felicia," he said looking down at her. Felicia was sitting low in her seat, her head hanging down. When I acknowledged the introduction, she raised her chin only enough to make eye contact, and said "Hi" with apparent reservation. She touched my heart. I saw her beautiful face clouded by emotional discomfort: her countenance by insecurity. Compassion filled my heart as I heard Mr. Cole say his wife had been in a bad accident and I started piecing it all together in my mind. Her eyes seemed to say. "I am a stranger here and no one knows my history."

I introduced myself to her and wished her a Happy Mother's Day. She spoke softly and shyly but for the most part, I could not understand what she said. My heart cried for her. I had such an urge to love on her. I did not know her story, but woman to woman, I hurt for her. On this Mother's Day, it seemed everyone had a smile on their faces, except Felicia. I knelt down in front of her and asked her if she would allow my husband and me to treat her to a Mother's Day lunch.

She gave me a shy smile and said yes, returning her head to the downcast position, her eyes to the floor.

I suggested a restaurant near the church, giving them directions and went to find my husband. When I introduced my husband, Ron, to Mike and Felicia, Mike again explained who they were. Again, he received a blank response. In explanation, we had recently moved to Branson and had been working long hours in an effort to get our business started. Television was at the bottom of our priorities list. They could have been the governor's family and we would not have recognized them. However, as Mike repeated their story, a dim light came on as I recalled a conversation with my daughter, telling me that some young kids in a talent contest on a TV show captivated our grandson, Hunter. As I thought about that, I realized whom I had just met.

The Cole kids, Michael, Avery and Nadia rallied around as we told them, "Let's go to lunch."

I explain all of this to say, I was not being a star chaser. I simply wanted to bless a lady who looked like she had been through a very hard time. Again, being Mother's Day, the restaurant was packed, so we were seated in a back dining room. To our surprise and delight, Mike asked the kids to sing. They performed "Holy, Holy, Holy, an earnest witness to the other diners in the room. They followed with an emotion evoking God Bless America. Ron and I were shocked, pleased and blessed.

After that day, we saw the Coles occasionally, watching them perform at local theatres a couple of times. Over the months, Felicia and I connected on a girl-to-girl level. I came to learn of her strong spirit, her vigor for life and overtime, her huge purse collection.

Several months later, on a by-chance meeting on the 76

strip, we ran into Voices of Glory. Ron was visiting with Mike beside our truck and I had gone to their SUV to talk with Felicia.

After visiting for about ten minutes, Mike walked up to me and said, "I want you to write our story." I noticed my husband coming up behind Mike and shrugging his shoulders. Mike continued, "Ron said you are writing a book. Our story needs to be told and in my spirit, I know you are the one who is supposed to write it."

Yes, I was helping a friend write her memoir, *I Thought You Had a Bigger Dream*, but I was not an author. I was flattered. I was intimidated. His statement that "in his spirit, he knew I was the one to write their story" blew me away. I felt less than qualified.

That is how I came to write the story of Voices of Glory. I feel honored to know this strong, loving family. It has been my privilege to record the struggles and victories of Mike, Felicia, their children, and all of their extended family; to tell their story to a multitude of their friends and fans whose lives they have touched.

I believe ours was a divine appointment that Sunday morning at Faith Life Church. I believe we all have divine appointments. We have only to recognize them and choose to come up to the challenge laid before us to fulfill our destiny.

When I see her now, three years later, Felicia is sitting high in her chair as she continues to heal, confident to take on the next challenge before her. In faith, I see her completely healed, walking on her own.

We have a plan, Felicia and I, to go purse shopping. She will drive. I will be her passenger, proof that she is totally restored.

Claudia Stewart Farrell

Acknowledgements

THANK YOU TO THE Michael Cole family for taking me into their lives in such a way that I was able to learn their spirits. Their family dynamics, their strengths and their weaknesses, their personalities, their humor, their love for each other, their dedication to the Lord Jesus and their focus on the Kingdom of God were revealed to me in an open and honest way, allowing me to record their story in as true a light as possible.

I also wish to acknowledge and honor Michael's brothers and sisters who allowed their selves to be vulnerable in the telling of the painful stories from their childhood, sharing with me personally, their struggles and their victories. Mike and Felicia knew that all of their stories would shout triumphant, showing the goodness of God regardless of the failures of people. The Coles wish to say that no dishonor is due Cybald and Jan Cole, but indeed, to give thanks to them for planting in their children good seed that proved worthy of a good harvest in all of their lives. Each of the Cole family members took a different path to get to where they are today...but it is where they are that counts...loving, nurturing, productive members of society who love God.

We also wish to honor Mr. and Mrs. Stanley, Felicia's parents, and all of her family for the many blessings they have brought into their lives and the lives of their children through the good times and the hard times over the years.

The Coles wish to thank all of the medical staff at Berkshire Medical Center, Helen Hayes Hospital, Northwest Center for Special Care and Wingate at Ulster Healthcare for all of the loving care given to Felicia and the special consideration given to the Cole family over the many months.

A huge thank you is due to many friends and family members who gave unselfishly of their time and resources to see them through all the hills and valleys of recovery after Felicia's accident, and next for jumping on the bandwagon and supporting Voices of Glory in their ministry. They know who they are and know that the hearts of the Cole family are full of gratitude toward them.

Thanks are given to a myriad of people who helped the children with their ministry through every possible avenue that was available to them, encouraging them and giving them a sense of accomplishment and value in their efforts.

Thanks to Sonia Brown, John Carroll, and Rosa Gross, for your contributions to the story.

Thanks are due to Sandra Vedane for proofreading, to my dear friend, Martha DeZwarte Rankin for the final edit, to Penny Robichaux-Koontz for her wonderful insights, and to all of my family who helped and encouraged me.

I give loving thanks to my husband, Ron, who always gives unselfishly, putting the Kingdom of God first. Thank you, Ron, for your spiritual leadership and direction involved in this writing, as a mentor to me and a good friend to all of the Cole family.

And most importantly, "But I thank God, who always leads us in victory because of Christ. Wherever we go, God uses us to make clear what it means to know Christ. It's like a fragrance that fills the air." (II Corinthians 2:14, GWT)

Introduction

ON JULY 21, 2005, a young man made a major life altering choice. He was free to choose as we all have dominion over our own personal choices. His dominion choice was to drink and drive. This choice not only altered his life course, but that of many others. He drank and had a good time with friends, then left the familiar hangout and drove home. However, that is not where this story ends.

The young man was under the influence of alcohol that impaired his ability to drive safely. A witness testified that he was following the young man at approximately 60 miles per hour, but then he picked up speed, pulled away, and the witness lost sight of him. According to the police report, as the young man under the influence rounded a curve, he crossed four feet over the centerline and hit a northbound van almost head on.

It was dark at the time of the accident, almost midnight. It was difficult to distinguish exactly what had happened. The witness came around the same curve, quickly braking, narrowly avoiding impact himself, and stopping only five feet from the heavily damaged van. He testified he could hear crying and screams. He did his best to check on the people in both the car and the van and then called 911. Others stopped as they too came upon the scene of the accident. The driver of the car appeared to be all right, with only minor injuries. The cries and screams were coming from the van. People tried to help, but little could be done. The minivan's doors were severely damaged. The van driver appeared to be in shock, asking where she was. After a while, the police and ambulances arrived. The jaws of life were used to free those trapped in the van, first the living and then the dead.

Five schoolteachers were the occupants of the van. That night they had attended a dance performance at Jacob's Pillow in Becket, MA, as part of their curriculum for an administrative course they were taking at Massachusetts College of Liberal Arts in North Adams. They were simply driving back to campus. It had been a good night for the girlfriends, dinner and then the dance performance. Felicia Cole especially enjoyed the performance, as she was a dancer herself. She had studied dance as a young girl and was the praise dance leader at her church. Now everything would be different.

The young man's life altering choice significantly changed the lives of Felicia, her husband Mike, and their children. This story, based on true events, regarding both the accident and the earlier lives of the Cole family, shows the love and faithfulness of God and the strength they drew from their heavenly Father when they exercised the dominion given to them by their Creator and followed His direction to… Choose Life. (Deuteronomy 30:19, KJV).

It was an accident. No one planned for this to happen. No

one wished harm to any of the individuals. Even though much harm did come, as the word of God promises, "His favor is for a lifetime and joy comes in the morning." (Psalm 30:5, KJV)

HIGHER THAN ME

The Story of Voices of Glory

CHAPTER 1

Send A Miracle

MIKE KNELT BESIDE FELICIA'S bedside, his head resting on his cold fingers. Warmth seemed like a thing of the past. This stark room, this lifeless body, dead dreams, emptiness…everything seemed cold except his warm breath as he whispered, "Lord, I'm asking you…send a miracle. We can't go on like this. I know you are still a miracle working God. I know you hear my prayers, Lord. Send a miracle today." Mike raised his head and stared out the window of Helen Hayes Hospital at the gray October sky. Fall was officially here. He had spent over two months in this room.

His thoughts returned to that humid July night that seemed so long ago. He had rehearsed these scenes so many times, and yet again, the rerun danced across his mind. He recalled lying on his bed; saw himself flipping his pillow over and feeling the welcome coolness of the linen pillowcase on his face and then immediately turning again, responding to the restlessness in his soul. Why didn't she call? When he agreed that Felicia should go to Massachusetts to continue her studies…he didn't mean for all normalcy of life to be lost. He wasn't expecting too much for her to call him tonight. After all it was July 21st—his birthday. Their last conversation had been brief and they had a lot to discuss, but he was patient to wait for her birthday call. He didn't know whether to be worried or hurt. Their 14-year marriage was founded on two things, the word of God and teamwork. That's how it had always been.

Felicia was so bright and ambitious, always ready to take on new challenges to improve herself and help her family. It was part of Mike's dream that Felicia realize her dreams. She had been so successful in her career already. Holding three degrees, Felicia worked as a bi-lingual biology teacher at Poughkeepsie High School in Poughkeepsie, New York. Now with the additional classes, she would earn an administration degree qualifying her for a position as a school principal. Even their children had been involved in the decision for her to go back to school. There was a family round-table discussion, knowing the time Felicia would spend away from home would be a sacrifice for all of them. Nadia and Avery were still so young, only four and eight and Mikey was just thirteen. However, they were united as a family in their long-term goals, knowing that together they could accomplish anything they set their minds to. *Teamwork* defined their marriage and their family.

He smiled to himself, thinking about the special relationship they'd always had. Then he chuckled with the thought, maybe the old adage "absence makes the heart grow fonder," wasn't really true. But, no, it just wasn't like Felicia not to take care of family. Family was first, always. He knew he could count on her.

It had been a good day with the kids. They had gone to the

Poughkeepsie Galleria Mall for an outing. Not all fathers would consider that a good day, but with the tough conditions he had grown up under, Mike knew what was important to him and thought he knew what was important for his children. They window shopped, and had Chinese for lunch in the food court. Yes, it was a good way for a father to spend his birthday... with his kids, he reflected.

Suddenly he remembered something Felicia had said to him during their last conversation. "Mike, I don't know what is going on. I feel like my head is full of static like on a radio. I am so confused. I don't understand what is going on." It seemed strange to both of them. Felicia was always so clear in her thinking, always so purposeful.

His thoughts jumped back to the present. Could her silence have anything to do with what she told me about her confusion? That was a worrisome thought. Something must have happened. But, what? There were no phone calls. No emergency alerts. Just silence. Just nothing. I guess she's just too busy to call, he thought, as he finally drifted off to sleep in their double bed, one side feeling very empty.

Alarmed, Mike jerked awake. The telephone. The telephone was ringing. He groped for the portable phone, but it wasn't in its cradle. Stumbling to the kitchen and lifting the receiver from the wall phone, he answered, "Hello" thru dazed confusion.

"May I speak to Mr. Michael Cole, please?" an unfamiliar voice was saying.

"Who is this?" Mike asked a little gruffly, not understanding the reason for someone to make such a formal request to speak with him.

The caller identified himself as a neurologist from the hospital. "Your wife has been in an accident. You need to come right away. She is at the Berkshire Medical Center in Pittsfield."

"Doctor, is she going to be alright?" Mike asked, hardly able to breathe.

"We don't really know much yet, we need to run some tests. Just get here as soon as you can," the doctor responded.

"Where's Pittsfield?" Mike asked, still confused.

"In Massachusetts, Pittsfield, Massachusetts," the doctor answered patiently, knowing his phone call had roused Mike from sleep. "I'll give you directions."

Mike fumbled in the kitchen drawer for paper and pen. "Okay, I'm ready," Mike said, exhaling his tension.

" Alright, when you get to Pittsfield, take I-20 North, then watch for Highway 7, it turns into North St. The address is 725 North Street. Have you got that?"

"Yeah, I think so. I'll find it. Thank you. I'll be there. I'll be there as soon as I can," Mike said softly.

"Is there anything more I can do for you?" the doctor offered.

Mike thought for a second, "What did the doctor mean, was there anything he could do for me?"

"Oh, yes," he then responded. "Will you please call Felicia's parents and let them know?"

"Yes, I can do that," the doctor replied. Mike gave the doctor the phone number. He was glad he did not have to be the one to make the call. He had enough to think about.

He looked at the clock on the wall. "Two-thirty," he said aloud. He stared at the clock in a trance. This clock was the one Felicia had chosen especially for their kitchen. She had wanted to redecorate and had chosen yellow for the kitchen walls. He had painted and cleaned up the mess while she went shopping.

She had brought home several new things, including a round, green and white clock with diamond shapes in place of the numbers: a perfect kitchen clock. It was perfect for their new kitchen just as Felicia had been perfect for him as a wife. Together they had worked to make their house a happy home he thought, as tears came to his eyes.

Time seemed to stand still as he considered what he had just been told, still not fully awake. Felicia's been in an accident.

"What should I do?" he asked himself. It's the middle of the night. The children are asleep. He ran his hand across the top of his head as if that would clear his thinking. Felicia needs me. Suddenly Mike rallied himself into action. He must get to the hospital quickly. Where did the doctor say she was....in Pittsfield, that's it.

He hurried into their son's room, but, trying not to alarm them, said gently, "Boys, you need to wake up. Mom's been in an accident."

Mikey, their oldest, rolled over in the bed and asked, "What happened, Dad?"

"I really don't know much, son, but we have to get to the hospital," he answered as Michael II swung his long legs off the side of the bed searching his father's face.

Avery awoke to the sound of their voices.

"You need to get up, Avery," Mike said again.

"Why Daddy? I'm tired," asked Avery, not really comprehending the words that had awoken him.

"Just go to the dining room table, son." Mike answered, patiently.

He went to Nadia's room and sat on the edge of her bed. Still so small, he spoke her name and then tenderly lifted her into his lap.

"What, Daddy?" Nadia asked in her sleepy voice.

"It's okay, Baby, I just need to take you to the table," he said as he rose with her in his arms.

Mike took a chair at the dining room table, the familiarity of their family meeting place giving him comfort. He stood Nadia on the floor next to him, his arm still wrapped around her. Nadia's head rested sleepily against his chest, her favorite pink flowered nightgown looking shorter than it did just a week ago. Mike looked into his son's anxious faces and again attempted the difficult task of explaining to the children that their mother had been in a car accident. The words came hard as he tried to keep his voice steady.

"Mommy was in a car accident and she's in the hospital."

"Is she going to be alright?" Avery asked, propped against the wall, his crayon blue pajama pants hanging from his slender hips.

"I'm sure she will be. You kids know what a strong person your mom is," he answered, trying to sound assuring.

"Where is she?" asked Mikey, fighting back tears, knowing he had to be strong for his little brother and sister.

"She's at a hospital in Massachusetts," Mike answered in a matter-of-fact manner.

Nadia snuggled in closer as tears filled her eyes, not sure of all she had heard.

"We need to get ready. We'll leave as soon as we're dressed," he instructed.

Just as Mike was heading for his bedroom, the phone rang again. "What now?" he asked himself as he answered the second unexpected call.

"Mike, this is Deacon Brown. Do you know our wives have been in an accident?" he asked speaking slowly, uncertain of just what Mike might know.

Deacon Brown's wife, Sonia, had called him from the hospital. She had a fractured pelvis, sacrum, right ankle and lacerations on her forehead. She had told her husband that she knew Felicia had been severely injured and she wasn't even sure she had survived the accident. She had been told her head was badly battered as their van spun around. Sonia knew one of their friends had died in the accident, but she didn't know who it was.

"The doctor just called me," Mike answered, "was Sonia hurt, too?"

"Yes, but, she'll be alright. She called me, but she didn't seem to know much about what had happened. I'm going to the hospital. I'd like for you to go with me." Deacon Brown tried to sound calm. He didn't know what Mike would find when he got to the hospital. Would his wife even still be alive? If she were alive, would she be able to talk to him? From what Sonia had told him, he didn't think so. He knew it wasn't a good idea for Mike to go alone.

"I'm taking the children with me," Mike responded.

"That's all right. There's plenty of room for all of us," Deacon Brown assured him. "I'll be there in about twenty minutes."

"We'll be ready." Mike said wearily. It was going to be a long night. He would be glad to get to the hospital and talk to Felicia. She was the only one he really trusted to tell him what had happened. She was the only one he needed to see. She was the only one.

CHAPTER 2

She Will Never Be The Same

DEACON BROWN WAS GOOD company for Mike as they made the long drive to the hospital. They had been friends for a long time, their wives best of friends. They attended the same church, Bethel Church of God in Christ in Poughkeepsie, New York. Mike was an elder and Felicia held the office of missionary, working together with the youth of the church. Their families hung out together. Yes, it was good to be with Deacon Brown.

They shared with each other what they knew about how and where the accident had happened. They didn't know much, but it was somewhat of a comfort to rehearse what they did know. Sonia was going to be okay. The accident must not have been too bad. Felicia would be okay, too, Mike told himself.

Since Deacon Brown had spoken with his wife, he had more information than Mike did, but he was careful what he said. He knew it wasn't his place to tell Mike much about Felicia. As they drove, there were long periods of silence. The children hadn't said a word after getting into Deacon Brown's SUV. They listened to the conversation in the front seat, but it seemed the same thing was just being said over and over. Soon the drone of the men's deep voices lulled them to sleep. Mike looked into the back seat. Avery, his head leaning against the window, seemed peaceful and Mikey's arm was tucked protectively around Nadia, sitting between her brothers and sleeping against Mikey's side. Mike turned further in his seat to see Mikey's head tilted back, his eyes closed. He hoped that he was asleep, too. The kids needed more rest. Who knew what was ahead of them?

Mike vacillated between faith and fear. He prayed that the Lord keep Felicia, heal her, and restore her. This is what he had learned from the Bible. This was how he knew to pray; this is what he expected. Then the fearful thoughts would flood over him. Deacon Brown said Sonia had told him Felicia had hit her head. Why hadn't Felicia called him? What am I going to find? Was she cut up? Just what has happened to her he wondered, but did not voice. They knew Sonia would be all right, but what about Felicia? He held it all in. There was no use speculating. He must believe for the best.

Suddenly, Mike said, "Deacon Brown, I just remembered that about two years ago, you and I were in an accident together."

"Yeah, that's right. Sonia and I were having a cookout with your family and she had sent me to the store for extra groceries. I had asked you to ride along with me. That guy ran a red light, or was it a stop sign… and t-boned my van. He was so intoxicated he didn't even know where he was. He just plowed right into us, flipping the van over on its side," remembered Deacon Brown.

"It happened so fast, I don't remember much. However, I do remember that just seconds before we were hit, I had fastened my seat belt. I am so glad I did or I may have been hurt, myself," Mike reflected. "As it was, neither of us was injured and we just crawled out the driver's window. He was really going fast to flip us like that."

"I know. Almost as soon as we got out, I saw Felicia and Sonia running toward us. They were so relieved that we weren't hurt. They were praising God and hugging our necks at the same time," Mike said, almost managing a smile.

"I can still see Felicia jumping up and down, one arm around your neck, the other waving in the air in praise," Deacon Brown laughed.

"Before the police took him away, I prayed with that man even though it was obvious he was intoxicated. I told him he needed Jesus; that he didn't know what might happen to him and it was time for him to give his life to Christ," Mike recalled. "Some people who had witnessed the accident scoffed at my attempt, but I could only hope that my words would mean something to him. He obviously needed to find a better path. I know it happened only a few blocks from your house and before we hardly knew what was going on, our wives were there," Mike added.

"Yes, I remember calling Sonia on my cell phone and it seemed they were there in an instant," chuckled Deacon Brown.

"Strange, now it is our wives together in an accident and we're going to them," said Mike as his thoughts drifted off to Felicia again.

Felicia had encouraged Sonia to go to college and earn her teaching degree. She had mentored her, advising what classes to take, and motivated her when she was challenged with new courses and difficult projects. Yes, Felicia was a tower of strength for all of them. That tower could not have fallen.

Mike sat in silence, looking out the passenger window, watching the white line against the shoulder of the highway. Why hadn't the doctor told him more? It seems like doctor's words were always guarded. He had often heard it said that doctors didn't want to give people false hope.

So many thoughts tore at his mind. What if she's hurt really badly? Maybe that's the reason she didn't call. So many what if's, yet Mike realized he really didn't know anything.

"I just want *some* hope, Lord. Any hope. I love my wife," he silently prayed.

He closed his eyes thinking it would be good to be able to sleep but sleep wouldn't come, only troubling thoughts, roller coaster emotions and then back to telling himself to trust God.

They were nearing the intersection that would take them onto Highway 7, and then to the hospital.

"I think it's the next exit," Mike offered as he had been studying the road signs, anticipating the end of this trip and the beginning of an unknown road ahead of him. Moving to the right and following the ramp, Deacon Brown merged onto Highway 7. The traffic was light, as it was not quite time for the morning rush hour.

"The doctor said this turns into North Street," Mike told Deacon Brown. Almost immediately, he spotted a blue hospital sign and knew they were on the right track. He let his breath out, not even realizing he was holding it until he heard his own sigh.

As they pulled into the parking garage, Mike spoke to the

children to awaken them. "We're here, kids. Try to wake up," Mike said with enough volume to get their attention.

Mikey squirmed in his seat, removing his arm from Nadia's shoulder. Just then, she slid sideways in the seat as Deacon Brown made a sharp right to turn into a parking space. Nadia scooted forward, pulling herself up with one hand on the back of her father's seat. "Where's Mommy?" she asked with childlike faith that her mother would be there waiting for them.

Mike avoided her question as he opened the door of the SUV and stepped out. The early morning air was warm and pleasant. He opened the back door, reaching for Nadia's hand as she crawled across Mikey's lap.

Mikey stepped out and followed closely behind Mike as he headed for the emergency entrance. Avery opened the door on the driver's side, moved at a snail's pace to get out and stretched his arms high above his head, not attempting to hide his yawn. Deacon Brown turned the key in the car door listening for the click to be sure it had locked. He and Avery lagged behind. He, too, needed to stretch after more than two tense hours behind the wheel.

Mike entered the hospital hallway, turning his gaze to each side attempting to get his bearings. He spotted a sign, "INFORMATION". As he approached the desk, a pleasant older man asked if he could be of assistance. Mike gave him Felicia's name, rambling through unnecessary information as he tried to gather his thoughts and get out the right words that would lead him to her. The older gentleman typed Felicia's name on the keyboard and found that she had been admitted to the intensive care unit. The attendant was courteous, expressed sympathy for the situation while giving warm smiles to the children and pointed toward the arrow signs in the hallway displaying the direction to ICU.

Deacon Brown relieved and grateful to hear that Felicia was still alive, asked for information regarding his wife, and told Mike he would come to ICU as soon as he had checked on Sonia, then headed toward the elevators.

Mike reached down to secure Nadia's hand and the boys followed them down the long hallway. Nadia saw the sign indicating the way to the restrooms and started pulling on Mike's hand to get his attention. "Daddy, I gotta go," she said, looking up at him with a pleading look. Mike continued down the hall, and then suddenly realized how long it had been since they had left home. "Boys, let's go to the restroom while they're handy."

"Good idea," Avery called as he took off ahead of the rest of them. As Mike stood outside the restrooms, waiting for Nadia, anxious thoughts about Felicia's condition rose up in him again. The doctor that called hadn't told him she was in intensive care. It all seemed surreal. Was this really happening? It seemed more like a bad dream than his life.

Mike again took Nadia's hand as she came out of the restroom and they continued to the ICU waiting room where Mike instructed the kids to stay until he came back.

As he stepped up to the nurse's station, he heard a man's voice ask, "Are you Mr. Cole?"

"Yes," Mike responded quickly then realized his volume was higher than necessary, due to his anxiousness, causing several nurses to turn away from their work to see what was going on.

A man in a white coat introduced himself as Felicia's neurologist. The doctor proceeded, describing Felicia's condition. He used medical terms which were difficult to follow, but from his tone and a too graphic description of her head injury, Mike knew Felicia had indeed, been hurt very badly. As he listened to the doctor, he looked down the long hospital hallway as though it were the entrance to a deep, dark cave. If he entered into it, he may not be able to find his way back out.

Mike knew he had missed some of what the doctor said, but certain phrases played across his mind. She was hit head-on by a drunk driver. She is badly injured. She is in a coma. We are doing everything we can. Then the doctor's words, "If she lives, your wife will never be the same," jerked him back to attention.

"You do know that, don't you?" the doctor queried, trying to be sure he was understood. "She will never be the same."

"What do ya' mean she'll never be the same?" Mike asked, his demeanor bordering on hostility.

Again, the doctor repeated the medical facts, sounding hopeless about the outcome. Mike stood there shaking his head "no" at what he was hearing, but meaning to convey that he understood. "Thank you, doctor," he said quietly, staring at the floor as he began walking away. He did not know where he was going, but he did not want to hear anymore. "This is just too much," he muttered. He looked back toward the waiting room where he had left his children, then wandered off in the opposite direction. They were lingering by the waiting room door, but he knew he could trust them to stay there. *I cannot face them, not yet.*

He passed another small waiting room. It was empty. *Good,* he thought as he turned back and entered into the quiet darkness as only the lights from the hallway shone dimly into the room; *I need to be alone. I need to think.* "What should I do?" he asked himself as he fell to his knees in front of a green padded chair. He covered his face with his hands and tried to calm himself. The doctor's words kept playing in his ears as though he were listening to a recording. Tears flooded down his cheeks as he sobbed for Felicia, for their children, for himself. The sobbing shook his whole body, but he had to let it out. He hadn't allowed himself to break since that first alert that woke him from sleep. With the emotion released, he felt a little calmer. Mike began to pray, "God, lead me to the Rock that is higher than I. I can't do anything, even if I knew what to do. I can't do anything. Please lead me to the rock. Yes, that is where my strength must come from," thought Mike. He closed his eyes and for just a few minutes, he enjoyed the silence, and appreciated the peace that had come over him.

Wiping away his tears, Mike stepped back into the hallway. All eyes were on him as he again approached the nurse's station. The doctor was still there studying Felicia's chart. Mike looked at him and asked, "Where is my wife?"

"Follow me," he said, as he gestured down the hall. "She needs a CT scan. We are getting ready to take her downstairs."

"Can I come along?" asked Mike, uncertain of the protocol.

"That'll be fine," the doctor replied. "It'll be about ten minutes."

Mike entered Felicia's room with hesitation. What he saw was both shocking and comforting. Finally, he was able to lay his eyes on her. She appeared to be sleeping, but he understood the reality of the coma.

"My poor baby," he whispered. Her face was so swollen and bruised he thought, "*I barely recognize her*".

He touched her hand as he reached the side of her bed. He didn't get a response; he didn't expect one. He stared at all of the tubes and monitors, the flashing lights, heard the hollow beeping, and tried to understand the digital readouts. It was overwhelming to see her like this. He leaned over and kissed her cheek tenderly. The doctor stood in the doorway momentarily, then left Mike alone with his wife.

"I'm here, Felicia," he said, as much to comfort himself as her. He hoped she could hear him. He hoped for much.

"Lord, she's in Your hands. I can't help her but You can. I'll do what Your Word says… to 'trust in the Lord with all your heart, and lean not on your own understanding; in all your ways acknowledge Him and He shall direct your paths'" (Proverbs 3: 5-6, NKJV), he recited the familiar passage.

"I don't understand why this has happened to us Lord, but I'll trust you." Mike let out a big sigh, feeling the pressure of near empty lungs. With God's help, he could make it through this. He again talked to Felicia as though she could hear and understand him. "The children are with me. They're in the waiting room. Your parents have been called. They should be here soon."

Tears again rolled down his cheeks. He felt so helpless. What could he do to make everything all right? Nothing—he had to acknowledge to himself. Only God can help us now.

CHAPTER 3

Two Places At Once

A NURSE ENTERED THE room and began preparations to take Felicia to radiology. Mike gently squeezed Felicia's hand, and then wiped his tears away. He moved out of the nurse's way and stepped back into the hallway. He realized he needed to talk to the children and let them know what he was doing. He squared his shoulders and attempted a calm appearance as he approached the waiting room. Keep a stiff upper lip…Isn't that how the saying goes? he thought to himself.

Nadia was the first to see him and ran to him calling, "Daddy." He swept her up in his arms, nuzzling her neck, enabling him to hide his face as he talked.

"Where's Mommy?" Nadia asked again.

"She's in bed," Mike assured her. That sounds like a safe place to be, he thought to himself.

"How's Mom doing?" asked Mikey. Avery, looking at a car magazine peeked over the top of it when he heard his father's voice and then waited for his brother's question to be answered.

Mike hedged. The kids didn't need to hear everything he'd been told. "Well," he started slowly. "She bumped her head so she's in a coma. It's kind of like sleeping. They want to take some x-rays. I'm going to go with her to the radiology department. Will you kids be okay by yourselves for awhile?"

The boys nodded their heads "yes." Mike sat Nadia down in a chair and asked her to be a good girl, telling her he would be back in a little while.

There was a TV playing, but with the volume turned down very low. Someone was sleeping in a chair at the far end of the room snuggled comfortably under a white hospital blanket. No one else was there. There were magazines to keep the boys entertained and he knew he could trust Mikey to watch after Nadia and Avery.

As Mike stepped out of the waiting room, he saw a gurney being pushed down the hall and realized it was Felicia. He followed, waiting until they were inside the elevator, then he stepped in. The male nurse fiddled nervously with the blanket that was covering Felicia, then stared at the buttons indicating the floor number. Mike stood with his head down, not wanting to make small talk. He couldn't force himself to look at Felicia's bruised and lacerated face. Then he could not will himself not to. A huge lump rose up in his throat and tears again filled his eyes as he looked at her once beautiful face, a face now swollen beyond recognition. The ride in the elevator was interminable, but finally the doors opened, allowing Mike to escape. It was too hard being so close to her and her so far away.

Mike watched as the nurse pushed the gurney out of the elevator and down the hallway, turning at the sign, *Radiology*. He trailed after them almost in a trance, not knowing what to do, just following, following. The nurse pressed the large button on the wall and double doors swung open, allowing Mike through at the same time. The gurney was rolled into the radiology department and his wife was gone from him once again.

Mike stepped into a small area off the hallway, and then realized he was in the technician's room. He watched through the glass wall as they placed Felicia in the CT scanner. It was as though there was no life in her at all. They moved her around like a rag doll. As the machine started running, images of Felicia's head appeared on the numerous monitors, one, then another, then another. Mike stood silently watching as the technician, his back to the door, operated the sophisticated equipment in front of him. After several minutes, the machine stopped moving and the technician stood to leave the room.

"Sir, what is that?" Mike asked.

"Who are you?" the technician wanted to know. "You're not supposed to be in here."

"I'm her husband. You... you just did that CT Scan on my wife," he stuttered.

"I can't tell you anything, sir. I could get fired for it." He hesitated as though he wanted to say something, but then just repeated himself, "I can't tell you anything at all."

"That's okay," Mike said, "I understand."

The nurse who had brought Felicia to radiology reentered the CT room. Mike stood outside of the doorway watching as they again moved his rag doll onto the gurney to wheel her back to her room. He felt someone tap him on his shoulder and turned. The technician spoke softly saying, "I will tell you that from what I see, it looks okay but the doctor will have to be the one to make that decision. I really can't say."

"Thank you," Mike exhaled his relief. This was the first good news he'd had since he got to the hospital. He smiled and again said, "Thank you," glad for at least a little hope.

Mike spent the rest of the morning back and forth between Felicia's room and the waiting room, thankful to have at least some time with his children. As he sat watching them, questions started coming to his mind. There were so many decisions to be made. Decisions about who would take care of the children, decisions about his work, decisions about Felicia's care; one decision at time he thought. I can do this with your help Lord, one decision at a time.

"Oh, no, it's seven-thirty. I need to call work," Mike said aloud, but speaking to himself. He had prepared a Power Point presentation for his department to be reviewed in the day's meeting. The program was ready, but he didn't think to bring his computer with him in his hurry to leave the house and he hadn't emailed the report to the office yet. He already had the day scheduled off to attend the memorial service for his mother who had passed away recently. His absence was not a problem but not providing the report could be. He had worked at IBM for 25 years. It had been good employment for him. In just the last six months, he had been transferred to the position of development technician. He did much of his work on a laptop and often times would take his computer home to finish a project in the evening if there had been too many interruptions during the day. He liked his job, preparing production reports for his supervisors and presenting them to a team of PhDs, who then reported to the department heads.

"Good Morning, this is Mike Cole," Mike said. "Can I please speak with Dale?"

"Hi Mike, this is Chris. Dale isn't in yet."

"I'd better talk to Andy then," Mike requested.

"Okay, no problem," Chris said with a cheery voice as he transferred the call.

As Andy lifted the receiver, Mike said, "Good Morning, Andy. I'm sorry to have to call you, but my wife was in a bad car accident last night and she's in the hospital. It happened in Massachusetts and I'm here with her now."

"Is she alright, Mike?" he asked with concern.

"We don't know yet. She has a bad head injury. I'm going to need to be here so I guess I will have to take some time off work," Mike answered, as though he wasn't sure what to do. "Also, I'm not able to send the report for today's meeting. I apologize. It's ready, but I don't have my laptop with me."

"Oh, that's okay. We will work around it. Is there anything we can do?" offered Andy.

"Thanks, but nothing for now. I really don't know what to expect. I'm sorry to put this on you guys. I know everybody already has a full work load," Mike apologized again.

"Don't worry about that. We have you covered. You just take care of your family."

"I'll call you later when I know more," Mike said.

"Yes, please, keep in touch and let us know how she's doing."

"I will," answered Mike as he hung up the phone and looked at his watch.

"Well, that's done, now what?" He felt like he was playing chess, trying to move the pieces around the board, but not knowing the right moves for each piece.

"I guess everyone is probably getting ready to go to Connecticut for Mother's memorial service," Mike pondered. He had called his brother Donald shortly after he had arrived at the hospital to let him know what had happened and that he would not be at the service. It had been a month since his mother's death and cremation. She was being returned to her roots; not her, just her ashes, her earthly remains, Mike reminded himself. He knew the spirit departed at death. But, for those who know Christ, to be absent from the body is to be present with the Lord. Such promises were a real comfort when someone close to you leaves this earth, he reflected, thinking first about his mother and then almost freezing in his thoughts with the renewed realization of how close his wife was to death.

When talking to Donald earlier that morning, he had asked for a favor. "Please don't tell anyone how badly Felicia is injured until after Mother's memorial service. Just tell them I'm not there because of the accident. It wouldn't be fair for them to feel like they should be in two places at once. When the service is over, tell them then. Anyone who is able can come later. It will be best that way. It's just too much to deal with all at once."

"Whatever you want, brother, that's the way it will be," Donald assured him.

"Thanks, Donald. Just call me later," Mike requested, ending the conversation.

Mike thought about his large family and was amused by how many things had to be juggled for all of them to be in the same place at the same time: work schedules, school schedules, daycare, and transportation. He was glad he was born into a large family. His brothers and sisters, nieces and nephews, were all very important to him. They had worked hard to be close. Much had happened in their lives to separate them. It has made us appreciate each other even more he reminded himself. Mike ran their names through his head, oldest to youngest: Christian, Mary, Monique, me, Donald, Gerard, Joseph, Francis, Joy, James, and Warrie. My mother gave birth to eleven children; my father had to provide for eleven children, he thought. Just imagine, there would have been thirteen of us if Mom hadn't miscarried with the twins, he recalled, shaking his head, knowing how full his and Felicia's hands were with just three.

"I will be glad when they get here. It will be good to have my family with me," Mike reflected. Even though he had a large family, they hadn't always been together. Their parents had difficulties and child welfare had intervened, breaking the family up and sending them to different foster homes and community shelters. Mike realized that it was remarkable that they had reconnected and rekindled their relationships as adults, considering how far flung they had all been.

Mike studied his own children. He knew they were tired, but they were such good kids. They were just sitting quietly as though nothing was wrong. They weren't pestering to leave or complaining about having to be there. He knew he was very blessed. He thanked God for his children. He too sat quietly. There was nothing to do but wait and go through the situation in as much peace and love and trust as he could muster.

He stepped out in the hallway to see if anyone was looking for them, then returned to the waiting room. Felicia's parents will be here soon. They will help take care of the children; that will be good, he thought. It wasn't long before Deacon Brown came through the door and dropped into the chair next to him.

"How's Sonia?" Mike asked, with hope that at least there would be a good report on her.

"She's pretty banged up. She'll have a long recovery time, but she's going to be okay," he answered, reassuring Mike.

"Does she know what happened," Mike asked, hoping for some detail that may cause this to make more sense.

"She said all she remembers was waking up to her friend Alleen's voice calling out to her and Felicia. Sonia answered her. Felicia did not. Sonia cried telling me how upset she was that she was unable to determine if Felicia was okay. Of course, it was very good news when I told her Felicia had not died," Deacon Brown reported.

"So how is Felicia?" he asked. He knew that being in ICU meant her injuries were more serious and was concerned about the report he was about to receive.

"It's pretty bad but I think she'll be alright. She's in a coma. Once she comes out of that we'll know more. They did a CT scan but it's too soon for them to tell me anything yet," he replied. Mike just couldn't give Deacon Brown the hopeless report the doctor had given him. It was too overwhelming. He'll see soon enough for himself, he thought.

"You know how we were talking about that drunken guy hitting us? Well, it was alcohol again," Mike said, shaking his head as he felt his anger rise up.

"That's what I was told," Deacon Brown concurred, also shaking his head in disbelief and sadness.

"I just have to believe she'll be alright. Do you want to see her?" asked Mike, trying to sound positive even though he really didn't have anything to base it on except a few words from the radiology technician who had encouraged him; that and his faith in God to take care of her.

The two of them stood and Mike again instructed the children to wait quietly until his return. Avery pulled several matchbox cars out of his pockets and he and Nadia sat down on the floor, running the cars up the chair legs and across the arms. They seemed like they were doing all right which gave Mike a sense of relief. He looked at his older son as Mikey scooted to the edge of his chair anticipating that maybe he would go, too.

"I need for you to stay with the kids, Mikey, and thank you, son," Mike said, giving him a few firm pats on the back. Mikey slid back in his chair and looked back towards the TV but didn't really focus on it. He didn't know what to do with himself. Several people were now in the waiting room, but he didn't want to talk to anyone. After his dad left the room, he watched his brother and sister play and wished he were little again. This seems to be easier for them, he thought.

CHAPTER 4

He's A Thief

MIKE AND DEACON BROWN returned to the waiting room to find Felicia's parents had just arrived. They were hugging the children and offering comforting words. Mike asked if they were ready to see Felicia. He took Sadie first, while Mr. Stanley stayed with the children. Mike then left Felicia's room giving his place to her father. They, too, were astonished at the severity of Felicia's injuries; to see their daughter in such a condition was almost unbearable.

As the morning passed, more and more people began arriving from Highland, Poughkeepsie and Long Island. The children were glad to see familiar faces. Throughout the morning, Mike acted as usher, taking one visitor after the other to Felicia's room. Friends and family members were stricken by Felicia's appearance and condition. They cried for her, and comforted each other with this-is-too-hard-to-handle kind of hugs and quiet whispers.

Mike had found a place of peace. He was no longer alarmed when he looked at his wife. He was now the strong arm for the others to lean on. He was quiet. He watched as people would come and go. So many people loved Felicia and only wanted what was best for her. Mike knew, however, that others were jealous of her because she was so talented, giving her all at school, at church, to her friends and family. From these people he sensed a secret satisfaction that something bad had happened to the one who always seemed to have it so good.

Mike learned firsthand how differently people deal with hardships and trouble. A close friend from church became so distraught over the severity of Felicia's injuries that he slapped the wall beside him.

"Don't take it so hard. We're trusting God that Felicia is going to come out of this," Mike said, attempting to hearten him.

"I hate the devil. He is such a thief. He steals, and kills and destroys," the friend retorted. "For Felicia to be struck down in the prime of life like this…our beautiful dancer, singer, teacher; how will we ever get along without her? She brings so much to our church…to all of us. It's just not right! I hate the devil."

"I hate him, too," Mike avowed, "but I know I have to be strong… for Felicia and for my family and I need for you to be strong for me."

"I will, Mike. You know I'm here for you," he said, resting his hand on Mike's shoulder. "I just can't believe this," he sighed, with renewed control.

Since they went to church together, many people visited both

Felicia and Sonia at the hospital. Two of their friends, Alleen Josesphs-Clarke and Pauline Elliott, suffered lesser injuries in the accident and were expected to make quick recoveries. However, they also learned that Lenore Silverbush, a teacher from Brooklyn, one of the passengers in the van had died at the scene. They all knew it was no coincidence that Felicia had just witnessed to her, leading her in a salvation prayer to receive Jesus as her Savior and Lord. It had happened within just a few days of losing her earthly life. "This was the grace and mercy of God who knew this lady would not survive the collision," they assured each other.

All Mike could do was praise God that Felicia was still alive and that Mrs. Silverbush would spend eternity with her Heavenly Father.

By late afternoon, Mike's family started arriving from Connecticut. He tried to tell them gently just how seriously Felicia was injured without alarming them. He wanted to prepare them before they saw her. Some of them were upset that Mike had asked Donald to withhold the details of the accident, not revealing just how critical her condition was. Joseph especially was hurt that Mike had not called him for help. Since he was a doctor, he could have been sure she was getting the best possible care. Mike, in an effort to make peace with Joseph and show honor to his brother as a doctor, gave his permission for Joseph to review Felicia's chart. After carefully studying the medical records, Joseph saw that everything possible was being done and his only job now was to reassure Mike that indeed that was the case.

Even though he had attempted to prepare them, seeing Felicia was still a shock. As each of them entered the room, reality sank in. This was no bump on the head. Mike came and went with each visiting sibling to support and comfort them even though that was what he himself needed. He knew the situation could not be understood with mere words. Only with their eyes could they fully comprehend her condition.

As Mike entered the room with yet another family member, he noticed that his brother-in-law Ron looked particularly disturbed. He looked to his sister Joy for an answer to her husband's demeanor, but he could not read her expression. As soon as Ron had seen Mike reenter the room, he had turned his face away and slipped out the door not wanting to add to Mike's distress.

Mike followed him down the hallway. "Are you okay?" Mike asked with concern, knowing everyone had to deal with their feelings in their own way.

Ron turned to Mike with tears in his eyes. "She just looks so bad, Mike, I can't bear it," Ron blurted out. "Felicia is the most charismatic person I know. I can't stand to see her so lifeless. You guys were just at our house on the Fourth when you went to Jones Beach for the day. She was so happy talking about how much she enjoyed the fireworks display. Now"…he choked… but the words wouldn't come. He swallowed hard. "So quickly her life has changed from vibrant to…to…" he didn't want to complete his thought. "Life is so fragile," he finished.

"She won't always be like this," Mike attempted to assure him. "You know God will bring her back," he encouraged. Mike knew Ron had strong faith and that was the best way to bring his thoughts back to center.

"Yes, I know," Ron nodded his head, "but I just never

expected her… to… to look like that… to be in such a bad way."
Again Mike thanked God for strengthening him as once more
he found himself as the comforter.

Other members of the family had similar reactions. How
could this have happened to Felicia? Where was the one who
always knew just what to say and do? The accident had turned
their world upside down. This time, they had to be the ones to
make things right for her. Mike knew his family would do everything within their grasp to do just that, for Felicia, for him
and for their children.

Mike's sister, Monique, sat in the waiting room with her family
as the others took turns going to Felicia. She had already made
her visit, but only briefly. One look brought doubt to Monique's
mind that Felicia could possibly live. She encouraged her brother with thoughts opposite of her real feelings.

"She'll make it, Mike. She's strong," she declared, hoping
her words did not ring false. Mike nodded his head in agreement, knowing his family was trying to keep him bolstered up.

Emile approached his Uncle Mike. "Can I get Mikey out of
here for a little while? I think he needs it," he suggested.

"Sure, thank you, Emile," Mike smiled appreciatively at his
oldest nephew.

Francis, one of Mike's younger brothers, left Felicia's room
knowing he must soon leave the hospital and go home. He
returned to the waiting room to say goodbye to Mike and the
kids. Monique and Francis spoke of possible arrangements to
be made for the children, feeling overwhelmed by the circum-

stances. Mike assured them everything would work out; he just had to take things a day at a time. Francis said goodbye to Monique and started to shake Mike's hand to leave.

"I'll walk you to your car," Mike offered.

"Okay," Francis responded, not sure how he could just walk away, leaving his brother with such a load. They took the elevator to visitor parking, exchanging small talk as they moved down the hallway and exited the hospital.

"Look, I want to help but I feel so incapable of making a difference for you," Francis said, pulling his hand out of his pocket and reaching for Mike's hand, then pressing greenbacks into his palm. "Take this, I don't know what else to do for you, and I want to do something. Perhaps…perhaps this will help," Francis said, feeling uncertain, but glad at least, to be doing something.

"Thank you, brother," Mike said with an encouraging smile as he gave Francis a quick embrace. "Everything helps. Every kindness makes a difference for us."

"I'll let you know how she's doing," Mike offered as Francis opened his car door. Mike turned back towards the hospital doors, thinking about his last statement. What report would he be able to give his brother, he wondered.

Emile and Mikey had taken the elevator to the ground floor. Emile knew that it would take them to the commercial side of the hospital and hurried through the already too-familiar, large hospital lobby.

"How about getting something to eat?" Emile immediately offered knowing teenage boys were always hungry. He was only nine years older than Mikey and was quick to pick up on his body language.

Emile went to the information desk and asked if they could find a good restaurant within walking distance. They were pointed in the right direction, and headed for the suggested destination several blocks away.

Settling into a cozy booth, Emile quickly ordered Philly cheese steaks for himself and Mikey. The cousins talked briefly about Felicia's condition, but Emile quickly changed the subject to guy talk to get Mikey's mind off his situation. They talked about how the Yankees were doing; that it was a good year for them. They talked about their favorite ball players and argued about who was better and why. Mikey laughed for the first time all day.

Soon their sandwiches were served and they greedily chomped into the crusty bread piled thick with succulent cheesy beef, grilled green peppers and onions.

"This is the best sandwich I've ever eaten," Mikey said, talking with his mouth still half-full. Emile laughed.

"Haven't you ever had a Philly Cheese before?" he asked in surprise.

"Nope and this is the best thing that's happened all day," Mikey grinned ear to ear, as the rich juices dribbled down his chin.

CHAPTER 5

An Uncertain Future

FELICIA'S PARENTS HAD TAKEN a hotel room in Pittsfield and kept the children with them, taking care of their meals and their every need. This was a great help and comfort to Mike. It allowed him to focus on Felicia. After several days, Grandma Sadie told Mike they needed to go home and offered to take the children with them.

"Yes, thank you," Mike answered. "I'll come home in a few days. We'll figure out what to do then."

Mike addressed his son, "Mikey, I found out you are old enough to visit your mother. Do you want to see her before you leave?"

"I guess so," he answered. He did want to see her, but all of the talk he had overheard made him afraid. It showed on his face.

"Come on son. I'll go with you," encouraged Mike, "It'll be okay."

Mikey entered her room cautiously. Even though he had had several days to prepare for this moment, it was still a shock to see the strong mother he knew lying there so weak and defenseless. Mikey stood beside his mother's bed, his father's arm wrapped firmly around his shoulders. Tears poured down his cheeks and ran down his neck. It was difficult to breathe and it felt as though there was not enough air in the room. He gripped the side rails of the bed hard in an effort to keep control of his emotions. Mikey had been in hospital rooms before with elderly family members. He had seen medical equipment and watched monitors working, but this was different. He could see that they had cut her throat and put a tube in it. He had heard of this, but had never seen it. It was very frightening. There were IV's in her arms and bandages on her head. Her face and neck were ballooned out of proportion to the rest of her body. She looked so small under the sheet that covered her. Was this his happy, vibrant mother? Mikey knew in his heart this person lying in the bed *was* his mother yet she looked nothing like her; her face so swollen, dark circles around her eyes, her right cheek so discolored with pools of blood. He just stood there in shock, not knowing what to say, so he said nothing at all.

Mikey looked away towards his uncle to avoid the pain of looking at his mom. His Uncle Donald and Aunt Tamara had been quietly singing to Felicia when they had entered the room. Felicia loved music. They hoped that hearing the melody of familiar voices and the words of favorite songs would help rouse her. It was a spiritual song of a loving God; the God they knew as a family.

Mike said, "Please keep singing. We all need to hear it." They stood at the bedside a short time more, and then Mike led his son out of the hospital room and back to his grandparents. He knew there was nothing to say that would make it any easier for Mikey. Their future was uncertain. "I know it looks bad son, but don't lose hope. For your mother's sake, please don't lose hope."

Mike watched as his family walked away from him. The kids needed to go home with their grandparents. He knew that was best yet it left him feeling lonely. He returned to his bedside vigil.

Deacon Brown had checked on Mike and Felicia again and asked if he would like to see Sonia.

"Yes," Mike responded. "I do want to see her." Together they took the elevator to her floor. As they entered the room, it appeared Sonia was sleeping but Deacon Brown spoke, telling her Mike was there to see her.

"Hello, Mike," Sonia greeted him weakly.

"Hello, Sonia," Mike responded. She laid there with her eyes closed for a few moments and then asked about Felicia.

"She's the same," Mike answered, knowing Deacon Brown had informed his wife of Felicia's condition. "But she'll be better soon, I'm sure," he quickly added.

"How are you feeling, Sonia? You took some pretty hard knocks yourself."

"They are keeping me comfortable. I'll be all right," she answered.

Deacon Brown offered Mike a chair that he gladly accepted. He was tired and was grateful to be able to sit down. They talked about Felicia's injuries with Mike sharing a little more of what the doctors had told him. They discussed the accident. Mike was curious to know more details. Since Felicia couldn't tell him anything, he was glad to learn what Sonia knew.

"I don't understand why Felicia was riding with someone. I had specifically asked her to drive herself wherever she went," Mike told Sonia.

"Felicia really shouldn't have been with us," Sonia said, explaining the circumstances. "The school had a bus scheduled to take everyone to Becket but there were too many of us. The bus wouldn't hold everyone. Felicia actually had a seat on that bus but she gave it up to someone else, knowing we had room in the van. I guess she did try to honor what you asked Mike, but circumstances caused her to make other choices. She was just trying to be helpful."

"Yes, Felicia would do that," Mike said thoughtfully, but wishing she hadn't. Sonia went on to tell him she thought Felicia had slipped her arm out of the shoulder harness and so she could lean forward in order to be able to hear better and take part in the conversation. She was in the third row of the van by herself. Sometime after that, the accident happened.

Mike tried not to react to the news about the seatbelt. He didn't want to say anything that might upset Sonia.

"I didn't know that," Mike responded. "I better let you rest now. I hope you are feeling better soon." He wanted out of the room. He didn't want to believe what he had just been told about the seat belt and couldn't understand why Felicia would do that. She was always so conscientious about things.

"I hope Felicia will be better too," Mrs. Brown said tiredly, as Mike stood to leave.

Mike drifted down the hall toward the elevators. Felicia had given up her seat on the bus. She wasn't wearing her seatbelt correctly. She hadn't followed my requests not to ride with anyone. That's why he told her to take the Durango. It was a heavy vehicle and if something did happen he knew she would be safer—and now the seatbelt. Maybe, this could have all been avoided. With just a few precautions, they may not be living this nightmare. Mike wanted to be angry. He wanted to scold. He wanted to scream. There was no one to be his target or his audience. He wanted to release his raw feelings. He wanted to vent.

He returned to Felicia's room deflated. Sometimes, it's best not to know why, he reasoned. He was exhausted. I'm not thinking right, he told himself. I must rest. I can't be weak. I must find that place of peace again.

Late one evening, Donald pleaded, "Mike, please come with me. You need to get out of this room for a while. It's not good for you to just sit here hour after hour, day after day. You know there are other hurting people here, too. Let's go share some light and hope with them. What do you say?"

Mike pulled himself out of his chair, giving Donald a doubtful look. Did he have anything good left to give to others when he was so drained, he asked himself as he attempted to cooperate.

Mike shuffled to the waiting room behind his brother and dropped into the nearest chair. He glanced around the room at people sitting in groups, obviously acquainted and quietly speaking with each other. Some looked as tired as Mike felt. One woman was crying.

A clergyman stood to leave, shaking hands with the woman who had been crying and with the young man beside her. After he left, Donald approached the family and introduced himself. Mike reluctantly joined him. They shared their stories. Mike and Donald telling about Felicia being in a coma, they telling of a suicide attempt by drug overdose. The young boy shared a few details, his mother listening as he spoke about his sister. Donald and Mike offered comforting words in an attempt to console them. They in turn asked questions about Felicia and expressed sympathy, realizing they were sharing similar heartaches.

"Donald had been right," thought Mike. Taking his eyes off his own situation was encouraging to himself as well as to this family. It was reassuring to know others were making it through crisis too. As they visited and became better acquainted, a young girl, the sister of the drug overdose patient came into the waiting room. She carried a guitar. Soon she was softly strumming a pretty, but unfamiliar tune. Mike leaned his head back against the wall and closed his eyes. As he listened, he again thought, I came to share what little I could and now I am reaping the reward for the small seed of comfort that we sowed. That is the goodness of God. We just can't out give Him. As I give to others, He gives back to me. Donald noticed the slight smile on his brother's face and knew he was right to get him out of Felicia's room, if only for a little while.

Mike returned to his wife's side and settled into a chair. The young girl with the guitar heard second hand of Felicia's plight from Donald and offered to go to her room to play for her. She stepped just inside the doorway, her guitar in hand and played softly. Mike was moved by the music and asked about its origin. It was unusual and foreign to his ear.

"It's Hebrew," she responded, "a Jewish prayer."

Closing his eyes, he waited for sleep to come. Why did this have to happen? How long would she stay this way? Maybe I should have kept the children with me. No, they are where they need to be, with their grandparents. Strength Lord, thank You for strength. Thank You for strength to minister to others when I feel so needy myself was his silent prayer as he drifted off to sleep.

z After this, Donald and Mike would keep their eyes open for opportunities to minister kindness and comfort to others in the hospital. One day while visiting the emergency waiting room, they met a lady whose niece had been shot in a drive-by shooting. The family was in shock. Everyone knew of drive-bys happening, but no one thought it would happen to them. The girl had just been in the wrong place, at the wrong time, while visiting the neighborhood of a friend. Normally, she would not have been anywhere near there. Suddenly they were the victims of horrific violence where innocent by-standers were caught in the midst of personal disputes.

The brothers were pleased that their attempts to console and pray for the family were received. They knew the value of strong arms of support in the time of crisis just as strong arms had been offered to them by so many.

Days passed and the doctor requested a conference with Mike. They told him she no longer required acute care in ICU, and they would soon be ready to move Felicia to a different unit. A ventilator had been started in the emergency room and it was still doing her breathing for her. It required monitoring by respiratory specialists so she was sent to that special unit.

Donald felt impressed to go around the respiratory unit and pray with other people for healing of breathing problems. They

ministered to the other patients often and were blessed knowing they were making a difference in people's lives. For those
who dared to believe, they knew healing belonged to them.

Often when they were sitting in the waiting room, new families would be there because a loved one had been admitted due
to an accident or illness. They shared the love of God and encouraged people with truths from the Bible. Others would join
in the conversation, giving thanks to God and talking about the
love of Christ.

On one such day, they were talking about Jesus' sacrifice
and his desire that all should be saved. After a time, a young girl
looked at Mike and asked, "Can I be saved?"

"Yes," he answered with excitement, "you can be saved right
now." A circle of believers formed around the young girl as she
was led through a prayer of repentance and salvation. She gladly received Jesus as her Lord and Savior.

"What a reward for a small effort on our part," Mike expressed to Donald later.

"I believe our pain is alleviated as we minister to others. I
believe that is God's intention and His way," Donald nodded in
agreement.

One day passed into another and still there was no change in
Felicia's condition. Mike had stayed at Felicia's bedside continuously. The hospital offered him a hospitality room but he did
not want to use it. He didn't want to leave Felicia's side. "I want
to be there when she wakes up," Mike argued with his brothers
and sisters. "I'm sleeping in the chair. I'm okay."

"You must sleep in a bed, Mike. This has gone on too long.
You will be no good for Felicia if you make yourself sick," they

argued back. Mike had finally given in by going to the hospitality room for just a couple of hours each night. There was a phone by the bed. If the nurses needed to reach him, they would call. He thought to himself, it's like the red phone we always heard about on the president's desk. If it rings, it means big trouble. Every time he awoke from a brief rest, and realized the phone had not rung, he would have the thought, she has lived for another day.

CHAPTER 6

The Doctor And The Dancer

HE ATTEMPTED TO THINK on good things during the long hours at Felicia's bedside. He forced dreaded thoughts out of his mind by replacing them with thoughts that were glorifying to God; thoughts that would lead him to speak praise instead of fear and worry.

As he sat there pondering his life, his thoughts went back to the office at IBM where he first met Felicia. She had graduated from college with a double major in biology and Spanish. She was working full time at IBM and on her master's degree at the same time. It was 1987. She had fit in well with his group of friends, occasionally gathering in the break room together. Mike was attracted to her because of her peaceful demeanor and Christ-like attitude. Mike thought Felicia was a great gal. She was his junior by nine years, more the age of his younger sisters. He was in a long-term relationship with his girlfriend, Roxie. He hoped to be married soon. He had made a commitment to Roxie and to God. Besides, Felicia wouldn't be interested in him. She was educated. He was the poster child for pulling himself up by his bootstraps. He had dropped out of college to support himself and so wasn't able to fulfill his personal goal of becoming an electrical engineer. Felicia had met every goal she had ever set for herself. His thoughts drifted off to his childhood and the reasons for his struggles, knowing his "bootstraps" thought wasn't correct. God had been at his side all of the time.

Looking back as an adult, he could see that turmoil had always been a part of his young family life yet he had some pleasant memories. His father was a quiet, gentle man. He still pictured him fondly, sitting in the living room talking with his children, puffing on his favorite pipe. If he closed his eyes, Mike could almost smell the sweet aroma that swirled out of his father's pipe and diffused into the air. He worked as a histologist at Mount Sinai hospital. He was good at what he did. His name was Cybald Luke Cole. He was an African.

Cybald's parents had died tragically when he was still very young. His maternal uncle, Emile Luke, an influential government official of Sierra Leone, West Africa, raised him in Freetown. The Queen of England had knighted his Uncle Emile, giving them the titles of Sir Emile Fashole Luke and Lady Sarah Christiana.

As a young man, Mike's father became involved with a girl from the Freetown area. When Cybald's uncle learned she was pregnant, he sent Cybald to the states. The plan was for him to study to become a doctor and then return to Africa to provide medical care in their home area. His uncle knew he would be gone long enough for the girl to make a life for herself and her child.

In later years, Mike and the others learned of their half sister in Africa. She had been named Queen. Some of them had met and befriended Queen, learning of the hardship that had been caused by Emile Luke not encouraging Cybald to take responsibility. They could only assume that he thought he was doing what was best for Cybald, even though the consequences could easily be seen in their half sister.

It was during the very early days of the civil rights movement that Cybald met Mike's mother, Jan Drake. They found a common interest in supporting the efforts to end discrimination against their people. They both had made career choices. Cybald was a student, working on his Bachelor's of Science degree in preparation for medical school.

Jan dreamed of being a dancer. She and her brother, Warren, were topnotch dancing partners aspiring to be professionals. They were raised in an educated family in Ansonia, Connecticut. Their father was the first black policeman in Ansonia. Shirley Janice Drake was raised to be a lady. She was light-skinned and found acceptance and even though Cybald was very dark, she saw a great future with him. She saw herself as a doctor's wife. However, not so with her family, who shunned him for his dark complexion and African roots. Prejudice within the family was only one of the battles that would derail their marriage.

After a short courtship, they married and almost immediately started their family. The babies came quickly changing Jan's focus from the dance floor to the playpen. In just over four years, they had four babies. Cybald wanted to continue his schooling but financial pressure caused him to need to work more and more hours and he eventually gave up on the idea of medical school and a career as a doctor.

In contradiction to Cybald's quiet nature, Jan was outspoken and fiery. She was very vocal about her disappointment of how her life had turned out and she blamed Cybald. She felt he had stolen her dream of dancing and his failure to become a doctor robbed her of her much desired social status.

They lived in reasonable quarters, a nice apartment, later a large house, but soon even the basics became more and more scarce. Jan had been raised Catholic. She considered having children a woman's lot and a privilege. She loved her children and yet resented her husband at the same time. Cybald adored his children, yet over time was worn down emotionally by his wife's harsh words and lack of contentment. He turned to drinking to ease his pain. The cycle of poverty had begun.

There were periods of calm, periods when they got along, but it was only a matter of time before there would be another flare up of fighting and abuse. Cybald tried to support his growing family, but over time, his drinking escalated in unison with his wife's verbal and physical attacks.

Jan's behavior indicated depression and perhaps even mental illness. She stopped caring. She stopped taking care of her children. She put the household chores off on her oldest daughters without teaching them how to keep house. Their environment went from bad to worse. Not only did she not take good care of their family or give proper attention to her children, she also did not protect them from her oldest son, Chris. He ran the house through tyranny and that led to their eventual downfall and the separation of the family.

Donald who had come to spend the day with him interrupted Mike's thoughts. Mike shared what he had been thinking about. For a long time, they talked as brothers often do, of things from the past; remembering some good times and some not so good times. They talked about how it had been as youngsters living on Riverside Drive in New York City and playing at Riverside Park when their family was still together. That is how their family's memories were delineated—before they were separated and after they were separated.

Mike was in the 5th grade when his family was split up and he, Donald, Mary and Monique were placed at the Mineola shelter in Long Island. His other brothers and sisters were placed in various foster homes. It was obvious to the shelter administrators that Mike had some problems to overcome. He had a speech impediment and it was apparent that he was not at the fifth grade level in his learning. Mike had missed a lot of school and there was no discipline at home for him to do his homework when he did miss. His mother had taken the path of least resistance when it came to her sons. She allowed Mike to lay in bed instead of getting him up and preparing him for school. She seemed oblivious to why he was so tired in the morning. It fell to his older brother, Chris. He would shake his younger brothers and sisters out of their sleep and send them on late night scavenger hunts to find empty bottles and cans to redeem for cash to buy treats and food for him. Often times it was well after midnight before they were settled back into bed. It was no wonder he had fallen behind in school. Even days when he did make it to school, he was tired and hungry and he couldn't focus on his schoolwork. It was easier to stay home and sleep. At least, he wasn't hungry while he was asleep.

Donald, too, remembered being on the streets late at night.

He recalled that if they did not cooperate, Chris would punish them with a belt or hit them with whatever was handy. Mike told Donald that once when he was unable to bring home a treat, Chris hit him across the head with a wire clothes hanger. The next day at school, a nun asked him how he got the red mark across his head. "I lied," Mike recalled, "because I was more afraid of Chris than I was the nuns."

He laughed to lighten the mood, saying, "And you know, Donald, everyone was afraid of the nuns."

Donald chuckled in agreement with Mike's joke. "It is still amazing to me that our mother and father didn't stop him from mistreating us," Donald mused.

"Mom always protected Chris. As her first-born, she just refused to see the bad things he did or admit there was anything wrong with him. Dad wouldn't confront him or he had to fight both of them," Mike recalled. "It was always the same."

"I know from talking to people that knew our family," Mike told Donald, "that once Mother became angry against our father, she didn't care what she said in front of her children. She would go on a tirade and tell him off, belittling his roots and calling him derogatory names that were slanderous against her own race. As a young child, Chris repeated the ugly words and the ugly attitude. It is as if he learned how to be angry from her. Anger then was the prominent disposition that developed in him. When Father tried to correct him, Mother would interfere, stopping any disciplinary action. She literally taught Chris to disrespect Father. He was barely out of diapers and the two of them had teamed up against Dad. I doubt that Mother realized what she was creating when she made a small child her ally against his father. As he got older, he treated everyone the same way he treated Dad. He abused Dad and got away with it, so he abused us, too.

They talked about other times they had been intimidated, punished and abused by their oldest brother. He was a bully and a brute. That was how they remembered him.

"Mom was tough, too," Mike recalled. "I remember once when we were very young, Mom and Dad had a huge fight. Somehow, Mother managed to lock him out of the apartment but he was determined to get back in. He went up the fire escape and broke out a window to crawl through. I think I remember that the fight was because Dad had attempted to discipline Chris but again mother wouldn't allow it. She was so angry, screaming and throwing plates at him. I remember the plates breaking and cutting him. I can still see the blood running down his face."

Mike continued, "Mom sent me outside to find a policeman. Back in those days, the police still walked their beats in New York City. I didn't speak clearly and I couldn't make myself understood so I finally just took the policeman's hand and led him to our apartment. The next thing I knew he had put handcuffs on our father. I will always remember that. I blamed myself. I was only five or six years old. I was too young to know what was about to happen when she sent me for the police. I was just obeying Mother but it was devastating for me. When he handcuffed him, I thought the policeman was mad at our father and it was my fault," Mike explained.

"Perhaps, when I went in search of him, I thought he was going to help Dad since he was hurt. I already had speech problems. I think that incident just made it worse."

"By then Chris was big and he would pick fights but Dad wouldn't hit back. He didn't want to hurt his son, so often times he took a beating. I can remember seeing Dad's face swollen and bruised from Chris pummeling him. He just didn't know how to deal with the hostility from Chris and then from his wife, too. You remember, don't you?" Mike asked. Donald just nodded his head. He was younger than Mike; but he had his own distinct impressions.

"The only time I really felt safe was when we would go to mass with Mother," Mike recalled. "I remember so clearly seeing her praying her rosary. I knew she loved God and I wanted to be close to her so I could be close to God, too. She did all she knew to do as a Catholic. She taught us to love God. We owe her that."

"I remember when things were really hard at home, when Chris was acting up or Mother and Father were arguing, I would find a corner to sit in and talk to God. I knew He could understand me even if nobody else could," Mike reminisced. "I realize now that talking to God made me feel safe when my world seemed like such an unsafe place."

"Still through all of that we always treated them both with respect," Mike reflected, knowing that indeed all of them except Chris had shown honor to their parents despite the circumstances.

Those thoughts led him to remember another vivid-but-sad memory that he shared with Donald. Mike saw himself as a young boy breaking white bread into small pieces and hiding it in the pages of his schoolbooks for a cherished snack. "Soon, you and Gerard caught on to what I was doing and started hiding bread for yourselves, too. Yes, it was no wonder I didn't do well at school," Mike finished.

He shook his head in recollection, knowing one reason his sister Mary was a good student. Chris had forced her to do his homework. She had to do school work above her grade level. Chris' bullying had actually worked to her advantage when it came to her education.

"Once we were placed at the shelter, Mary, Monique and you were sent to public school, but the staff knew I would not make it in the mainstream. They attempted to school me themselves, but I only got further behind," Mike reflected, knowing Donald understood it all.

"Things probably could have gone a lot differently for both of us if I hadn't been so insistent we stay together. I still remember what happened after we were sent to the Susquehanna Valley Home," Donald admitted.

"I know what you are remembering," Mike responded.

Arrangements were being made to place in foster care as their siblings had been, except they weren't going to be sent to the same family. One day Mike walked into their room and saw that Donald was crying. "What's wrong?" Mike asked his younger brother.

"They're going to send you to one place and me to another," Donald answered, catching the big tears sliding down his cheeks with the back of his curled hand. "I don't want to be by myself," he cried out in pain. "I want to stay with you, Mike," he said with pleading in his voice, as though his big brother could make everything all right.

"It'll be better if we're in foster homes instead of a group home like this. We need to have parents to take care of us," Mike tried to explain with wisdom beyond his years.

"No," Donald insisted. "I don't want to go anywhere if you're not going too. Please, Mike, tell them we have to stay together," begged Donald.

"Alright, I'll tell them we want to stay here," Mike said, responding to Donald's appeal. He felt bad for his brother. Mike knew he would miss Donald, too. At least, we know they will feed us here and we are away from Chris and everything that wasn't right at home, Mike reasoned.

"So we asked to stay in the group home until they could find a home that would take both of us," Mike stated, "but of course, that never happened. Maybe it was for the best anyway," Mike told his younger brother. We turned out alright, didn't we?" he asked, playfully poking at his brother.

"Well, I did anyway," Donald teased back.

"I remember something else about that time," Mike said. "I remember you coming to me and telling me that you thought we should kneel beside our bunk bed and pray every night and that we should do eight pushups every night."

"Pray and do eight pushups, huh? I was a deep thinker!" Donald laughed.

"I guess you were concerned about not only our spiritual but our physical health, too," Mike ribbed. "I don't know why I remember that. It's funny that you settled on eight pushups. Maybe that was all you could do without collapsing," he said, poking at Donald. "I know God saw our hearts were tender toward Him even then."

CHAPTER 7

Not So Incognito

SOMEONE COMING INTO THE room caught their attention. It was their brother, James. This day was truly going to be a mini-family reunion for the brothers. After saying their hellos, James went to Felicia's bedside and took her hand.

"She's the glue in our family; she's adhesive," James smiled. "I know I'm not the only one who feels this way. There is just something about her. I always feel good in Felicia's presence." Mike was touched by his brother's tenderness towards his wife. They all truly loved Felicia.

"I told you she was a keeper—and she still is," James said, reminding his brother about the conversation they'd had the first time James met Felicia.

"Remember, I told you—you had better hold onto her," James playfully reminded his brother.

"You were right about that," Mike agreed. "Felicia has been my best friend—an excellent wife."

"We were just talking about when we were kids at home with Mom and Dad," Donald said, drawing James into their conversation.

"I don't have a lot of memories about that time," James interjected, "except I do remember the day the social workers came to our house and took us away."

"I remember me and Warrie going to our new foster home and they had Smarties candy and I remember asking if I could have some. You know, things that were important to a three year old," James laughed. "That scene is burned into my memory."

"I know I had it pretty good. I had a normal childhood. Church, basketball, track, student government; same as everybody else we knew," James related.

Mike and Donald looked at each other and laughed. "Yeah, just like everybody else, but not like us," Mike assured him.

"That was a bad day for us older ones. No one knew what was happening. These people just came into our house and took us away. I remember Mother was crying but she let us go. Later we learned the truth, but Mother still had her own story."

Mike shared what their mother had told him; that she was just overwhelmed with so many children and so little money to care for us and she had asked for help until they could get things worked out. That is what she wanted me to believe when I got older.

"The other side of the story, of course, is that Chris had molested two of our sisters. They told our aunt who reported it to child welfare and they investigated our family and declared our parents unfit. Dad wasn't, but I think he just gave up. I don't know about Mother, but I know her handling of Chris is what ultimately split us up. He was out of control. He got mixed up with a bad bunch of kids at school. They were his peers, a bad influence and no one held him accountable at home. Of course, it complicated all of our relationships for years," Mike mused as his brothers nodded their heads in agreement.

"I'm not sure who was a bad influence on whom from some of the stories I've heard, but I do know Chris' behavior was violent and controlling to the extreme," Donald added. "Going into military service was the best thing he could have done for himself. I know it helped him. He did well there."

"And at least he did repent," James interjected. "When he came to me with his apology, he took responsibility for all the trouble he had caused our family. He knew much of it was his fault. I think I was about sixteen at that time. The years in the military were good for him, taking the focus off himself and teaching him self-discipline. He had worked hard and gained status as a sergeant in the army. I know when he was diagnosed with cancer he was scared. He wanted everyone's forgiveness. He did not want to leave this earth with so much unfinished business and hard feelings toward him. At the end, he wanted to be sure that things were right between himself and us, and with God. Some of us found it easier to forgive him than others did. His atrocities towards us younger ones were less direct," he reasoned.

"Yes, Donald and I had the opportunity to pray with him. I believe he truly was sorry. He had a lot to be forgiven of, but we knew we had to show mercy. We knew too much of the word of God to deny him that," Mike confessed.

"Hmm…," Donald nodded agreement. "Colossians 3: Forgiving each other even as Christ has forgiven you. It is sobering to know that we must forgive in order to be forgiven.'"

"As tough as he was, he did come around. He did soften. Remember Mike, how he seemed to change? " Donald questioned.

"We really didn't have any brotherly relationship with him for all those years, but near the end he opened up to us."

"Yes, I remember. There was a total change in his demeanor and his attitude. He even seemed to welcome our prayers," Mike said thoughtfully.

"I remember the day he called and asked if we would come and visit him in D.C. He didn't want to believe what the doctors had told him. I know he hoped for better. He welcomed our prayers then," Donald told them.

"It was a good thing to go to him. Mom went with me so I wasn't able to stay with him very long," Mike clarified. "He was staying at a hotel. I don't remember the reason, but it seems like he didn't want to die at home. I recall lying on the bed and praying with him. His body was so frail. He did seem to rally. I think he was strengthened by our presence and our faith," Mike said in explanation to James.

Donald recalled, "I stayed longer, but I was running out of vacation days at work and felt I had to leave, so I did. I didn't get very far up the road before I felt the Holy Spirit was telling me to go back. I obeyed. I went back in spite of feeling pulled to return home. I am glad I did. Chris was pleased. He knew he didn't have long to live and in fact, he died the next morning. I was glad I was with him," Donald shared.

"Well, I am glad I have other older brothers," James offered. "I remember the day I met you, as an adult, Mike. I was in my last year of high school. We met at a city bus depot. I remember sitting on a bench and talking. I was impressed with your demeanor, your character. I remember thinking about what an honest person you were and that you had a good heart. It appeared you were doing well, but there was nothing pretentious about you. We went to your apartment and I stayed the weekend. You were seeing some girl at the time."

"Hmm, yes. Roxie. That story is for another time," Mike chuckled, feeling his face flush.

"Well, you were the brother I wished I had always known and was glad to know then," James said, biting his lip to control his emotion.

Donald reached over and patted Mike on the shoulder. In spite of everything, they were family. God had reunited them on a level that only He could do. They did not grow up in the same homes yet they were all brothers to the core, the three of them and the others.

"I remember the first time I met you, too, Donald. It was after we were all grown. We went to the Drake family reunion in New Haven, Connecticut, with Mother. I was wearing a bracelet my foster grandmother had given me. It was leather and said 'I Love Jesus.' I questioned whether I should wear it because I didn't want my brothers to think I was soft. I wanted to be a minister, yet would I deny Him before men? I remember deciding to wear it, but I wore a long sleeve shirt to hide it. At one point, my sleeve pulled back and you saw the bracelet. You looked me in the eye and smiled. I don't remember exactly what you said, but it was an emotional moment, a bonding moment for us. I know now the soft aren't the ones who stand up for Jesus, but the courageous," James declared.

"That's right, Brother," Donald grinned at James, reaching to give him a high five.

"Through it all you are worthy of praise, Lord," Mike whispered his thought, "we are bonded together through our mutual love of Christ."

The brothers visited about many other things; how some of their siblings were doing, what was ahead for Mike and the children with Felicia's future looking so unsure.

"Life is uncertain for everyone," Donald reflected. "It seems strange to think about Chris and Warrie both dying." At the mention of Warrie's death, James' countenance fell. Warrie dying so young was heartbreaking for all of the Cole family. It was especially painful for James. He knew her best. When the welfare department separated the family, they were sensitive to do it in pairs. James and Warrie had grown up in the same foster home.

To add insult to the injury of her early death—was the way she had died. She was simply attempting to walk across the street. The only explanation the family had of her death was the report of the eyewitnesses.

Warrie had stood on the curb and watched the traffic. The street was busy as people weaved their way between cars and buses that were negotiating for parking places and picking up passengers. She saw her opportunity as a car swung into a parking space near her. How could she have known the driver would immediately change his mind about parking and quickly swing back into the traffic lane? His car knocked her down and then ran over her. People screamed at the sight as the driver realized he had hit someone or something and backed up, crushing her body a second time.

The details became known as local people talking to local people got the details from those involved. The man driving the car was not from the neighborhood. He, in fact, was there because he had picked up a prostitute and was taking her back home. He had offered to stop and buy her something to eat, pulling towards the curb, but when she declined, he jerked back into traffic without caution. Had he taken more time, he probably would have seen someone in front of him, but in his haste, he reacted to his own situation without thought.

It cost a young lady her life. It cost a family a loss that could never be repaid. It cost James his hero. Warrie had called James her cheerleader. When she was gone, James told a family member that he didn't realize how much he relied on Warrie for validation. She was his hero not the other way around. "The slats have been knocked out from under me," he acknowledged. They had a big family, but in many ways, it was just the two of them. He wrote a poem about her that came to him within an hour of learning of her death. He kept it close to him, only sharing it with a special few.

James had wanted to retaliate. He knew who was responsible. He knew where he lived. He knew he came to a poorer part of town to do his dirty work and then returned to his nice neighborhood thinking he left his secret lifestyle behind him. Only this time, he wasn't so incognito. This time he left a blood trail. James thought about all of the things he wanted to say to him. He thought about how he wanted to punch him in the face. He planned his revenge. He would enlist a couple of his brothers to go with him. He planned his revenge, but he stopped himself. He stopped the plans and then he stopped his thoughts. This was not who he was. This was not an action he could take in good conscience. He would not go to the man's home. Nothing he could say or do would bring his beloved sister back. James prayed for grace to forgive. That was his new plan.

They changed the subject to more lighthearted memories. Time passed quickly and soon the morning was gone. "Thanks for coming today," Mike said, rising from his chair as James stood to leave. He shook his brother's hand and then encircled him with a hug. It means more than you'll ever know to have this kind of support.

"We're family," James smiled, returning Mike's hug

CHAPTER 8

Ballet Shoes, A Tambourine And Kanya

FELICIA'S PARENTS HAD COME for another visit, but had gone to the hotel to rest while the kids spent time with their dad. It was good to see them. Good to hug his boys, good to hold Nadia on his knee and hear about all of the things they had been doing. They looked well. Mike knew he did not have to be concerned about their well-being when they were with their grandparents. He was thankful it was summertime so they didn't have to deal with school schedules but he realized that would change soon.

Friends and family had brought small gifts to the children to keep them entertained while they were at the hospital. A friend of Felicia's, Ms. Gwen, gave them playing cards which seemed to be a favorite, as they now sat playing a game of War. Mikey played with his younger brother and sister, but it was mechanical. "I don't want to play anymore," Mikey said discouraged, dropping his cards on the table.

He flipped through the TV stations and stopped on a cartoon. He willed himself not to think about whether his mother would live or die, or whether she would stay in a coma forever, but his days were long and monotonous. He should be enjoying his summer with his friends, riding his bike, going swimming, but instead, he was sad, scared and lonely for his mother's playful ways. He missed his mother. Even though she was just a few doors down the hall, to him, she wasn't really there.

"I'm here, Mike," Joy announced, as she entered the waiting room. Mike was staring at the television, but seemed to be looking beyond it. Mikey was seated beside him watching a cartoon. She took the chair on the other side of her brother, smiling as she watched her younger nephew and niece, playing cards and enjoying some joke between the two of them.

"Hi, Joy. Thanks for coming."

"I'm yours for the whole week. I'm here to do whatever I can to help," Joy stated.

"Just having your company will be great," her older brother confessed. The hours at the hospital were long and lonesome yet Mike didn't want to be anywhere else.

"Mikey, Joy and I are going to Mom's room. Please keep an eye on Avery and Nadia. If you need me, just tell the nurse."

"Okay, Dad," Mikey agreed, not taking his eyes from the television. They had gotten into a routine. He had heard the same instructions many times.

Joy felt compelled to pray for her sister-in-law once again as she stood at her bedside. She laid her hand on Felicia's arm and prayed for healing for her and peace and strength for her brother, as Mike sat in his usual chair, his head bowed.

"Thank you, Joy. Come, sit down," Mike pointed toward a chair near the window, "and tell me what is going on in your life." They visited about her work with the Brooklyn Police Department and that she worked as an officer with the court section. Even though she didn't use specifics regarding names or cases, she often had a humorous story of something that had happened on the job. They talked about her husband and children and what they had been doing. The morning passed quickly and it was soon time for lunch.

"Let's get something to eat," Mike suggested. "There's a good restaurant close by and I know the kids are probably hungry."

"Sounds good to me," Joy agreed.

Mike checked to be sure that everything was okay with Felicia before he left the room. He didn't ever want to leave her in need if even the slightest gesture would make her more comfortable.

They headed for the corner coffee shop where Mike and Donald had already eaten several times. Joy herded Nadia into the girl's restroom, making sure her hands were clean for lunch. Hospitals weren't exactly germ free and Mike sure didn't need the kids to get sick.

Mikey, Avery and Nadia enjoyed their visit with Aunt Joy over lunch. She was always interested in what they thought about things and took every opportunity to give them good information and good advice. She kept it at their level, making it fun. She complimented Mikey. It was obvious he had taken a leadership role with his brother and sister to help his father and make things as easy as possible. Avery, too, displayed a mature attitude not arguing with his big brother and encouraging Nadia to cooperate with whatever they were asked to do. The kids smiled in appreciation. They were very fond of her.

Returning to the hospital, the kids resumed their activities of television and game playing and Mike and Joy went again to Felicia's room.

"I want to be in her room as much as possible," Mike explained. "I don't like for her to be alone. I think it will help her to hear our voices and maybe we will say something that will help rouse her."

"I agree. Keep life stirring around her," Joy confirmed.

Mike settled into his chair and closed his eyes, sleepy from a full stomach. Jerking, he soon realized he had taken a short nap.

"Sorry, I didn't mean to go to sleep," Mike apologized.

"No problem," Joy said, turning away from the window. "I've heard reports that you haven't been sleeping much. That's one reason I'm here—so you will go to the guest room and actually get a full night's rest."

"Thanks, Joy. You know we are all lucky to have each other considering how we were split up and had so little contact over the years. I know I didn't see some of you for nearly twenty years. Some of you didn't even make it to our wedding," Mike lamented.

"I know, I think about that, too, how very fortunate we are," Joy agreed. "I am grateful to God that He preserved our family in spite of all the challenges, all the wrongs, all the pain and separation we have suffered."

"Francis was always there for me, but I even lost contact with him during my college years. I don't recall much about our home life. The memories of a five year old can be vague," Joy shared. I think I have impressions more than actual memories but I do remember some things. I've heard it said that I lived in my own world. I do remember singing to myself. Maybe that was my way of being comforted. I think I've always enjoyed music. It seems I remember Mother playing the piano and the violin."

"Do you remember playing with her tambourine? Mom had a tambourine and she let us play with it. I, also, remember being particularly fascinated with her ballet shoes," Joy said, as a smile appeared on her face from the pleasant thought. "Do you remember those?"

"I remember her shoes, but not the tambourine. I probably wasn't interested in playing with it, but she made much of her ballet slippers," Mike recalled.

"I really haven't ever talked to any of you about that time in our lives before," Joy said with hesitation, not sure how deep he would want to go. She knew other members of the family wanted to leave the past in the past, not rehearsing their painful history.

"I've talked about it some," Mike responded, "but there is a lot in my life that most of you don't know about. Personally, I think it is good to get it out. We might be able to shed a helpful light on each other's perspectives."

"I guess each of us has to deal with our pain in our own way," she replied.

"I think it is a blessing for me that I don't remember much," Joy continued. "I don't have hurtful memories. I do have a vague impression of being uncomfortable around Chris and even Mother. I guess I knew something was off yet I was too young to piece it all together. Nevertheless, I also had a sense of being loved, especially by our father, but Mother too. I remember her praying."

"And I remember being hungry. Am I thinking right about that?" she quizzed her older brother.

"Yes, unfortunately I think we were hungry a lot," Mike said, verifying her memory. "I remember going to the rectory with Dad. The priest would give us vouchers for food at the local grocery store. I remember him charging food there too, so we would have something in the house to eat. I am confident he did everything he could to keep us fed, warm, and with a roof over our heads. It broke his heart when we were taken away from him."

"Yes, I'm sure it did," Joy agreed, and then went on with her own thoughts. "I know one day, I found a jar of peanut butter and ate it straight from the jar. I remember thinking I wonder when we are going to eat again."

"The only other memory I have about that is Mother giving me saltine crackers which I liked and she put syrup on my eggs. Maybe I didn't like them, so she sweetened them to get me to eat, and I remember Father making some kind of dish I ate with my fingers. I don't know why I remember that; maybe I was hungry or if he didn't cook often, it may just have stood out to me," she mused.

"You were so little, you probably ate everything with your fingers," Mike teased. "Father made several things. I know he made pig's feet and rice."

Joy wrinkled her nose at that. "And he made a chicken curry dish," he said, ignoring his sister. "Oh, I bet I know what you are remembering. Kanya."

"Kangya?" she questioned.

"Kanya," he corrected. "It was made with roasted peanuts and sugar. There was something else in it, too, rice, I think. I'm not sure, but Dad would make it for us…and yes, we ate it with our fingers. It was sweet. That's probably why you remember it so well even though you were so little," he laughed.

"Probably so," Joy grinned, pleased to have a happy memory to share with her brother. "It sounds strange. What was it? "

"It was like candy. As I understand it, it was an African recipe. Something Dad ate as a child."

"Well, that makes the memory even more fun," she smiled. Mike nodded in agreement.

"There are pictures in my mind of the day Francis and I went to our new foster home," Joy said, almost in a daze. "I remember the people coming and taking Francis and me away. I know I was crying. I think the best way to say it is that I was confused because I didn't understand what was happening. When we left the house, the people, I guess they were social workers, took us shopping for new clothes. I remember feeling good about that…about getting something new, I mean. When we were taken to the foster home, I recall thinking how nice and clean their house was. I remember we had spaghetti that night for dinner. Spaghetti is still a comfort food for me. I guess it comforted me that night. Maybe I remember those things because they made me feel like everything was going to be all right. I'm sure the fact Francis was there helped. I probably didn't realize it was permanent." Joy reasoned.

"I remember hearing that you and Francis were in a good home, but that's about all I know," Mike interjected.

"Our foster mother was a loving person," Joy explained, "but her husband wasn't very easy to get along with. He drank a lot and that affected his behavior. I know that as I got older, I learned how to deal with him to keep out of trouble. I remember our foster parents arguing, but they didn't fight, not physically. He was a good man, but when he had been drinking, he seemed to stir things up. He would pick at what the kids were or weren't doing and Mom would intervene in an attempt to protect whoever was unfortunate enough to attract his attention on any given day. She was sensitive to our spirits as well as providing for us physically."

"Alcohol causes so much trouble. It really is a curse on society," Mike said, dwelling a moment on the thought. Alcohol had certainly changed his life, possibly forever.

"Yes, it is, but all in all they were good parents," Joy continued, focusing on her foster father rather than realizing the full implication of Mike's statement. "They opened their home to several foster children plus they had two of their own. At least, that is what they told us, but we found out much later that they were adopted as infants. I know you have heard me speak of them. Some of the kids didn't believe they were their children, but I had no reason to doubt it. Mom had their baby pictures. They are twins, Dennis and Diane."

"We all got along with each other. Nevertheless, even though they did a great job creating a safe, happy, family environment for us there was an obvious division between the foster children and their own. It was an unspoken rule to stay in your place. I remember once sitting in my foster father's lap and being told by Mom that he was Diane's dad, not mine. Yet, they weren't ugly about it. After all, I did still have a father of my own. It was just that an invisible line had been drawn. I guess I learned to cope with the situation. I have always been able to focus on the positive things in my life and dismiss the negative. I'm sure that is how I came through."

"You still keep in touch with them don't you?" Mike asked.

"Oh, yes, I consider them family. We are close. I remember when my foster mom was in the hospital and I was concerned if my foster father was being taken care of because he was sickly at the time, too. Francis and I went to his house to check on him. He didn't look good and admitted his medicine was not being given to him properly. Francis took his pulse and he could barely sense it. We decided to take him to the hospital immediately. We were walking him to the car, one of us on each side of him, helping him along. Suddenly, he collapsed to the ground. I ran into the house and called for an ambulance. But, it was too late. He died before the paramedics arrived. There was nothing that could be done. His heart had just stopped."

"That must have been a shock for him to die like that," Mike offered.

"Yes, it was, yet we knew he was very ill," Joy responded.

"I'm just thankful Dennis and Diane are able to take care of their mom since she decided to move to Alabama after Dad died. I wish she was closer so I could do more for her, but it is good to know that they are there."

"You were fortunate to at least have a stable environment. We didn't all fare so well," Mike commented. "But even in the group home I knew I could count on regular meals and clean clothes and a clean bed. I was appreciative of that, knowing it was better than what I had at home and God saw us through it all anyway. I struggled, but I feel good about what I have accomplished with His help," Mike shared. "But I had a lot of trouble in school and that made life harder for me," he admitted.

"When I was young, I didn't do very well in school either," Joy confessed. "I didn't speak clearly and I remember being embarrassed that I had to go to speech therapy."

"You know Father spoke with a strong accent. I don't know if that played a part in some of us not pronouncing our words clearly or not. But, I have wondered about that. I remember mom saying she had trouble understanding him when they first met," Joy advised.

"He did carry an accent, but I think, at least for me, the speech problems stemmed from an emotional basis. There was just too much stress for us to handle as young children," Mike offered as a possible answer for Joy.

Mike's mind wandered off to their early days, too. "I guess one reason we have been able to reconnect is that the welfare people did see to it that there were regularly scheduled visits even though I wasn't there very much," Mike allowed.

"Our foster parents were good to take Francis and me to those meetings. On one visit, Father gave me a microscope. I'm not sure why he singled me out for it. I remember Francis was disappointed he didn't get anything and that made me feel uncomfortable even though I was very pleased with it and I did share it with him. Dad took time to teach me how to use it. I spent a lot of time looking at different objects under the microscope and learned the intricacies of common items that are not obvious to the naked eye. I believe it helped me in art and in other parts of my life. I realized there was more than one way to look at things. I began analyzing things from a different perspective and that knowledge to look deeper developed an introspective view in me that I don't know that I would have otherwise had." Joy imparted this information to her brother with significant emotion, realizing the depth of her statement.

"I'm sure I was happy to see everyone on our family visits, but the thing I remember best is how Monique made me feel. She showed us so much love and kindness—more than anyone else did. She was always so happy to see us. Since she was older, I have no doubt that she missed her younger sisters and brothers. She was a pillar of strength to me. I looked up to her. She was so beautiful. I remember on one visit that she had a new hairdo, an afro. I went home and asked if could have my hair done like that because I wanted to be just like her."

"Another thing that stands out from those visits is that Mother always pushed education. Do you remember that?" Joy asked. "She would tell us we needed to work hard at school and that we should all find a way to go to college."

"Oh, yes," Mike agreed. "I think that was a big reason it was so hard to drop out after my first year of college, even though I knew I had to," he explained. "I tried to go, but it just didn't work out for me," he answered again, with a hint of regret in his voice.

Joy glanced at her brother's expression of pain, understanding that each of them had had different struggles. "When I was in junior high, one teacher seemed to connect with me on a different level. I guess she saw potential in me that others had overlooked or ignored. She encouraged me in my schoolwork. It gave me new hope and I started doing better. I think I wanted to prove to her that she was right about me so I probably tried harder," Joy admitted.

"It doesn't take much to encourage another person, especially children. I see that in my own children. They seem to want to prove that my confidence in them is justified. It's a small investment with a big return," Mike smiled.

"That's it," Joy agreed." I had a similar thing happen in high school. An art teacher saw talent in my work. I know that my projects were just mediocre, but his encouragement moved me forward on that path. I didn't go to art school, but I did study art in college and I don't think I would have done that if he hadn't given me confidence in my ability."

"But I almost didn't go to college either," Joy admitted.

"I didn't know that, why not?" Mike asked with interest.

"Diane was very bright, but was not a success at college and she told me I shouldn't bother to try. I didn't know how I would be able to pay for it anyway. At the time, I had an interest in cosmetology and was considering going to school to learn the trade. She said I should just be a beautician. She insinuated if she couldn't make it, I wouldn't be able to either, implying she was smarter than me." I don't think she was trying to insult me. I think she was trying to be helpful. I took it as a personal challenge though. My first year of college was paid for through a minority grant. I did pretty well and that qualified me for student loans so I put myself through school that way."

"I followed my high school art teacher's advice and enrolled in art classes. I excelled in sculpture. I remember a well-known artist, John Ahern, was particularly complimentary of my work, but he told me I would need to choose. He said that it was difficult to maintain a relationship and be true to your art: art is so demanding on your time. I was young and impressionable and took his words to heart. I knew I wanted a family of my own. I wanted children so I chose a course of study to include education as well as art. I wanted to know I could help support a family financially. I knew I couldn't raise a family as a 'starving artist.' I graduated with a Bachelor of Fine Arts Degree. My first job was teaching art therapy classes at a private school for the multi-handicapped."

"Do you remember when I came to visit you, while you were in college?" Mike asked.

"Yes, now that you mention it, I do remember. We went out dancing and had a good time. It meant a lot to me because I was really alone at that time. My foster father told all of us that when we were eighteen we had to take care of ourselves. I knew

I didn't have any idea how to do that. I went on to college and when Christmas came, I had nowhere to go. I really felt unwanted. I called my foster mom and she told me it was all right to come home. Once you made contact with me, I knew I didn't need to worry about being alone anymore."

"I'm glad you told me all of that. There was a lot I didn't know and I realize that's not your whole story. Maybe you can share more with me later. Now, I better check on the kids," Mike said as he stood up, giving his sister a hug of appreciation.

CHAPTER 9

Together They Were

FELICIA'S PARENTS CAME BACK to the hospital to check on her one more time and to pick up the kids. They talked about Felicia's care, questioning some of the choices that had been made. Even though he knew he could trust his in-laws to take good care of his children, they had not returned that trust in regard to his decisions about taking care of Felicia. Mike sensed tension between them.

They had had their own plans for Felicia's life. They had brought her up well, giving her every opportunity. The Stanley's had worked hard to give their family a good life. Mr. Stanley was a welder by trade, working in West Point, New York at the US Mint. Later, after his retirement, he had taken a job as a custodian at Temple Hill Academy in Newburgh, New York. Mrs. Stanley was a lab technologist, also earning a good income. They had bought a nice place in the suburbs, making their home in the town of Newburgh where they raised their family.

Sadie had groomed Felicia from early childhood, starting her in dance lessons at age four, learning tap, ballet, point and jazz by age 17. She taught her to love music and Felicia began singing at a young age, but she was also a tomboy at heart.

Her paternal grandparents lived on a small farm in North Carolina. Felicia cherished her summertime visits. There she taught her younger brothers, Richard and Brian what a farm was all about. Grandpa Stanley raised corn, tobacco and hogs. He had a tractor but was old school in his preference to use his workhorses. Each day of her visit, Felicia would ask, "Grandpa, can I ride the horse today?" Her favorite one was caramel colored with a blond mane, Mackie. Since he was a workhorse, she didn't run him. Felicia was happy just to saunter around the big barnyard atop the giant mount.

Grandma Annie was a great gardener. She set her summertime table with all the fruits of her labor, rosy red tomatoes, fresh green beans, spicy collard greens and golden sweet corn; canning her produce for the unavoidable winter ahead. What great memories were made on those sunshiny visits for the little city girl.

Mrs. Stanley had great stories to tell about Felicia as a young girl. She was a great organizer, always putting together ball games for her cousins and the neighborhood children, later playing on the town softball team. In high school, she excelled at track earning the nickname, "Fleet." She was selected as a cheerleader at her school, Newburgh Free Academy, donning her blue and gold uniform in style. All the years of dance lessons paid off as she helped choreograph their stunts even teaching her squad dance steps to spice up their routines. Chorus, marching band

and the school orchestra were a big part of Felicia's high school life. She started out on the clarinet, then, one by one learned to play each of the wood wind instruments.

Felicia was also a serious student earning good grades throughout her school years. By the time she was ready for college, Felicia had firm goals in mind. She knew she wanted a career. She wanted to be a teacher. Mike marveled at all Felicia had accomplished; not only was she a teacher, but she was now working on her fourth degree. Plus, she was fluent in two foreign languages, Spanish, and Jamaican Patois (Patwa) and could hold basic conversation in French and Creole. He remembered her telling him, she never cared about making a lot of money, but she was glad she was able to help care for their family. She didn't want the full financial load to be on him. What a good wife she is, he smiled to himself.

How different Felicia's early life had been from his. There came the rub. The Stanley's saw Felicia married to a doctor or lawyer or a successful businessman; someone of consequence; not to him. Sometimes he wondered himself how they had ever ended up together.

The reminiscing Mike had done the last few days had refreshed the visions of his own childhood; the tough times at home when his family was still together. It seemed there was never enough food. Their home lacked peace and joy. Somebody was always fussing and fighting, whether it was his brothers and sisters or Mom and Dad. They just weren't in a good place; not a safe, nurturing place for a child. All the turmoil had taken its toll on them.

Yet, he had done well. He was a good husband, a good father and a good provider. Together they were, despite anyone's objections. He believed it was by divine providence that they were together and together they would stay. This tension was just a thorn in his side. What bothered him most about it was the distraction it created when his focus—everyone's focus—should have been to get Felicia whole again.

"We must get united in our efforts. That is the stand I will take," Mike assured himself. He was walking a tight rope to keep it all together. He couldn't allow his temper to flare, or the anger and hurt he felt to cause him to say something he would regret. Angry words would only complicate his life. It was complicated enough the way it was. He kept his thoughts to himself even though he could have vented to his sister. He knew to leave it in God's hands.

"Bye, Daddy," Avery said, leaning his slim body over to embrace his father. "Grandma says it's time to go."

"Alright, I guess it is getting late," Mike said with regret that he had so little time to be with his children. He stood up to give his son Mikey a strong hug. It was obvious to Mike that Mikey was not handling things very well. He seemed despondent. "Would you like to stay here with me for a couple of days, son?" Mike asked.

"No, Dad. I want to go home, he responded." Mikey didn't want his dad to know it, but he wanted to avoid being in his mother's room. He hated seeing her that way. The less he had to face the situation the better. When he was in her room, he tried not to look at her. He would talk to others, but he just couldn't make himself talk to her as they did. It was just too painful and it didn't make any sense to him. They didn't even know if she could hear or understand what they were saying. It was like his mother was dead and he was the only one who knew it.

"All right, son, you do what you want," agreed Mike.

"I want to stay with you, Daddy," Nadia said, wrapping her arms around his knee and clinging to him.

"Grandma needs your help at her house, honey. You take care of Grandma, and I'll take care of Mommy. Okay?"

"Okay, Daddy. But I want to see Mommy."

"You can see her soon, but not today. Go with Grandma now. I will see you in a little while."

Joy had stayed the week. She had helped with the kids, stayed in Felicia's room at night so Mike would go to the hospitality room to get a full night's sleep and had kept him company. Mike enjoyed her presence. He appreciated her concern for him. "Thanks so much for coming. You have been a gift to me this week, Sis."

"I am glad I was able to come," Joy said. "It's been nice to have so much time to talk and share our history."

Joy and her husband, Ron, sat by the window, watching as Mike massaged Felicia's feet. It was amazing to watch the attentiveness and care he showed to her. He had faced this horrible situation head on, taking responsibility that surpassed anything they'd ever seen. He hadn't just left her care up to the nurses. He helped bathe her, put lotion on her arms and legs to be sure her skin did not dry out, combed her hair and brushed her teeth. He did all the things Felicia would be doing for herself if only she could. He did everything in his power to make his wife more comfortable and attractive.

Mike had told Joy how upset he had been one day when he went to Felicia's room and found someone had put her hair up with little braids and barrettes all over her head just like a little girl. He felt she looked ridiculous. He wanted to get her hair cut to make it easier to care for, but he got resistance from family members. Still it was his decision. He had her hair cut and groomed into a pretty style that Felicia would have approved. He would do what he knew his wife would have wanted done.

They sat in the waiting room for their final visit before Ron drove his wife back to Long Island. Donald popped in just before lunch and suggested a meal at the coffee shop. His unexpected visit was a nice surprise for Joy, as she had not seen him since the day of the memorial service and because of the accident, they had not had any time to visit. The kids were on their way back home with their grandparents and Joy was glad Mike would not be alone when she left.

The four of them settled into a booth at the coffee shop. They discussed the doctor's latest reports on Felicia's prognosis. They had nothing encouraging to say, on the contrary, they had given Mike absolutely no hope that Felicia would ever be functional again. Joy had been present in the room when Mike was first given the doctor's opinion. Amazingly, he did not seem to be moved by this report. It wasn't that he was ignoring or disputing the doctor's words, he just had a sense that God would do something. He refused to believe she was hopeless.

"God is faithful," Mike said with confidence, as their food was served.

CHAPTER 10

Something You Hoped For

OFTEN TIMES, MIKE KNELT beside Felicia's bed to pray. It was not uncommon for a nurse to enter the room to perform a simple task and find him there. Mike would look up and smile—no exchange of words was necessary and he would again bow his head. Mike talked to the Lord continually. He knew the Word. Many scriptures were committed to memory like Psalm 46: 1, "God is our refuge and our strength; A very present help in the time of trouble." (NKJV) Thank You, Father, that You provide help for me in my trouble. Thank You for loving brothers and sisters, and in-laws who have taken our children away from the sadness here and are showing them a good time at Disney-World. What a blessing that is for me to know they are having fun and are able to see Your goodness in the midst of all this trouble. For this, I am truly grateful.

Donald was constantly at Mike's side. It touched Mike each time Donald would appear at the door, but it did not surprise him. He was just moved by Donald's devotion to himself and Felicia. One day while both Donald and his wife, Tamara, were visiting, Mike expressed his gratitude to them. Mike knew the huge amount of time Donald was spending at the hospital was sacrificial for both him and his family, not to mention his job.

"Tamara and I discussed it from the beginning," Donald explained. "She knows my heart. My heart is to be here with you and Felicia. She knows I want to be here to pray and intercede for the two of you."

Tamara nodded her head in agreement, reaching out and patting Mike on the knee. "We love you and Felicia," she almost whispered, touched by her husband's words.

"But, what about your job?" Mike asked, in sudden awareness of just how much time his brother actually had been at the hospital instead of at work. "I've built up a lot of vacation time. Tamara and I agreed this was the best place to spend my earned days off. I want to be here. I want to make a difference. My boss is very supportive. It's my time. They know this is my choice and they are so good to work with me."

Mike found it difficult to speak as Donald said, "You would do the same thing for me if Tamara was the one lying in that bed."

Mike knew that was true. Even though they came from a large family, Mike and Donald had gone through some tough times together in the children's group home when they were separated from the rest of the family. They had only each other to lean on during that time and it had formed a strong bond between them.

"I don't know how I could get through this without all of

you.'" Mike choked out the emotional words. "I just can't give up on her regardless of what the doctors think."

"What? What do they think?" Tamara asked a little guarded, uncertain of what Mike was referring to.

"That Felicia's brain injury is so severe that she won't regain her mental faculties even if she does come out of the coma. They tried to be gentle in telling me, but they think she is going to a vegetable, unable to talk or even think. Not Felicia. Not my girl that is so smart, so able to learn and do everything. It just can't be like that. I refuse to believe it," Mike said, trying to control the quivering of his voice.

"Tamara, will you sing for us?" Donald requested, attempting to change the course of conversation. Tamara rose from her chair and walked to the side of the bed. Laying her hand on Felicia's head, she prayed a brief silent prayer and then began to sing. The song, "He Touched Me", came softly from her lips.

Mike and Donald sat in silence as they listened to the healing message and experienced the joy described in the lyrics knowing that indeed through the touch of the hand of God, Felicia would be made whole. They would have to remain patient. They would have to stay in faith, but they knew their miracle was on the way.

Mike scheduled a quick trip home to check on the house, take care of business, and to visit the guys at work, letting them know how Felicia was doing and to see the kids. It was odd walking back into the house after nearly three weeks of absence. The house was silent, not just quiet but empty; empty of their family, empty of their laughs and good times, empty of the smells from Felicia cooking their favorite meals of baked macaroni and cheese or barbeque ribs, stuffed shells or sweet potato pie. Mike wandered around the house, telling himself he was checking to make sure everything was all right, but really just wanting the comfort of seeing familiar things. He carried a bundle of clothes to the laundry room. Family had brought a few changes of clothing to the hospital for him and he needed to do laundry before he went back to Massachusetts.

He wandered down the hall and leaned against the door of his sons' room taking in the bunk beds, the blankets hurriedly tossed aside, Avery's chess trophies looking dusty on the wall shelf, his soccer ball dropped in the middle of the floor, Mikey's baseball bat leaning against the chest of drawers, his cleats kicked to the side. He took a deep breath. Fighting his emotions, he turned and walked down the long hallway. Pausing at Nadia's bedroom door, he looked into the room he had painted pink and hung with a Noah's Ark border while Felicia was still in the hospital recovering from the Caesarean section of Nadia's birth. Felicia's doctor was leaving the country for an extended trip and Felicia did not want to change doctors. So she had convinced her obstetrician to deliver Nadia on Felicia's birthday, October 26; a special day to celebrate each year for mother and daughter.

Mike looked around his daughter's room at the white bedroom furniture, the huge pile of dolls and stuffed toys, a picture of her best friend taped to the wall. He spotted her Dalmation puppy with the red fireman's hat still lying next to her pillow.

Mike sat down on the edge of Nadia's bed, picked up the stuffed Dalmatian, and turned the favorite toy over in his hands as a troubling thought grabbed his mind. Our little Nadia, how can I raise you without your Mommy's help? How will I raise a daughter alone? He stared at the floor, stewing over the question, but as was his practice when fear tried to creep in, he sought for something pleasant to dwell on. "I remember that beautiful Sunday morning"…he said aloud even though he was the only one in the house.

If only I could turn the clock back, Mike pondered. He thought back to a few Sundays earlier when there had been a special music program at church. Their kids, as well as several others had performed special numbers. Listening to them perform, he realized they were getting pretty good. With a little training, they may be able to sing very well together. Felicia was already working with Avery, giving him voice lessons at home. Music was important to their family, a big part of their lives. If only things could have gone on as they were, he wished. The thoughts of that day took him back to another Sunday morning.

Sundays were special. Mike and Felicia always looked forward to church service knowing God's love for them and trusting Him to speak to them through His Word. One particular Sunday, they were not scheduled to serve at their home church. They had decided to visit somewhere they had never been before and drove around until they spotted a little church that seemed like the right one for that morning.

Mike, Felicia and the boys stepped through the doors of the sanctuary. It was a small congregation, only about thirty people. A visiting prophetess was conducting the services. She looked in their direction as they were searching for a place to sit. Something had captured her attention and immediately she announced, "I am stopping the service. I have to minister to that couple who just walked in."

She instructed the parishioners, "You know where I am at

in the scripture and you know where I am going. I want you to study these scriptures for yourself at home. I must minister to this couple."

She spoke with urgency and with purpose. "Come to the front," she directed. They looked around and saw that all eyes were on them. There was space at the end of a back pew and Mike told Mikey to sit down and wait for them as Felicia sat Avery next to his older brother. They made their way to the front of the church bewildered as to why they had been singled out. They stood before her at the altar. Mike reached for Felicia's hand as the prophetess began speaking over them.

Mike closed his eyes and tried to concentrate on every word. "You are going to have a great ministry," she was saying; "a traveling ministry, evangelistic and powerful. You will have children that will travel around the world with you and they will be ministering to many people, many, many people. There will be much traveling."

Felicia was struck by the intensity of the prophetess' delivery. She had often times been in services where a prophecy was spoken over someone. Perhaps it seemed more powerful when they were talking about your own life she had reasoned.

"You will have a daughter," the prophetess was saying. "The daughter you always wanted. She is coming to you and she, too, will minister." Felicia squeezed Mike's hand. She knew Mike wanted a daughter. She had given him two sons, now they were being told they would have another child, a daughter.

"You are going to have the daughter you always wanted," she reaffirmed. She then prayed over them and dismissed the service. They knew they were late arriving but had hoped to catch at least some of the teaching. Obviously, that is not why we were supposed to be here today, thought Mike quietly.

He found it hard to keep his attention on the people around them as they left the altar and headed for the door to go home. He nodded and spoke with courtesy as people welcomed them, but he was in a hurry to get to the car and think about what had just happened.

At first, Mike and Felicia were quiet with their own thoughts as they drove home. The prophecy had been both overwhelming and confusing. "Were they to have a traveling ministry?" Mike wondered. Yes, they were active in their church, taking part in every opportunity to serve, but they had never thought they were supposed to have their own ministry. Mike smiled to himself about the thought of Felicia being pregnant again and having a baby girl. They already had two children, Michael II and Avery. "Would they really have another child? A baby girl? Yes, that would please him," he was thinking as Felicia's words interrupted his thoughts.

"Mike, what do you think all that means?" asked Felicia searchingly. She too had been deep in thought and yet she was full of questions. "Why would she call us out from all of those people? She says we're going to travel around, going from one place to another. I'm a teacher. How can I travel and keep my job? I want to do what God wants, but how could I teach? And what did she mean that the children would minister? How do children minister? They are just little. And she says we are going to have a little girl! Wow, she really gave us a lot to think about, didn't she?" she laughed. "I wonder when all that is going to happen," she said, sinking back into her own thoughts.

Mike chuckled aloud. Felicia was always thinking on her feet. Analyzing, planning, being sure she was prepared.

"Well," he started. "She doesn't know us at all so if any of that is going to happen, God must have told her. I don't know what it means either. I like what she said about us having a little girl though. You know I want a baby girl."

Felicia smiled her best flirty smile at Mike. "Avery's only two. Do we want to add another baby to our family already? "

"Any time is fine with me," Mike grinned.

The prophecy played in their minds and was raised in their conversations frequently for the next several weeks but as time passed they thought of it less often. Life went on. The boys were keeping them busy, as were their jobs. Mikey was now six years old and they had just had Avery's third birthday party. Felicia was enjoying her teaching job and Mike was doing well at IBM. They had a good life –balancing jobs, the kids and friends, and keeping busy with church activities every week.

"Mike, I am going to make a doctor's appointment. I think it's time to check and see just what is going on with me," Felicia had teased.

"What do you mean? What's going on with you?"

"Well, I hadn't said anything to you because I wasn't sure, but I think I might be pregnant. I didn't want you to be disappointed so I hadn't said anything yet, but it has been over two months so I think I might as well get checked."

"But I thought the doctor said after two caesarean sections you probably couldn't conceive again."

"Yes, he said probably but not absolutely," Felicia quipped, putting her arms around his neck and giving him a quick kiss.

"Now, I need to get Mikey on the bus and Avery to the sitter before I am late for school," she laughed happily.

At work that day, Mike kept catching himself with a big smile on his face as his thoughts returned to the news Felicia had given him that morning. "Can it really be possible?" he asked himself. He hoped they wouldn't have to wait too long to find out. He had pondered what he and Felicia had discussed that morning as they thought back to that very little church and the very huge prophecy over their lives. Felicia had said, "You know Mike, when something significant happens in life, there is an excitement, a stirring, and then things go back to normal. Until I realized I might be pregnant, that prophecy had totally faded from my thoughts. Now I'm back in expectation of what it all meant."

"Good news," Felicia announced as she was fixing dinner that evening. I called the doctor's office and they said they could get me in next week."

"I'm glad. Now that you have told me, I'm like a kid waiting for Christmas."

"We just had Christmas, Daddy," Mikey said, hearing what his dad had said, but not really understanding. They gave each other gleeful smiles.

"What was I thinking?" Mike said, throwing his arm around Mikey's shoulders and leading him away to the family room.

Mike remembered the grin Felicia just couldn't hide when she came in from her doctor's appointment the next week. "Well, what do you want the report to be?" she taunted.

"I want it to be 'Yes!'" he quickly answered.

"Well, yes, it is," Felicia, said happily. "But Mike, we need to talk about something," Felicia continued with caution, knowing her husband would not want to hear her next words. The doctor thinks that perhaps we should abort the baby. He says it is risky for me to carry and try to deliver this baby since I have had two caesarean sections. I don't want to do that, Mike. Do you?"

Mike was stopped. He was so full of joy hearing the confirmation that indeed Felicia was expecting. Now that joy was being robbed from him, as he had to consider the health and welfare of his wife if she had another baby.

"No, that's not right," Mike blurted out. "Did he say you had to have an abortion?" Mike questioned his wife further.

"No, he just cautioned that there were risks and we should consider it carefully," Felicia responded. "But I'm not worried, Mike. I think I'll be all right and I want the baby. We just need to trust God to take care of the baby and me," Felicia concluded, offering a smile of comfort to her husband.

"That's right. We will trust God. I want the baby too. We can't abort our child. Everything will be alright," Mike said, wrapping his arms around his wife. "God is faithful and true. We do not need to be in fear."

"And it is going to be a girl, just like that prophetess said," Mike announced very matter-of-factly.

"We'll have to wait and see about that," Felicia said, secretly hoping he was right. It will be awhile before we know," Felicia reminded him, "so you may as well relax."

He hadn't thought about the prophecy for several months, but with Felicia's announcement, he had hardly been able to think about anything else all week. Even though the prophetess had been so strong in her statements, everything had stayed status quo. They still worked with their church the same as they had. Their ministry hadn't changed. They had the same jobs. The news of Felicia's pregnancy was the first connection to the word spoken over them. "Could this be the beginning?" he wondered silently.

As Felicia prepared dinner, she too daydreamed about their new baby. They loved their boys and doing boy stuff together as a family. For six years, it had been all about snakes and snails and puppy dog tails. It would be fun to have another lady in the house. Fun to shop for lacey little dresses and white patent leather shoes, and pink…I want lots and lots of pink and other pastels too, Felicia thought to herself.

Time passed quickly. Their days were always busy and full until bedtime. Felicia's usually trim figure had yielded to predictable thickening making it obvious there was to be a new member of the Cole family. When Mike and Felicia told their sons that there would be a new baby at their house, they took the news with limited excitement. After all, what did they want with a baby? There were more important things in life to two little boys like playing and watching ball games with Dad.

After a few months of not-so-patient waiting, the doctor did an ultrasound. Felicia came home saying their baby was indeed a girl.

"Wow, the doctor said it was a baby girl? Just like the prophetess said. It was just meant to be," Mike concluded. "I can't wait for her to get here." He smiled the world's biggest grin, giving Felicia a gentle bear hug.

"Well, what shall we name her?" Mike asked with enthusiasm. "No, never mind, I want to name her."

"Oh, no, you don't. I'm going to name her," Felicia chided playfully. Over the next few weeks, they suggested names to each other, but did not come to an agreement.

"You're going to have to keep trying," Mike said one day as Felicia was looking through a book of baby names. "I will know when the right name comes up."

I remember the very first time I heard her name," Mike continued to reminisce. We were at Felicia's parent's house. I was sitting in the family room in the basement by myself. Out of nowhere, a name came to me. It just popped into my head. It wasn't a name I was very familiar with even though I'm sure I'd heard it before. *Nadia*. I remember running upstairs calling, 'Felicia, Felicia, a name came up to me. *Nadia*. I just feel that name in my spirit. *Nadia*.

Felicia had answered, "Yeah that seems like a really nice name. Let me look it up. I want to know what a name means before we choose it."

Felicia fished in her purse and pulled out the little book she had been carrying around, <u>The Best Ever Baby Names and Their Meanings</u>. She turned to the page listing the "N" names for girls and ran her finger down the page until she came to "Nadia."

Mike smiled to himself as he could still remember the look of astonishment on Felicia's face and the wonder that he felt as she read the meaning of Nadia—"something you hoped for."

"It has happened just as the prophetess at that little church had spoken." Mike smiled in confidence, knowing they had found just the right name for their hoped-for daughter. Tears again welled up in his eyes, "I miss my family. What has happened to our lives?"

He let out a deep sigh and shuffled on to his bedroom, dropping down on the bed. The dresser mirror reflected his need for a haircut. "Wow, I don't look so great," Mike thought, as he ran his hand around the back of his neck. "I'll have to find some place to get my haircut. Woman was there any part of my life you didn't touch?" he mused as his mind drew a picture of him straddling a kitchen chair as Felicia cut his hair. A weak smile played at the corners of his mouth as he allowed sweet memories to dance across his mind.

He reached over and picked up the portable telephone lying on the dresser to make a call. No dial tone. He punched a few numbers and listened again. "Oh yeah, I remember, its dead. That's why I had to answer the doctor's call in the kitchen. Guess I better charge it," he said aloud as he nestled it back in its cradle on the nightstand. Mike moved the phone aside and pulled the answering machine towards him. The red light was blinking. He pushed the play button. The tape was full, with messages from family and friends, condolences and offers of help. Mike listened to every message, making notes of things he needed to do, people he needed to contact. At the end of the tape, he heard her voice. "Hi. It's Felicia: happy birthday, Mike." She went on to say "Hi" to the kids and to tell them she loved them. She *had* called on his birthday. She'd called before he got back from the Galleria, but somehow he'd missed it. Mike played the recording several times. It was the first time he heard his wife's voice in what seemed an eternity. She had been faithful to call. "*I knew it*," Mike said to himself. Felicia has never failed me and she never will. He listened again just so he could hear her voice. "My sweet Felicia"...just the sound of her voice renewed his hope and his strength.

CHAPTER 11

Alone In A Room

MIKE KNEELED BESIDE FELICIA'S bed to pray, just as he had done so many times before. The now, so familiar voice of Yolanda Adams sang the words that exactly expressed his thoughts and feelings; indeed his very own circumstances. He had bought a CD player to have in the hospital room, picking out some of Felicia's favorite gospel songs from her CD case. He hoped the sound of the music would help stimulate her mind and wake her up. He listened for what must have been the hundredth time, no, seemed more like the thousandth time to "Open My Heart".

> *Alone in a room, It's just me and you*
> *I feel so lost cause I don't know what to do*
> *Now what if I choose the wrong thing to do*
> *I'm so afraid, afraid of disappointing you.*

His mind wandered as the music lolled him into a brief nap. He opened his eyes, knowing sleep came quickly because he was so exhausted. He knew he was not getting enough rest but he would rest later. For now, he would stay at Felicia's side. Again, he focused on the words of the song.

My hopes and dreams
Are fading fast
I'm all burned out
And I don't think my strength's gonna last
So I'm crying out
Crying out to you
Lord I know that you're the only one
Who is able to pull me through

Felicia was in the room, yet Mike felt all alone, lost. He didn't know what to do except pray and keep on praying. He just kept playing the song repeatedly; singing it to himself, singing it to Felicia, singing it to the Lord.

There were so many decisions to make. They had always made important decisions together as husband and wife, now he was on his own. He had the whole load, and felt so incomplete, so uncertain. They had always talked things through, shared ideas and were comfortable with their decisions as they almost always drew the same conclusions. Now Mike missed the guidance Felicia always offered. He was treading on new ground of making decisions alone. And he was afraid, afraid of making the wrong choices for her as he saw their hopes and dreams fading away from him as day upon day passed with Felicia still in a deep coma. Yet he knew he wasn't really alone. He knew God was with him. "I will never leave you or forsake you," Jesus said. Mike knew it was true.

It was time for another CT scan to check Felicia's progress and be sure there was not another build-up of fluid putting pressure on her brain. The doctor had explained that Felicia had what they call a hygroma, which was a collection of cerebrospinal fluid. He had explained if it grew too large, it could cause problems, especially neurologically. They had to keep it monitored and drained as she healed. Mike again followed the nurse with Felicia on the gurney to the radiology department. As he stepped into the technician's room, ready again to watch the procedure, he was abruptly stopped.

"You can't be in here. You need to go back to the waiting room. The doctor will give you the results later," he was told as the door was pushed closed on him.

"Wow, that was different," Mike thought as he looked down the hall and saw the waiting room sign above the door. He now realized the tech room was off limits, and he'd been given special favor that first night. "Thank you, Lord, for encouragement when I needed it most," he smiled.

Mike had planned another trip home to get the kids enrolled in school. He had to figure out where the best place was for them to stay. They may even need to change schools. IBM had been great to give him so much time off work. He needed to go to the office to give them an update.

Since Felicia was still in a coma, but soon would not need special medical care, the doctors had talked about moving her to a rehab hospital. No one knew how much longer she would remain in a coma or even if she would ever wake up. He would have to decide which facility would be best. At least, he reasoned, he could find some place closer to home to take his precious wife. He felt sad and lost and the doctor's words played as a dull, painful noise in his head: "Your wife will never be the same; she'll never be the same."

"Donald, they are talking about moving Felicia to a rehab hospital soon," Mike announced one day as Donald slid into the chair next to him in the waiting room. "I was thinking I would like to do something to show our appreciation for the amazing care Felicia has received and all the kindness that has been shown to me and our family. I was thinking about having a plaque made; a thank you plaque that would include all of the staff."

"That's a really nice idea, Mike." Together the brothers worked out the wording they wanted, the true expression of their heartfelt gratitude. The plaque was ordered and in just a few days it would be presented and hanging on the hospital wall.

Once the plaque was in hand, Mike and Donald went back to the ICU to thank the staff. They were very pleased with the way the plaque had turned out. They had chosen one with a clock at the top and the words printed under it read:

"Caring Hands Are the Instruments of Loving Hearts"

With Thanks, The Cole Family

The nursing staff graciously received the Cole brothers attempt to express their appreciation and show honor for all of the hard work and loving care afforded to Felicia. The brothers recognized it was only a symbol of thanksgiving, which they could never fully repay.

A couple of weeks later, Mike told Donald he wanted to give a plaque to the respiratory unit also. They ordered the second plaque and excitedly gave it to the staff as soon as it was ready.

"Hi Rosa," Mike greeted the ward secretary as he leaned on the nurses' station counter. Rosa looked up to see Mike and Donald smiling at her.

"We brought something we would like to present to all of you. Everyone has been so kind and attentive to Felicia. Thank you just doesn't seem adequate so we had a wall plaque made," he said, handing her a tissue wrapped package.

The staff that was within earshot heard what was being said and gathered around Rosa as she unwrapped the thank you gift that revealed a polished black engraved plaque with their words of gratitude.

"Gracious are the hearts that love unconditionally,
And lovely are the hands that serve with care.
Thank you for extending your love to Felicia."

The Cole Family

"We hope you will be allowed to hang it on the wall," Donald said with questioning in his voice.

"Oh, sure, that's no problem," one nurse readily assured them, as others responded with "yes, we can," and others nodded their heads in agreement.

"It is so nice when people find a special way to say thank you that tells us they really mean it. So many people come and go, but some people stand out in our minds. Your family will be remembered," Rosa said, expressing her appreciation, "and this will be a nice reminder of your family's faithfulness."

"Thank you," Mike answered with a big smile. He knew that not all the staff had faith that their prayers mattered, but he was sure some did.

One day a doctor stopped Mike and Donald in the hallway. He explained that he had attended Felicia, but was just in the fore shadows of her treatment. He said that he had observed the brothers, how they had ministered to other hurting people all over the hospital even though Felicia was in such a dire situation. "I want you to know," he said, "because of the two of you; this hospital will never be the same." The doctor thanked them, shook their hands and departed.

"Wow, what a great thing to hear," Mike said, wiping the tears away from his eyes.

"I didn't realize people were even aware we were ministering," Donald responded. "It is nice to know we are making a difference. But, it's not us. It's the anointing of the sweet Holy Spirit. That is what that doctor is seeing, what the people are sensing," Donald told his brother.

Mike knew Donald was absolutely right. "To God be the glory. We are just his messengers," he stated humbly.

Several days later, driving home from Massachusetts, Mike thought about all that had happened since that crucial birthday night. He played back in his mind the talk he'd had with his brother. "You know, Donald when the accident happened I knew I had a decision to make. Felicia was such a force in our lives. She was passionate about everything she did. Some people may have referred to her as an over-achiever. But, I know her. I know her heart. She isn't an over-achiever. She's a constant achiever. She has faith in God and she knows whatever she sets her mind to she can accomplish with His help. I knew I could count on Felicia no matter what happened."

"Now the one who I turned to, my helpmate, my sweetheart, my friend was no longer at my side. I questioned myself. Am I there for Felicia no matter what happens? Can she count on me? I had been told by the doctors—first that she probably wouldn't make it, and then if she did make it, they didn't know if she would ever come out of the coma. They were sure she would never be the same. She would be different. I didn't even know what that meant. Different how? Every report I got for weeks was only negative. I knew I could walk away and live my own life; not spend it beside a hospital bed with an unresponsive body. I knew these were selfish thoughts. I knew they were wrong thoughts. It was as if I had to give myself some space, to get some relief. I guess it was just self-preservation, kind of like a flight reaction to relieve the pain, to give my mind a break. I knew it didn't even make sense. I asked myself, do you believe in God or do you not? You know, the Lord's your shepherd or he's not your shepherd, I reminded myself. I knew I had a decision to make. I had children. I had a wife I loved very much. What did I want to do? I knew I had options. I just didn't have answers. But as I thought it through, I came to an understanding and to a conclusion. I knew the God we served and my decision was not to deviate from that. I knew He was able. I knew

He was willing. Because He was able, I was able. Because He was willing, I was willing. I would stand by Felicia no matter what—just like I knew she would stand by me if our places were reversed; if she were the one standing over my unresponsive body with her heart broken."

Mike stood in Felicia's room, waiting for the doctor to come to discharge her from Berkshire Medical Center. The decision had been made and everyone agreed that Helen Hayes Hospital was the best place for her to go for rehabilitation. Her facial wounds were healing well with most of the facial swelling gone. Yet, even though she was still comatose, she no longer needed acute medical care.

Felicia's primary doctor entered the room, shook hands with Mike and announced, "We've done everything we can for your wife. She is stable. Her stats all look good. Now it is just a matter of time, a matter of waiting. She still has some internal swelling, but that will reduce over time.

"The paperwork is all done and transport has been arranged. She'll be going in a couple of hours," the doctor announced as he picked Felicia's chart up from the bed. "Do you have any questions?"

Mike shook his head no.

"Let us know if we can do anything," he said with sincerity, patting Mike on the back as an offer of encouragement.

It was August 16, 2005. It had only been a little over three weeks since the accident, yet it seemed much longer. It seemed a lifetime since he had come home from work, had seen his children seated around the kitchen table, Felicia preparing their evening meal while supervising homework. That was his most common memory of their life together.

He stood over her bed, his mind almost blank. He had gotten in such a routine he hardly knew what to do with himself. I guess I should prepare to leave he thought. Mike began gathering up the few things that were lying around the room, packing them into a black duffel bag that he kept tucked behind a chair. He pushed the play button on the CD player one more time. Softly, the words came back to him that he knew by heart; alone in the room. Now they were moving to a new room in a new hospital. Even though Felicia was still in a coma, he wouldn't lose hope he told himself as he stared at her seemingly lifeless body. Maybe, just maybe, it won't be much longer…then I won't be alone in the room anymore, Mike prayed under his breath.

By late morning, a gurney arrived in the doorway giving Mike the signal it was time to leave. "I will follow you to the hospital in West Haverstraw. If you lose me, I'll find my way. Thanks for taking care of my wife," he added as he reached out and touched Felicia's hand, and tried to offer a friendly smile to the paramedics.

As Mike left the floor, he stopped at the nurse's station to say a final goodbye. Several nurses wished Mike well as they watched the gurney rolling down the hall. Rosa, the ward secretary, who had received the plaque on behalf of the respiratory unit, was among the nurses to see them leave. She, too, expressed her well wishes for Felicia, but in her heart, she questioned if their prayers would be answered. She had witnessed the faithfulness of the family and friends to keep prayers lifted up, yet there appeared to be no improvement, no hope. Her heart broke for them. Would she even live? If she did, would it matter if she were going to stay like this?

With Felicia settled at Helen Hayes Hospital, Mike turned his focus to making different arrangements for the kids. He asked himself the same question he had asked so many times over the last few weeks, what would Felicia do? That was his guide. Where would Felicia want the children to be? Who would she want to care for them? The kids were pre-enrolled in school thanks to Felicia. Avery and Nadia were to attend Clinton Elementary in Poughkeepsie. Felicia was no longer working at Newburgh Free Academy but was now teaching at Poughkeepsie High School. She had enrolled the two younger children in the Poughkeepsie school system so she could drive them to school and they would all be on the same schedule. Mikey was to start the eighth grade at Highland Middle School.

Many people had offered to help with the children. For some it would be too difficult, for others it was just too much to ask. Of course, Felicia's parents were spending a lot of time at the hospital and when they weren't there often times the children were with them. He couldn't ask them to do anymore than they were already doing.

Mike considered all the offers and thought about all of the friends he and Felicia had who would have been glad to help. He just kept coming back to the same question. Who would Felicia want to take care of her children? An idea popped in his head. There was one person who seemed like the perfect fit, someone who Felicia admired, someone who she had described as being just like herself; Julie Falco. Julie, like Felicia could be described as high energy, intelligent, fun loving, a real go-getter, a positive influence on their children. The Falco's had children near their boys' ages. They were friends and played soccer together.

Tony and Julie Falco had opened a community music hall.

Mr. Falco had constructed a large building on their property using aged wood from an old church; with interesting décor, he had created a fun atmosphere. They brought in talent from all over the area, bands, and performers featuring jazz, rock, gospel, classical, and reggae music. They named it *The Falcon* playing on their own name. Felicia's love for music drew her and the family there often. Julie was also a teacher at an elementary school in Poughkeepsie so she and Felicia always had a lot to talk about. Yes, he would ask the Falco's to help care for their children. That would please Felicia. Mike felt good about his decision. The Falco's readily agreed and everything easily fell into place. Julie could pick the kids up from school on the days Mike wasn't able to and care for them until he was available. Her schedule allowed her to make last minute adjustments; that would give Mike the flexibility he needed to keep everything coordinated. It was decided Mikey would continue to go to school at Highland, as he was able to ride the bus and was old enough to look after himself after school. That was a big piece of the puzzle worked out. He knew others would help him too, but the arrangement with the Falco's gave him the extra support he knew he needed and the sense of normalcy his children so badly needed.

Mike was glad to get back to work and to at least some semblance of a normal life. He was so grateful to have a job that permitted him to work from home part of the time. He still went to the hospital every day, but since Felicia was now closer to home, he was able to schedule visits instead of being there twenty-four-seven. Now he would be able to bring the children to visit more regularly.

Avery and Nadia had not been allowed in their mother's hospital room at Berkshire because of their young age, but the rules were different at Helen Hayes. Mike prepared the two younger children for their first visit to see their mom. It had been over a month since they had seen her. As Mike drove to the hospital he said, "Now remember kids what we told you. Mom is still in the coma. It's like she's asleep and can't wake up. She won't be able to talk to you, but you can talk to her and tell her you love her. It's okay to touch her...she won't always be like this. She's resting now so her body can heal. Right, Mikey?" Mike questioned, looking for his oldest son to help put the little ones at ease. Mikey nodded in agreement, trying to believe his dad's last statement—that she wouldn't always be like this.

When they arrived at the hospital room, Avery stood beside his mother's bed and studied her. It was just like his Dad had said; she looks like she's sleeping. Avery didn't say anything. He didn't ask any questions. He was always a quiet natured child. Mike watched as Avery spotted a chair and sat down. He pulled an action figure out of his jacket pocket and played with it, periodically sneaking looks at his mom.

Nadia climbed up on her dad's lap and chattered, asking simple questions, but did not appear to be upset. "Is that Mommy?" she asked. The pain of her question struck deeply into Mike's heart. Nadia was right. Even though Felicia looked better, she still did not look like herself.

Mikey leaned against the wall and stared out the window. He too had nothing to say. Mike knew his sons were disturbed, but he also knew something else. He knew Isaiah 54:17, "No weapon that is formed against thee shall prosper." (KJV) Mike believed it was only a matter of time and his children would have their mother back.

CHAPTER 12

Life Saving Intervention

STILL THERE WAS NO change in Felicia. She just laid there not responding to their voices or other attempts they made to stimulate her. The staff explained that the movements she did make were mostly involuntary muscle movement. However, it seemed she would move her fingers on her left hand. Mike took this as a good sign and studied Felicia's face as she moved her fingers to see if there seemed to be any conscious thought about it. Still the days passed with no progress, no real change, except that suddenly Mike did notice that Felicia had stopped moving her fingers. He questioned the doctor as to why there would be less movement. Mike had learned enough about her condition to know that any increased pressure on her brain would result in further neurologic impairment.

"Can we recheck the pressure to be sure she isn't having a problem?" Mike asked. The doctor's response was that there was no pressure problem; she had just stopped moving her hand.

Mike was not satisfied with this answer and so he questioned the doctor again the following day, still getting only a negligible response. Mike was deeply concerned, but since he had no medical training he didn't feel he had any grounds to push the matter any further.

He sat beside Felicia's bed with his head in his hands wishing there was something he could do. Feeling helpless, he wandered into the hall.

"Hi, Mike. How's it going?" asked Chris, the father of another comatose patient who was heading for his son's room.

"I don't know," Mike responded. "I'm worried. I feel like the doctor's should be doing something more."

"I'm glad I saw you today. I wanted to tell you that I know of a man who prays for people with head injuries. He has prayed for our son. He seems to have a special discernment for head injury patients. I have his name and phone number if you want to call him," Chris offered.

"Yes, I'll call him. I have to do something."

That evening Mike called the number on the scrap of paper Chris had given him. John Carroll answered the phone. Mike explained who he was, that Chris, Matthew's father had referred him. Mike explained that his wife had been in a bad car accident and had a severe head injury and was still in a coma after many weeks.

"I understand you believe in healing. Would you come to Helen Hayes hospital and pray for my wife?" Mike requested.

"I would be happy to," John responded. "That's about a two hour drive. People usually help pay my gas expense. Would that be alright?" John asked.

"Sure, that's fine," Mike agreed. I will be glad to help with your expenses. I am pleased you are willing to come."

The following day, John came to Felicia's room. Mike and John visited briefly, reviewing the facts of the accident. John went to Felicia's bedside. He stood quietly, listening and waiting. He stood behind her, reached out and placed his hands on Felicia's head. He prayed the Lord's Prayer aloud. Carefully, he moved her head; drawing his hands up along her jaw line, then back again to the base of her skull. John prayed silently for Felicia. He prayed to receive wisdom from God. He prayed for discernment and he prayed for healing.

Mike watched. He believed in the power of prayer. He did not understand the movements of John's hands around Felicia's head and along her jaw line, but he chose to trust him because he had no other answers. The doctor's were not satisfying his questions. Felicia seemed to be getting worse instead of better.

Yet, he questioned if he had made the right choice by calling him. He knew Felicia did not agree with some of the teachings of the Catholic Church and John was Catholic; but what harm could it do? Mike judged that John had a good heart simply through his willingness to help. What harm could prayer do? None, Mike concluded. Prayer was what was needed, regardless.

He would trust God to intervene through this man; this man, whom others had trusted with their loved ones. Chris' son Matthew had fallen from a ladder from a height of three stories. He had broken his neck and was now in a coma. Chris, too, believed in the power of prayer and wanted his son back as much as Mike wanted Felicia back.

It seemed John stayed by Felicia's bedside and prayed for a very long time. He kept doing the same thing over and over. Finally, John turned to Mike and said, "I think she is going to be okay. She has a lot of brain activity but she also has a lot of pressure."

"I thought so," Mike interrupted excitedly. He explained to John that Felicia had been moving her fingers, but had stopped. He shared with John that when he had told the doctor about it, he didn't think there was any significance, but Mike knew in his heart there was.

"You have confirmed just what I thought," Mike told John with a big smile. "I'm going to talk to the doctor again. "Thank you, thank you so much," Mike repeated, shaking John's hand.

Mike reached into his back pocket and pulled out his wallet. He took out several bills, offering them to John for his expense and time.

"No thank you, Mike. Usually, I would accept it, but God told me not to take it this time," he smiled. "I am glad God used me to help your wife. Be encouraged. Do talk to the doctor again. Everything is going to be all right."

The next morning, Mike asked at the nurse's station to see the doctor when he came to make his rounds. He waited anxiously for the doctor to arrive, knowing he was going to have to be forceful for Felicia's sake.

"Good morning, Doctor," Mike said courteously as the doctor entered Felicia's room.

"Good morning. The nurse said you wanted to talk me."

"Yes, I do. I just know pressure has developed on Felicia's brain again. I sit here with her everyday and I have seen the change in her. I want you to run another test to check. If you won't do it, I will have to take action. I will contact my attorney. I don't mean to be rude, but I can't just sit here knowing something is wrong and not do anything about it. Check her records. You'll see the doctors at Berkshire were keeping a very close watch on the pressure. Please Doctor."

"Well, I'll see what I can do, but I've seen nothing in her records to indicate a pressure problem. But I'll make some phone calls," he said leaving the room.

Mike was incredulous. They had been there for many days. How could they not know to watch the pressure? His wife was being treated without complete medical records; not treating her was more accurate he realized. It wasn't any wonder the doctor wouldn't pay any attention to him. Mike knew more about Felicia's medical condition than the medical staff did. The doctors had explained if the fluids built up too much, causing too much pressure, it could be fatal. I'll keep quiet for now, Mike thought to himself—for now.

That afternoon Mike got word that Felicia was to be transported to Good Samaritan hospital for a CT scan. Mike was overjoyed. Finally, something was going to be done to help her before it was too late. He praised God for sending John Carroll. He praised God that he had finally gotten the doctor's attention.

Mike climbed into the back of the ambulance for the ride to Good Samaritan hospital. He held Felicia's hand as he talked with the paramedic. He explained the circumstances of the accident causing Felicia's head injury and briefly reviewed some of the things that had happened over the past many weeks.

Arriving at the hospital, once more, Felicia was wheeled to radiology. Another CT scan was done. They returned to her room at Helen Hayes hospital and waited for the results. They weren't long in coming. It was just as Mike had known. Medical science confirmed what Mike had known in his spirit and the

Lord had confirmed through John Carroll. The fluids had built up again and were putting pressure on her brain.

Now they were on their way back to Good Samaritan Hospital. On September 9, 2005, the doctor did a procedure called "burr hole intervention" to drain the fluid and save her life.

After the procedure, the doctor came into the surgical waiting room to give Mike an update. "Everything went well. We have it back under control," the surgeon reported.

Mike stayed that night at Good Samaritan Hospital. He had too much invested to leave Felicia now. He wasn't going to trust her to anyone but God. As he rested in the chair beside Felicia's bed, he kept thinking about what the surgeon had said, "There was so much pressure, the fluid actually squirted out. It didn't just drain out. There was a force behind it."

"Thank you, Lord. Her healing is back on track," Mike smiled, his eyelids getting heavier and heavier.

CHAPTER 13

It Marked Our Lives

FELICIA REMAINED AT GOOD Samaritan Hospital several days and was then readmitted to Helen Hayes Hospital. Once the pressure on her brain was relieved, she started moving her fingers as she had before. This gave Mike great encouragement. His wife really was recovering. He was convinced she would come out of the coma. He stayed by her side as much as possible between work and caring for their children. He was constantly on the run, from home to the hospital, to school, to work, back to school, back to the hospital, to a friend's house to pick up the kids, home for a meal and rest and off again.

One morning, an aide came in to bathe Felicia. She asked Mike if he would like to do it, as he sometimes did. He loved washing his wife's face, smoothing her hair, putting on a little make-up; doing everything he could to make his beautiful wife look as nice as possible. Sometimes Felicia's eyes were open even though it didn't appear that she was actually looking at anything.

This particular morning her eyes were closed. Mike slipped his arm under Felicia's head, lifting her slightly off the pillow, talking to her as he always did. He began washing her face, when suddenly Felicia's eyes popped open and then rolled back in her head. Mike gasped and jumped. "Felicia, Felicia." She just laid there, eyes open with the irises barely visible. "What's happening?" Mike cried out. He started to lay her head back on the pillow so he could run for help when she closed her eyes and then slowly opened and closed them again. Mike checked the pulse in her neck and laid his hand on her chest. "She's still breathing," he announced. "She's okay." he assured himself.

Later, as Mike related this story, he confessed, "I admit it scared me. I thought she had died. I thought I'd had lost her. When I knew she was still breathing, that her heart was still beating, I was quickly at peace again. I just had an inner knowing that she was going to be alright if I didn't give up," he said again, knowing that was what he truly believed even if it didn't look like it sometimes.

There was so much to be grateful for. There were still daily visitors to the hospital to show their support. So many people cared about what happened to Felicia, so many showed love and concern for all of the Cole family. Mike was constantly encouraged by family and friends. One of his friends from work, Mike Kurimshak, came to the hospital and sat with him for two full days. Such loyalty and display of concern was unmatched by anything Mike had witnessed. His heart was full of love and appreciation. Mike understood how sacrificial it was for his friend to be there with him.

He was so thankful for all the help he was receiving, not only from family, but also from the community. Felicia's colleagues had asked what they could do to help and Mike expressed concern about the children getting behind on their school work since they had such disruptive schedules, between frequent hospital visits, being cared for at friend's houses and being almost constantly on the move. "You know how important education is to Felicia. I just can't neglect that. I need to find a way to know that Mikey is keeping his assignments turned in and the little ones are staying up with their class. If there is anything you could do to help in that way, I know it would mean everything to Felicia." This plea did not go unheeded. Several teachers from Poughkeepsie volunteered to tutor the children after school, taking turns, coming to the house and even fixing the evening meal. Often times, one of the kids would show Mike a small gift from one of the teachers, given with love and a word of encouragement.

He also owed a big thank you to a gentleman who worked at the school with Felicia. He was the director of the science department at Poughkeepsie High School. It came to his attention through the grapevine that new flooring was needed in the Cole's kitchen. Pat offered to help Mike replace the flooring. Mike purchased new tiles and together they replaced the worn out floor with a new one.

"Felicia will be pleased," declared Mike. "That was the last thing we needed to do to complete the kitchen redecorating. Then the accident happened and everything stopped," Mike stated, shaking his head at the thought of how life had changed so suddenly.

So many people blessed us in so many ways Mike reflected. There were volunteers at every turn. With Felicia's medical cost rising into figures he could barely relate to, all the expense of travel, extra meals eaten out, so many things to be seen to, it was overwhelming to think about. Again, Mike reminded himself who was at his side and of the scripture, "Keep your lives free from the love of money and be content with what you have, because God has said, never will I leave you; never will I forsake you." (Hebrews 13:5, NIV)

"I am so thankful I know the Word," he sighed as he recited Philippians 4:19 in his head—"But my God shall supply all your need according to His riches in glory by Christ Jesus." (KJV)

"I must stay in faith," Mike preached the Word to himself. "If I look at the situation, I will crumble, but if I keep my eyes on Jesus, I know we will make it through."

Sitting at the hospital, Mike shared with his brother, Donald, the goodness of God in all their circumstances. "I would like to write a letter to the people who have helped us so much, giving so generously of their time. I want them to know how grateful I am, how grateful we are as a family."

"That's a great idea, Mike," Donald responded. "Tell me if there's anything I can do to help you with that."

"I would appreciate your help, Donald. Let's do it today." Mike shared his heart:

"Too often we underestimate the power of a touch, a smile, a kind word, a listening ear, an honest compliment, or the smallest act of caring, all of which have the potential to turn a life around." - Leo Buscaglia

September 10, 2005

To Whom It May Concern:

I personally believe that no one is ever prepared to embrace tragedy, and I am quite sure that tragedy is not foreign to anyone. Yet, I am convinced that no one should have to experience it alone. How do I know? I know because of the difference your love and support has made in the life of my family and me. Without God and the support of those he sends to cushion the impact of our pain, the hard times become unbearable.

It is comforting to know that there are people like you in our world—people that can feel the pain of others and respond with caring hearts; people that know what it means to give unselfishly of themselves for the good of others; and people whose hearts are driven by love and compassion.

On behalf of Felicia, myself, and my family, I would like to thank you for extending your hands to help our family through such difficult times. I know that God's provision has been made available through your thoughtful deeds. You have shown us that caring hands are the instruments of loving hearts, and that the impact of tragedy can be softened by the supportive hearts of people like you.

Sincerely,
Michael A. Cole

Over the next couple of weeks, the doctors decided to start some passive therapies. They exercised Felicia's arms and legs, and her hands. Since she seemed to have no comprehension, the "exercise" was done to her, rather than by her. It was a step-by-step process and Mike could only hope it was making a difference.

One evening Mike looked up as he heard Felicia's hospital room door open. He had closed it earlier, desiring relief from all the activity in the hallway. As Gerard entered the room, Mike stood up and offered his hand, but instead Gerard encircled him with a bear hug.

"Thanks for coming," Mike said, knowing his brother had a busy life of his own.

"I have wanted to come," Gerard admitted. "I'm glad you are closer to home. It will make our visits easier," he said, smiling at his older brother.

They visited for a long time as Mike shared many details about Felicia's progress and all that had happened in the past couple of weeks.

"We have all been through a lot," Gerard stated, "yet we always seem to make it."

Yes," Mike agreed. "Life has definitely had its ups and downs yet God is faithful to keep us."

"It's our turn to take care of you," Gerard stated. "You've always tried to be there for all of us. I remember when you first started working at IBM and you had your own apartment. Mom found out about it when I was just a couple of months away from high school graduation. She sent me to live with you hoping it would keep me off the streets of New York City. You probably did help me stay out of trouble," joked Gerard.

"Right after that I volunteered for the Army National Guard and was sent to Fort Knox, Kentucky for basic training. I'm sure that kept me on track, too," he added, with sarcastic humor. "Actually, that is something I can give Chris credit for. I was always drawn to him when he was in uniform. He wore his uniform respectfully representing America with pride. I wanted to be a paratrooper just like him, but you'll remember that the army doctor said because I had the sickle cell anemia gene, I couldn't do that. It had something to do with the altitude, as I remember it," Gerard finished.

"Yes, I do remember that," Mike acknowledged. "Later, Mom and Monique stayed with me for awhile," Mike recounted, "and I was happy to help out, but I remember it got to be too much. One day I came home and announced, 'I'm moving to the YMCA.' By the time I was ready to move, they had found somewhere else to live. I just needed to get some of the responsibility off my shoulders," Mike said, justifying his decision. "I was still very young myself."

Mike sat contemplating that time in his life. He was forced to be independent, but he had fared pretty well. He had to grow up quickly, but he didn't see that as a negative. "We've had some interesting experiences in our lives," Mike commented.

"Yes, we have," Gerard chuckled." That reminds me of something I was thinking about the other day. I don't really know what brought it to mind, but I wondered if you or Donald would remember," Gerard laughed mischievously.

"What's that?" Mike asked. "I could use a good laugh."

"Do you remember when we were kids and we somehow got the idea to hang out at the neighborhood grocery store and help people carry their groceries to the car. We would stand there and wait for them to get through check out and then offer to push the cart to their car and unload the groceries for them. Of course, we were trying to earn tips and if I remember right, it turned out pretty good for us. We would pool our money together and take food home. Most of our customers were white," Gerard said, as though he was telling the story to someone who didn't already know.

"Sure, I remember that," Mike nodded.

"Well, do you remember the day we got a big scare when Harry, the store manager called us aside? We thought we were in big trouble and he wasn't going to allow us to do it anymore. I remember thinking one of those white folks had complained about us and that it was ruined for us. Here we were, three little black boys, looking up at this giant of a white man. We were shaking from head to toe."

"Oh, yes," Mike grinned, as the corners of his mouth turned up, knowing where Gerard's story was going.

And then, as we were standing there, our heads hanging low, we heard him say, "I want each of you boys to take a grocery cart, and go around the store and put anything in the cart you want," rehearsed Gerard, evoking the old memory.

By then the store was closed and he had locked the doors behind us. "You come and see me when you're finished. I will bag it for you," I remember him saying, continued Gerard.

"Oh boy, did we have a time! We headed straight for the cookies and candy. We had more sweets at our house for the next couple of weeks than we'd had in our whole life. I suppose we had other food in the carts too, but all I remember are all those cookies and bags of candy," Gerard laughed again.

The brothers agreed that good old Harry would always hold

a special place in their hearts. "His generosity to meet an obvious need showed love at its best," Mike declared with a full heart.

"What may have been received as a kind gesture by some truly marked our lives," Gerard agreed.

"And I remember we didn't get punished by Chris again for awhile," Mike recalled. "The mean ogre had been appeased," he snickered, trying hard to remember his older brother with a little humor.

"I know Chris was angry a lot," affirmed Gerard. "It seemed when he came home upset about something he would take it out on us. It seems like he would find a reason to punish us to show his control. Like, he would say, 'Why hasn't this house been cleaned up?' and then he would call us into his room one by one to punish us. But, what you may not know, Mike, is that he would tell me to fake it. He would speak harshly but he would tell me, scream and cry like you are being punished. I don't know why he showed me favor. I remember, too, he would take me along to Kennedy Park with him to play basketball with his friends. I don't remember him being mean to me, but I know he was very mean to you older ones."

"I guess maybe that's why I do have some good feelings from that time in our lives," Gerard mused. "I remember times coming home from school and smelling fresh baked cookies and baked beans on the stove. I don't know if it happened very often; maybe that's why I have a memory of it," he admitted.

Gerard went on sharing other memories, "I know when we visited our grandparents in Rockville Center, we always had a good time. They were very glad to see us and always had sweet treats for us and plenty to eat."

"I also have memories of Mom playing the piano. She liked

to play, 'To Dream the Impossible Dream.' I suppose, in her mind it took her away from her hard situation."

"It seems like there were two sides to Mom, one normal, the other out of control," Mike interjected. "I hated it when she would scream at Mary and Monique. It seems like she would fight with them rather than parent them. There was a lot of anger in both Mom and Chris. Perhaps today, doctors could have helped them more, but back then such problems were secreted away inside the family."

Gerard agreed, "I know it created a painful environment for all of us. It's a wonder we haven't had more problems than we have."

Gerard sighed and then said, "I remember the police started coming to our house for some reason, and it seems like it wasn't long afterwards that our family was split up and Joseph and I were sent to a foster home in Amityville. I guess I was pretty lucky. Right from the start, I adapted to my new home. The first day we walked in, there was a hot meal on the table and I can remember my foster mother saying that there was more if I wanted it. That was something we never heard at home. I guess I just knew I was in a good place, but Joseph didn't do so well, maybe because he was younger. He was very upset by the separation, to the point our foster parents asked for help from social services and they took him for regular sessions to South Oaks Mental Hospital. I remember teasing him when he was admitted there and yelling to him, 'You have to go to the crazy hospital'. I didn't understand him. Not that I didn't miss everyone, but I was comfortable and thought having three meals a day and new clothes was nothing to cry about. Later, I regretted saying those things to him. He wasn't crazy. It just disturbed him that much that we weren't all together. It's amazing that he ended up becoming a doctor. He was able to do so much for all of us including connecting us to our father's family in Africa."

Mike stated, "It was actually Mom's idea to take Dad's ashes back to his homeland. When he died, there wasn't much money for a funeral. I was talking to Mom about what we should do."

"Why don't we have your father cremated? Someday, you could take his ashes back to Africa. I know he would like that," she suggested.

"That sounds like a good solution," Mike agreed. "It would be much less expensive and you're right. Dad would like that."

"It was a couple of years later when Joseph came to me and told me he wanted to go to Africa. He had such a hunger to know more about our African roots and wanted to meet Dad's family. It's amazing that he was able to save enough money from his stipend since he was still in college, to finance an overseas trip. He asked if he could take Dad's ashes with him. I handed the urn over to his safekeeping. He had his heart set on it and he made it happen."

"It was nice to hear how our people in Africa welcomed him into their lives. Remember Dad's cousin Nerissa even gave him an African name," Mike recalled.

"Yeah, that's right. She said he should have the same African name as Dad. If I am remembering right it was 'Oluwah,'" Gerard smiled.

"God is good," Mike pondered the words which their cousin had translated "Oluwah" to mean in the African dialect that was native to their family.

"It's good to know that our father's ashes were buried in his parents' vault, returning him not only to his native country but actually to reunite his remains with his parents. There is comfort in that closure for me," Gerard mused.

"For all of us, I believe," Mike agreed.

"Who was the other man that Joseph found out about?" Mike asked, hoping Gerard would remember.

"Oh, yeah, the Civil War guy," Gerard recalled, "That was on Mom's side. He was James Drake, Sr. of Oxford, Connecticut. I know that because I was talking to Joseph about it recently. We were talking about his passion for genealogy and how he went to Nova Scotia several times searching graveyards for headstones."

"How did he know to look there? Mike asked.

"He said he paid the Black Loyalist Heritage Society to do genealogy searches. I guess he got some information from that. He also talked to some of our elderly relations but I don't who," Gerard said.

"Anyway, I think that's how he found out that James Drake, Sr. served as a soldier in the Civil War and then eventually was able to get great-granddad inducted into the African-American Civil War Memorial. Actually, he dug out a very rich family history. Stephen Croxton Goosley was our great-great grandfather who was born in Nova Scotia."

"That's the funny name I was trying to remember," Mike interrupted.

Well, that's where they found the link. His father was James Goosley, a former African/Mulatto slave from the Williamsburg, Virginia area. It is known that he ran away from his captures' plantation to become a Black Loyalist during the War of 1812, with the promise of freedom when Britain won the war. When the British were defeated, there was an agreement made between the States and the Crown that the Black Loyalist would be allowed to leave the States once their service had ended. That's why they ended up in Canada. He also learned that James and Stephen were both well- known African Methodist

Episcopal preachers in their communities in both Canada and the United States. "

"How can you remember all of that?" Mike laughed.

"Because I'm brilliant!" Gerard chided his brother. "That and as I said, Joseph and I just talked about it."

"Oh, yeah. You're brilliant and you just heard it recently. That's helps," Mike teased.

"So, Stephen Croxton Goosley's daughter Irene was our great grandmother, mother of Irene Moore, our grandmother who married James John Robert Drake, son of James Drake Sr. So, you see, I have brought you full circle," Gerard smiled.

"Yes, I recall most of that now. I am so glad Joseph did all of that. It's going to be important for our children and grandchildren to connect with their roots—African and American," mused Mike.

"Speaking of Dad being from Africa, it reminds me of the story of the visits the welfare department arranged for our family. I remember how Dad would get upset when it was time for the visit to be over." Gerard knew they had rehearsed this scene before, but it was on his mind and he told the story again.

"He was a proud man and was usually very quiet, but I remember once he shouted at the social worker, 'These are my kids. I am from Africa and I leave when I feel like it; I should be allowed to visit my kids,'" Gerard related with emphasis.

"It was hard for Dad. He loved his kids, but he lost control of his family along the way and was never able to get it back," Gerard said, summing it up.

"Yes, I remember you telling me that and now being a father, I can imagine how he must have felt. It would have been both humiliating and frustrating," Mike said, responding to Gerard's recollection.

"I have been thinking about Dad a lot," Mike said. "Do you remember that day you called and said you wanted to go see Monique and asked if I wanted to go with you?"

"Yeah, we went to New Haven, Connecticut. She had been living in an apartment, but in the short time, before we got there, she had moved out and we didn't know where to find her. We talked to her neighbors and one of them told us where she might be. She had moved in with Dad to take care of him. They were in a house that should have been condemned if it wasn't already. When we saw Dad, we knew he wasn't well, but it didn't seem like we could do much for him. It was a very depressing environment. It was so upsetting to see them like that."

"A couple of weeks later, Monique called to tell me that Dad was in the hospital and that we needed to come. He had colon cancer, but he didn't want anyone to know," recalled Gerard. "I wasn't much more than a kid at the time, about eighteen, I think," Gerard said, guessing.

"Yes, it was very upsetting," Mike agreed. "I went back to Connecticut to see him. Mom went with me. I remember being in his hospital room and getting a very strong impression that I needed to get a Bible for him. I looked all over the room, but I couldn't find one. It was a Catholic hospital so l thought there should have been a Bible there. I was so sure I was supposed to get a Bible into his hands that I went in search of a priest. The priest told me there was one in his room, but I assured him there wasn't, so he promised he would take one to Dad before the end of the day."

"When Mom and I were ready to leave that day, I hugged Dad and told him I loved him. He asked Mom for a kiss. He knew he was dying and probably thought he would never see her again. It hurt so bad to see her deny him such a simple request, yet she did. I wanted to stay longer, but Mom said, 'no, she wanted to go home,'" Mike said, swallowing hard to get past the emotion.

"That was the last time we saw him. Within just a couple of weeks more, Monique called to say Dad had died. She comforted me by telling me that he had read the Bible continuously from the time the priest brought it to him until he was no longer able. He read it all the time Monique had said. He didn't want to put it down. I knew that between reading the Bible and talking with the priest that Dad had confessed his belief in Christ as his Savior and that we did not need to be concerned about his eternal home. We will see him again someday," Mike said confidently, turning his head and looking directly at Gerard. "Just like it says in the Bible, that Abraham, Issac and Jacob were gathered to their people, so will we be."

"Where is that?" Gerard asked. "I don't remember."

"In Genesis, you can read about how they died and then were gathered to their people. It will be the same for us," Mike stated again, with confidence.

"It's good to know we can count on that," Gerard nodded his head with a look of peace and thoughtfulness.

"I just remembered something else about that time," Mike said, hesitating at the memory. "When Monique called to say Dad had died, Mom rode back to the hospital with me. I don't remember exactly why, but they took us to the hospital morgue. There was Dad's lifeless body lying on the gurney and what did Mother do but lean over and kiss him! I was shocked and grieved. Why now? I wanted to ask her. Why didn't you do that for him when it would have meant something? Why did she do the kinds of things she did?" Mike asked his brother the rhetorical question.

"I guess we will never know what triggered her off-the-wall behavior. There are plenty of stories about some of the weird things she did that I don't even want to repeat," Mike confided to Gerard. "It's best to let those things go. She did the best she could."

CHAPTER 14

Just Do Something

THEY HAD SUCH BUSY schedules, the days and weeks passed without notice. During one early morning visit, Mike was in the room when the doctor made his rounds.

"Mr. Cole, I'm glad you're here. I need to talk to you. Your wife has been receiving therapy for over two months now and we aren't seeing any progress. I know that isn't what you want to hear, but what I want to recommend is for her to be transferred to a facility that specializes in brain injury rehabilitation. You probably aren't familiar with it, but it's Northwest Center for Special Care in Lake Katrine. It isn't too far. I am hopeful that they can help your wife there."

"If you think they can help her doctor, that's what I want. What do I need to do?"

"Just agree for her to be moved and we'll make all the arrangements."

"Yes, of course," Mike nodded. "I want to do whatever is best for Felicia."

"Good, we'll get things set up," he said, reaching to shake Mike's hand and then departing.

Mike felt like he was on a merry-go-round that wouldn't stop. Here was another change, but that was okay if it would be a good change; if it would help Felicia recover. Mike let everyone know that she was being moved to Lake Katrine. He was glad it was closer to Highland and he would be spending less time on the road.

It was October 23, 2005. They settled Felicia into the new facility, did their evaluation, put together a treatment plan and made ready to bring her back to health. Mike was encouraged. They were specialists in brain traumas. Their approach was different. They would help her. Mike prayed daily for Felicia to wake up. It had been over three months since the accident and she had shown little sign of regaining consciousness.

Every day the therapists worked with her. They exercised her limbs, performed various routines designed to stimulate her body and mind. From Mike's perspective, he saw little progress, but the therapists were noting small changes and felt it was worthwhile to continue the therapies. Felicia was keeping her eyes open more now, even though she didn't seem to focus and gave no response to verbal commands or conversation. She had responded to the therapies enough that she was at least sitting up harnessed into a wheelchair. Even though she sat slumped over and apparently was unaware of her surroundings, at least she was upright for the first time in months. She was free from all the medical paraphernalia except the feeding tube. They had successfully weaned her from the ventilator and she was breathing on her own. The swelling and bruises were gone, only a long scar remained on her forehead. The doctors had explained that coming out of a deep coma was a process that took time. Surely, the process had begun. Surely, this would be over with soon, he thought trying to cheer himself. He would not give up on her. Not now.

How many hours had Mike sat at Felicia's bedside? How many hours had Donald sat beside him? Together they sat, sharing their thoughts, sharing the word of God. It was a time of strengthening, not of despair. One day Mike told Donald, "I have come to understand it is while you are in the middle of the thing; that is when your faith is evident—that is when your faith has to be shown. It's not when it is over with and you can say… oh, she is well. It is while you are going through the process that your faith is important; that is when God can see if you trust Him, while you are in the hard place. This situation has brought trusting God to a whole different level for me." Mike sighed, knowing he had stayed the course.

"Yes," Donald agreed. "It reminds me of Abraham when he went to sacrifice his son, Issac. He knew the God that he served. He knew that God would not let him down. Even though that was a hard task, in his heart he knew that God would prevail. With our physical eyes, it is hard to go through, but with our spiritual eyes, we are confident that our Father will bring us through and He will use this situation to glorify Himself. Felicia's story, your story, your children's story will be a testimony to the world."

One good thing has come out of all of this, Mike thought one day as he was sitting alone in Felicia's room. It has allowed me time to spend with my family, learning more about their lives, current and past. It has given us an opportunity to delve into lengthy stories that could not be shared at normal family gatherings. At least for him, he felt less judgmental about people, especially his siblings, knowing the circumstances that had formed them into the people they were today. He thought about his recent visit from his sister Monique and some of the things she had shared with him.

She had stirred up sympathetic emotions as she told stories from her perspective. He knew that she and Mary had done a lot of the housework and caring for their younger brothers and sisters, but he may not have realized just how much responsibility had actually been put on them as young girls causing them to miss much of their childhood.

"Donald and James and Gerard and I have been talking about a lot of things that happened to us, too," he had told Monique.

"Do you remember how we worked for tips at the neighborhood grocery store?" queried Mike.

"Yes, but my memory about that store isn't quite as honorable," Monique admitted. "I know one time, Mary and I went to the store wearing Mother's coats. We knew we could hide food in the pockets and it wouldn't show. We didn't get caught and I think we only did it once or twice. I know I felt so guilty. I'm sure that's why I remember it to this day," she confessed.

"You were motivated by hunger, I'm sure. Who knows how long it had been since you had eaten when you got that idea?" Mike said lovingly.

"I wish we had better childhood memories," he offered with compassion. "You know we have all had different battles to fight, but we are all winners. Regardless, of our choices we are now in good, safe places by the love and mercy of God. Through it all, even though it was hard, I know God protected us. We could say we were victims, and as children we were, but look how we have risen above it. I am proud of who we are. We all can be," Mike stated with conviction.

Still days passed with no apparent change. Mike was at peace yet eager to have his wife back. "Just do something," he implored her as he sat next to her bed studying her. Her expression remained the same. Her eyes were open yet she seemed to just stare straight ahead. He moved his hand in front of her eyes; there was no reaction. He slouched back in his chair. Maybe she just needs a little more time; yes, that's right, more time, and more therapy.

In Felicia's semi-private room there was another patient; an older lady. "How long did they say she had been here…in a coma? Five years? Ten? It was frightening to think about it. Could that be what happens to Felicia? No, I will not accept that. Felicia has improved. They said this lady had remained the same for years. Felicia has only been this way a short time. I won't give up hope. But, what I will do is pray for this lady. Mike felt sorry for her. She had been there for so long, she no longer had visitors. He was sure it was too hard on the family to continue visits when there appeared to be no hope. But, I have hope and I can pray.

There are so many people praying for Felicia. The least I can do in return is pray for this one who seems to have no one else.

Mike came to Northwest everyday; sometimes two or three times a day. One day as he settled in the chair next to Felicia's bed, movement caught his eye. Felicia had appeared to move her hand. Not just the finger movement like he had seen early on, the finger movement that had stopped when the pressure on her brain increased, and then started again when it was relieved. No, this was different. This seemed to be more intentional. She moved again. This time it was her arm. Mike questioned the nurses.

"Have you noticed Felicia moving her hands and arms?" Mike queried, looking for a good report from the professionals.

"Yes, her activity has increased," the nurse agreed.

"That's a good sign, right?" Mike asked, seeking confirmation but intentionally stifling his hopes.

"As a person starts waking up from a coma, we will see more movement in the limbs. So, yes, it's a good sign," she replied.

In fact, soon the activity increased so much that it became a problem. Felicia was getting bruises from hitting her arms and legs against the side rails of her bed. She still was not responding to commands, but she did seem to be waking from that deep sleep she had been in for so long. They moved her mattress from the bed to the floor. The worst thing that could happen was she would roll off the mattress dropping a few inches. That seemed a small price to pay to avoid the bruising which was now a continuous occurrence. Even though Felicia was not responsive, things were definitely changing. It was speculation, but it appeared she was becoming more aware. There was a new restlessness that was not only physically manifested, but also seemed to be coming from deep within.

One night, Mike was again startled out of sleep by a ringing telephone. He sat up on the edge of the bed and answered the phone. "Mr. Cole, I am sorry to disturb you so late, but we wondered if you could come in. Your wife is so restless. We don't want to medicate her, but she seems disturbed. We thought it might help if you were here with her. Would you mind?"

"No, I don't mind. I'll come," he agreed. Hanging up the phone, he looked at the clock. It was almost one. I will just have to trust that the kids won't need me, he thought. I'm glad we have friends staying with us. Mike had opened their home to friends who were in need of a helping hand. They had been occupying the basement of the house for the past couple of months. He hurried to dress and then went to the boy's room to let them know what was going on.

"I'll be back in the morning before you're awake," he assured them. "Go back to sleep now." The boys sleepily acknowledged what their father had said and seemed to be back to sleep before he had even left the room.

Mike lay down next to his wife on the mattress on the floor. He put his arm around her and moved closer to her. It seemed that there was a slight response from her; a familiarity that would have come from her subconscious. Quickly she relaxed and it seemed she almost snuggled up next to him.

It felt familiar and strange at the same time to be lying next to her. "This is good," Mike said to himself—another step toward "normal".

At the first light of day, Mike awakened and realized where

he was. Felicia seemed to be sleeping peacefully. I had better go home now, he thought or I might oversleep. Mike slipped slowly away from Felicia being sure he did not alert her that he was leaving.

After that first night, it was as if Mike slept with one eye open, waiting, listening for the call for him to come to Northwest and comfort his wife. They called frequently. It did seem that his presence soothed her. He would hold her and talk to her, assuring her everything was going to be all right. He had to believe that himself, to continue to walk out what would have been a total nightmare had he not had the rock to lean on… Jesus, the One he had called on from that first night; the One who is higher than me he considered again with confidence and a smile.

It seemed that each day, she was a little more alert, that her movements were a little more intentional. One day at work a co-worker asked Mike how Felicia was doing. "She seems to finally be waking up. Little by little, she's coming out of it," he was happy to report.

CHAPTER 15

She Squeezed My Hand

MIKE TOOK THE KIDS frequently to visit Felicia. They were more relaxed with the situation now. One day he suggested they sing to their mother. Mike had been playing CD's at Felicia's bedside almost since the beginning. Now he had the idea that it might help if Felicia could hear her own children singing. At first, they were hesitant, feeling awkward about singing somewhere other than church. That was easy for them. They had done it so many times. Much to Mike's satisfaction, they soon became comfortable and thought of more and more songs they could sing to her. Mike was pleased. He just knew it would make a difference. It was good for him too. He sat peacefully beside his wife, as his children's voices ministered the Word of God to them both.

Hearing their singing from the hallways, people started asking if the children could sing for them. At first, there was reluctance. Avery was shy and didn't want to have attention drawn to him nor did he want to talk to strangers. Mikey took Felicia's condition very hard and closed in to protect himself from further hurt. It just wasn't in his perspective to reach out to others. Nadia, still being small and loving to sing didn't resist. She enjoyed the attention and seemed to know it was a good thing to do. With their father's encouragement, they started singing in the waiting room near their mother's room.

One day, a lady asked if they would go to her mother's room and sing to her. Mike agreed, saying they would be happy to if it was all right with the nurse. While she was asking permission, Mikey whispered to his father, "I don't want to sing for anyone but Mom." Avery overheard Mikey. "Me neither," he complained.

Mike encouraged his sons, telling them to watch the people and see how the songs blessed them. "You are singing songs that praise God and encourage the people. You don't want to be selfish boys. If you can do something to help others, God will see to it that other people help your mom." They weren't convinced, but they did cooperate. The more they sang, the more they saw what their father had meant by the reactions of the people.

"They really do want to hear us," Mikey said. As in most everything, the boys warmed to the idea and blessed many people with their God-given talent, not realizing the seed they were planting for their future. But, Mike thought about it. He couldn't help but consider the prophecy about the children ministering. Felicia had asked, "How can they minister? They are just children." Perhaps this is how, Mike reflected.

One day, some teachers from Newburgh Free Academy where Felicia had worked, visited the hospital. They talked about making a CD with songs and messages from the students and words of encouragement from her friends and co-workers. "It might just help," they concluded.

"The children could record some songs on it for their mother too," Mike suggested. "I believe it will help her.

"If anyone has the inner strength needed to fight their way back to health, it's Felicia Cole," one of the teachers stated emphatically.

"And soon she will be able to thank you herself," Mike offered encouragement back to them.

After the teachers left that day, Mike thought about the statement made about Felicia's inner strength. It pleased Mike and buoyed his confidence. "She will get up off this bed," he cried out from deep within his soul.

Entering the room, Donald sat down beside Mike and reached in his pocket withdrawing a small stack of index cards. He handed them to Mike. I had the idea to post healing verses on the wall beside Felicia's bed. Everyone that visits can recite the cards. They will give encouragement to the reader and Felicia will repeatedly hear the healing scriptures straight from the Bible. Mike looked at the first card on the stack. It read Felicia (Fortunate), then the word—Joyful—referencing the scripture John 10:10. Mike smiled. He hadn't remembered that Felicia's name meant fortunate and said so to Donald.

"Indeed, Felicia does seem to have been fortunate in everything she did," Mike agreed, "and I must trust she will be fortunate in the outcome of this trial also."

"Her name also means happy or joyful," Donald said. "That certainly describes the Felicia I know.

Mike looked back to the card in his hand. On the right side of the card, Donald had written a mini-sermon. It encouraged Mike as he read it. It was good to read about the goodness of God and the promises that He makes to His children. He flipped to the next card. He caught his breath as he saw a picture of Felicia taken not long ago. The image bore little resemblance to the woman lying in the bed. Even though her face was healing, there was a strange lack of life which was so obvious in the photograph. Donald had referenced the familiar chapter of Psalm 91… "Because she has set her love upon Me, therefore, I will deliver her."

"These are great, Donald. Thank you so much for doing this. I know every word of God is true and it will be so good to have it before my eyes all the time."

Donald reached in his pocket again and pulled out a small plastic bag of stickpins. "I think we can get away with using these," he said as he rose to pin the cards on the wall.

Mike continued to watch his wife for signs of increased alertness. It seemed when the children were in the room, that she was even more restless. She was keeping her eyes open more now, but she still didn't seem to focus. Even though there were no major breakthroughs, Mike's faith was high. "We've come so far, I just know the road will not end here," he told himself.

He would sit at Felicia's bedside and talk to her as though she understood every word. "Work is going well. I really like what I'm doing. I'm able to keep up with work and be here with you a lot, too. That's really good. IBM has been just great. The kids are doing well. They are spending a lot of time at the Falco's but they miss you, Felicia. We all miss you so much. We love you. We want you home with us."

One morning when Mike was sharing with her, he thought he saw the slightest smile. Yes, there was a difference in her expression. Hope, new hope. He almost giggled with joy.

"I have to go now. I have to go to work, but I will be here this evening," he told her almost bouncing out of the room.

On that evening's visit, Mike continued to speak to his wife, telling her about his day. He took her face in his hands and kissed her briefly. "I love you. I know you are coming back to me," he said confidently.

Over the next few days, it seemed Felicia was continuing to improve. "Is it my imagination, or is she starting to comprehend?" he questioned himself. He continued to get that faint smile from her when he was talking and he wondered if she was actually looking at him.

The doctor's reports were positive in regard to neurologic progress. They recommended that the therapies be continued. She is definitely responding, they advised.

That was all good, but Mike was not fully satisfied with the care Felicia was receiving; or the lack of it seemed more appropriate. Other than the regular therapy sessions, it seemed there wasn't much attention paid to her. Especially at night, they seemed to be short-staffed.

Sometimes, he would be in the room and a nurse would come in and say, "Oh, I didn't know you were here." He wasn't surprised to hear that. Often times, there was no one at the nurse's station. The facility was open to visitors twenty-four hours a day so the families could come and go, as they needed.

He was concerned about the security, especially for people in Felicia's condition who were totally defenseless. People just seemed to come and go as they pleased with no monitoring. Many times Mike would get out of bed and go to the facility just to be sure Felicia was all right.

In spite of these concerns, Felicia was improving and that was enough for now.

"Let's sing to Mom," Avery interjected, as Mikey finished telling his dad about something funny that had happened at school. Nadia and Mikey were standing at the foot of their mother's bed. Mike was sitting in his usual place and Avery was standing on the other side of the bed. He playfully reached for his mother's hand and held it in his.

"Hi, Mom, what do you want to hear today? What about 'Mary, did you know?' Or would you like a little Donnie McClurkin? We know you love 'Walking in Authority.'" On that suggestion, Mikey starting clicking his fingers to set the rhythm he could hear in his head. Nadia quickly joined in. They sang it together at church, so they were quick to perform it. As they finished the first song, Mikey immediately led them into 'Tis so sweet to trust in Jesus.' Avery still had ahold of Felicia's hand. He looked down at his own hand as he thought he felt a sensation on his fingers. He concentrated and watched as he saw his mother's fingers lightly grip his.

"Dad, Mom just squeezed my hand," he yelled.

"What?" Mike answered in disbelief. "Let me see," he said as he took Felicia's hand and held it as Avery had been doing. He felt nothing.

"For sure, she squeezed my hand," Avery said again, looking at his brother and sister, wanting them to believe him.

"Sing again. Keep singing," Mike cajoled his children.

Slowly the children began singing the same tune, "'Tis so sweet to trust in Jesus.'"

Focusing and waiting to feel the squeeze of his hand, Mike looked to his children, "Wow! I think you're right, Avery. I think I felt it too." Her expression did not reveal that possible smile, but it indeed could have been perceived as one of concentration.

Again, Mike felt Felicia squeeze his hand, stronger this time. This time he knew. He knew it was a purposeful squeeze.

"It's a miracle, children. Your mother is trying to tell us she hears you—she just can't talk to you. Yes, we have our miracle… just like we've been believing for," Mike grinned from ear to ear.

Mike and the kids were convinced that Felicia was trying to communicate with them. Yet, there was nothing perceivable to convince the doctors or nursing staff.

Each day Mike saw slight changes in Felicia. She seemed to be looking around. Her eyes were open now unless she was asleep. She didn't respond to voice, but she did seem to be responding to her environment. She was aware when a spoon was put to her lips and she had started taking soft foods by mouth. Even though it seemed very mechanical, she was improving every day. Progress was slow, but Mike stood in faith knowing it really was just a matter of time.

CHAPTER 16

Now I Had No Doubt

MIKE ASKED DONALD, "YOU know when James was here the other day, he mentioned the girl I was seeing at the time he came to stay with me. Did I ever tell you that whole story?" Mike questioned, as he and Donald sat in the waiting room watching for an opportunity to minister a cheering word.

"I don't know that I know the whole story," Donald answered, "but I know you were together for a long time."

"At the time that relationship first began," Mike explained, "I was active in church and evangelism. I was going to a Catholic church. I attended a non-traditional mass and played guitar as part of the worship team," he said with a faraway look in his eye. "I was sold out to God. I thought I wanted to be a monk."

"I think this is going to be a long story," Donald interrupted. "I'm hungry. You can tell me your story while we eat." They headed for the corner coffee shop near the hospital. It had become a regular hang out for the two of them. They often ate the breakfast special—omelets and fruit salad.

After they were settled in their booth and had given their orders, Mike continued. "I've always been sensitive to God, even as a very young child, so becoming a monk seemed like the natural order of things to me. Yet I didn't submit myself to the church and pursue that course. I remember I was twenty-four when Roxie and I met. I was alone and lonely and tired of not having a girlfriend. I told God, if You aren't going to send me a girlfriend, I am going to pick one for myself. I talked to God like that all of the time. It was a habit that developed in me as a child and it was strong in me. I realized later that I had taken my own course instead of waiting for God's plan. I had taken a detour through my own will and way. I started hanging out on campus at the University of Binghamton in search of a relationship. I met someone whom I thought would make a good wife and asked her for a date. That was Roxie. We dated for about six months and then the relationship evolved into a physical one."

"I wasn't comfortable with the circumstances, but I let my need for companionship and my flesh overrule any conviction I had about it. I knew God had told me not to be intimate with anyone until I was married. I reasoned that we were going to get married, but it just wasn't the right time yet. I will make her my wife," I told God.

"I was working at IBM at the time. I had a good job considering I only had a high school education. It hadn't been easy to get that job; not because I couldn't do the work, but because of a health issue, which I didn't even know, I had. After the first interview, I was hired subject to passing the required physical. But I didn't pass. The blood test showed I was anemic. I didn't know exactly what that meant except it was a reason for them not to hire me. I don't know if you know this part either. I had contacted our father because I knew he would understand the medical implications. Dad got me an appointment with a colleague who determined I was anemic due to malnutrition. This news did not come as a surprise to me. It all made sense based on what I knew to be the mainstays of my diet. Fruits and vegetables were not on the list of affordable groceries and even good meat was only an occasional luxury. With help, I changed my diet, started eating better and it wasn't long before I was retested and IBM hired me. I was always grateful to Dad for knowing just what to do. I sure didn't know how to help myself."

"I was working full time and trying to go to classes, but there just wasn't enough study time to pass the college courses; not the way I had to do it. I was not a good speller or reader, but I could sight read. If I had to write an essay, I would search newspapers and magazines for the correct spelling of a word I wanted to use and copy it. It took hours to do my homework. If I got a C on a paper, I was happy. So, I gave up. I dropped out of school. I just didn't think I had any choice. With more rest, I could give my all at work and that seemed like the right thing to do. I was disappointed that I couldn't be an electrical engineer, but I was used to adjusting and this was just one more change. You know how our lives always were."

"When IBM needed to fill temporary positions at the East Fishkill location, I was offered the opportunity. Even though it meant leaving Binghamton, I assured Roxie it would be good because I would be making more money and we could have a big wedding."

Mike went on telling Donald his story. Looking back, Mike could see the move to East Fishkill was part of his destiny unfolding. Soon he made new friends at work. One was a gentleman by the name of Donald Allen, who attended the Seventh Day Adventist Church. Mr. Allen was involved in prison ministry in the area. After becoming better acquainted, and learning of Mike's interest in spiritual matters, he encouraged Mike to become part of their prison ministry team serving at the Downstate Correctional Facility in East Fishkill. Mike teamed up with Don. He helped plan the ministry time, played his guitar and sang as he had at Saturday night mass.

"I remember playing "Seek Ye First", a great teaching song especially for new Christians. It was straight from the Word of God," Mike told Donald with a smile.

Before long, he became friends with Earl McKinley, another co-worker, and started ministering with him at Camp Beacon in Beacon, New York. During this time, he had formed close relationships with several evangelists and prophets in their church circle.

"About a year after I started seeing Roxie, a man of God approached me saying, "The girl you are with is not your wife. She isn't the right one," he had warned. I didn't like what I was hearing and answered, "Yes, she is my wife. I am going to make her my wife. She was the first girl I was intimate with and I am going to marry her. I was so convicted by the man's words I really stewed over the situation. The way I was living wasn't right and I knew it. We had to get married. At the first opportunity, I went to Binghamton and proposed marriage to Roxie, but she turned me down."

She said, "No, I'm not going to get married. I'll get married when I'm done with school."

"We'd had this conversation before and I knew Roxie was resolute. If I wanted to make her my wife, I would have to be willing to wait."

"Okay, when you get done with school, we'll get married," I told her.

"I convinced myself waiting was right even though it would be another couple of years before she would graduate from college. Sometime later, another prophet gave me the same message. The girl you are seeing is not to be your wife. This was hard to accept. I thought I had a deal with God. I thought I could make the relationship right by marrying her. It was the right thing to do and it wasn't difficult because I liked Roxie, even though I wasn't confident that she felt the same way about me. She seemed content to have just a casual relationship without making a commitment. I stayed busy with work and ministry and just left the situation alone. I was living in East Fishkill; she was at school in Binghamton. I didn't need to press it either way.

Things were going well at work. After the temporary assignments were over, IBM offered me a permanent position at the East Fishkill facility that included a pay raise. Since I was already living there and involved in ministry, it was an easy decision to accept the promotion.

Don and I ministered frequently at the prison. I remember so many times before services, I would drop to my knees asking for forgiveness for my impure relationship with Roxie. I didn't feel worthy to preach His word when I wasn't being obedient myself. I would promise God that I wouldn't be intimate with her and then the next time I saw her, I would be weak and give in. It happened over and over. I would return home so disappointed in myself.

This next part may seem like it has nothing to do with Roxie but believe me it does. I became friends with another IBM coworker by the name of Eddie Briggs, who attended the Baptist Church. Even though we grew up in the Catholic Church, when it came to ministry denominations were not important to me. As long as they taught Jesus as Savior, I knew they were in one accord. We even found out that we lived in the same neighborhood. Often times Ed and I would carpool to work. One day driving home, we saw a man hitchhiking. He had a severe limp and dragged his right leg. I asked Ed if it would be okay if we offered him a ride. He readily agreed and I pulled onto the side of the road. Rolling down the window, I asked, "Would you like a ride?" The man grinned and reached for the back door handle.

As he was climbing into the back seat, Ed asked, "What happened to your leg? How come you're limping?"

"I was in a motorcycle accident a few years ago," he answered. "I hate it."

My daughter cries saying, " 'Why do you walk like that, Daddy? No other man walks like that. Why do you walk like that, Daddy?' "

"It makes me feel really bad, man," he sighed.

I asked him, "Where are you going?" He didn't give an exact destination, but said he needed to get farther up the highway.

"Okay, we'll take you as far as we can," I said, handing him a gospel tract, " 'How to be born again.' " It was quiet in the car. I remember checking my rear view mirror. The man appeared to be reading the tract. He looked up and saw me watching him.

"Can God really save me?" he asked.

"Yes," Ed and I answered simultaneously.

"Even if I tried to kill someone?" he asked with hesitation.

We again said, "Yep," nodding our heads and smiling. He continued to ask, what if I did this thing or that thing, giving examples of all kinds of bad things he had done.

Again we said, "Yes, God will forgive you and He will save you."

I asked him, "Would you like to come to my house or Ed's house? It's only a short way from the highway. We'll pray for you for salvation, then for healing. Will that be okay? "

"Yeah, yeah, I'm blessed!" he answered excitedly. "A guy gave me a coat today and some other people gave me money. Now you want to pray for me!

We decided to go to Ed's house. We told the man about God's love for him. We explained that when he believed what Jesus did for him on the cross, taking the punishment for his sins, and if he confessed and repented for his sins, he would be forgiven and saved. When we knew he understood and believed, we began praying for him.

He received gladly and said, "Wow! I feel completely different. I don't know what's going on with me. I just feel different."

"I knew that was the Holy Spirit all over him," Mike confirmed.

"Now I am going to tell you something that will excite you. This man was supernaturally healed. I don't know if you have ever witnessed anything like that first hand, Donald. I can't help but wonder if God allowed me to see it so I would have faith to believe for Felicia's complete recovery. God's word says He never changes, so why do people think He no longer heals? I believe He does.

"Anyway, Ed looked at me and said, 'I want you to pray out loud for this man's healing.'"

"At that time of my life I was very shy about praying aloud, but I forced myself and starting speaking to God and asking Him to heal the man's leg. Almost immediately the man responded saying, 'Oh, my God, my leg! I can feel tingling back and forth. I can feel the circulation!' He didn't know what to think and kept repeating himself."

Ed and I were praising God. We were thrilled that God was working in this man's life. He had definitely felt something happening in his legs.

Ed looked at his watch and hurriedly announced, "I have to leave. I have to pick up my wife from work,"… and he walked out the door.

We followed Ed outside. I said, "Come along with me. I'll take you to my house. It's only two blocks away. I've got a Bible I want to give you."

We had walked about a block when the man said, "I feel like running. I feel like I can run."

I encouraged him, "If you feel like running, run."

He ran a few steps and then said, "Nope, I have too much pain."

I answered, "In due time, God will bless you and God will heal you completely. Just trust God. Let's go to my house."

There were about twenty steps up to my second floor apartment. He climbed the stairs although it was still difficult for him. I offered him a seat and began searching for the Bible. We visited about different things while I was looking. Finally, I gave up. I couldn't find the Bible I wanted.

"I'll tell you what," I said, "Since I can't find the Bible, I would like to take you to the mall and buy you a new one, then I'll take you back to the highway. Will that be okay?"

"No problem. That'll be great," he grinned.

He walked back down the stairs. About half way, he stopped. He stepped down with his right foot. It held him. He stepped again. He stepped again. I watched as this was happening. The man was amazed. Suddenly, he was able to walk properly with his right leg. His right foot was no longer dragging! He was no longer in pain.

"How could this happen? I just can't believe it! I'm so happy," he said, looking at me and almost crying.

I was just as excited as he was. I took off running for Ed's house, hoping that he had returned home so I could tell him what had happened. But when I got there, Ed was still gone. I ran back to my house realizing I had left the man at the bottom of my steps. I had witnessed healings before, but this time I was the one who had prayed so I was even more excited and a little amazed, too.

Hopping into my car, I said, "Let's go to the mall."

He was crying again. "Man, I can't believe it," he said, shaking his head. "I can't believe it. I can walk right. I can really walk right. Just wait until my little girl sees me now! She ain't gonna be ashamed of me anymore."

"Oh, you can believe it," I said laughing. "It's just like the Bible tells us: Just trust God."

We went to the mall bookstore. I bought a newer translation of the New Testament with Psalms and Proverbs. I knew it would be easier for him to read and to carry.

As we were walking through the mall, I began reading Psalm 139, telling him God knows everything about you. No matter where you go, He is always present.

"No, no. I'll take it home and read it," he said, reaching to take the Bible out of my hand. You don't need to read it to me." I wasn't sure what to think, but I handed the man the Bible.

I said, "Okay, you want to take it home and read it. That's fine. In the meantime, I know you must be hungry. Let me get you something to eat."

I ordered a couple of slices of pizza and sodas while he

found a vacant table. We talked just a few minutes as we ate, but he seemed anxious to leave.

"Come on, I'll take you back to the highway," I said, heading for the parking lot.

As we drove, he began to open up, telling me about his family and his life story. Out of the blue, he started talking, but I couldn't understand what he was saying.

I asked him, "What are you saying?" I knew he was speaking in tongues; speaking through the Holy Spirit.

"Romans 12: 1," he responded.

He turned and looked at me and said, "*I beseech you therefore, brethren, by the mercies of God, that you present your bodies a living sacrifice, holy, acceptable to God, which is your reasonable service.*"

I was stunned. I pulled off the road and into a gas station. It was getting dark and I parked under a light. The Bible was lying beside him on the seat. I handed it to him and said, "Find that verse for me." I had to know why he would quote that scripture to me. He couldn't know anything about me, yet he had probed deep into my soul. Was it possible that God was speaking through this total stranger?

"I don't know anything about the Bible," he said. "I went to a Jehovah's Witness church once or twice but that's it. I don't even know what I said."

I was very familiar with the verse being convicted by it countless times. I took the Bible back and turned to Romans. He had quoted scripture without having memorized it. That's why he didn't know what he'd said.

When I told him he had been speaking through the Spirit, he didn't really react because he didn't understand spiritual things. However, I was aware that this was one more time that the Lord was speaking to me about ending my relationship with Roxie. How many times did I need to hear the same thing before I would acknowledge it? I was pretty shook up, but he wasn't anyone I could talk to about it.

"I'll take you back to the highway," I offered. I remember turning on the windshield wipers because it had started to snow.

"Wow, it's too cold for you to hitchhike tonight. I will drive you a ways, and then get you a room in Middletown. That way you'll get farther down the road."

During the drive, the man shared more about his life. He relished the thought of getting a shower, revealing the fact that he had been released from prison not long ago and was now hitchhiking his way home.

I made arrangements for a room at a motel alongside the highway so he could easily thumb a ride the next day. I spoke reassuring words to him, encouraging him to read the Bible, then left, feeling good that I was able to assist the man.

As I was driving home, understanding came to me. I thought God was using me to help this man but in fact, God was using him to help me. Now I had no doubt. I couldn't continue to be with Roxie. I was not able to do what the Lord had asked me to do as my reasonable service…to present my body a living sacrifice, holy and acceptable to Him as long as I was with her. I knew I had things out of order. I thought about the song I had played and sang at the prison from Matthew 6:33, "Seek ye first the kingdom of God and His righteousness and all these things will be added unto you." (KJV). I had been more interested in seeking a girlfriend…a wife, than I was in seeking the Lord. I had been living in disobedience ever since I got into that relationship," Mike said shaking his head.

"I am through with this," I told myself. "This message was too clear to miss."

I went back to Roxie and told her what God had done. I told her, "We've got to get married. We've got to make this right."

She said no; she didn't want to make it right. She just wanted to leave things the way they were. I got weak and gave in again. She wasn't making this easy.

"You're right. I didn't know all of this," Donald said, laying his fork down and reaching for his coffee cup.

"Oh, there's more," Mike muttered through a quick couple of bites. He had been talking so much his food was getting cold.

"There was a special service advertised at a local church and I decided to attend. After the service, a man approached me. His name was Prophet Jonah. He told me, "'You've got to let her go. You are a mighty man of God, but God will not preserve a family for you if you keep this up.'"

There it was again. It seemed each time the message was getting more pointed, a little more blunt. I will do it, I told myself. I'm going to tell her it's over. I purposed it in my heart. I had to follow through.

It was summer break for Roxie. I went to Long Island to see her. I cried all the way there. We had been together for six years. I thought she was going to be my wife. I didn't want to be alone again. I purposed to recite the scripture Proverbs 3:5, "Trust in the Lord with all your heart and lean not on your own understanding; in all your ways submit to Him, and He will make your paths straight." I carried it in my heart to give me courage and strength. I'll be strong this time. I said. I'll take her out to a nice restaurant and tell her there. That way I won't be tempted.

I told Roxie it was over; that we were no longer compatible. She was upset and didn't want to accept the break up even though she still didn't want to get married. I took her home and dropped her at her door. It was done. I wouldn't go in and go backwards again.

I drove back home feeling good about finally being obedient but dreading being lonely again. I remember I was almost home. I had cried all the tears I could. I can still picture the exit for Newburgh. That is where I started feeling stronger. I started talking to God and asking Him to send me a wife. I am committed to You, Lord, and I need a wife who is committed to You, too. I want a wife who will love You with all her heart and all her soul and all her might just like it says in Deuteronomy. And I want our children to be committed to You, too, I added.

"Wait a minute. Felicia is from Newburgh," Donald inserted in amazement.

"Yeah, quite a coincidence, huh?" Mike chortled, grabbing another bite.

"Well, two weeks later Roxie called and wanted to come see me. She drove to my apartment. She said she wanted to talk. We visited for a while but it didn't seem that she had anything in particular she wanted to tell me. I offered to fix us something to eat. While I was in the kitchen, she slipped into my bedroom, but I didn't know that. Everything was quiet for about fifteen minutes. I was busy cooking when Roxie called out for me to come into the other room. I realized she was in my bedroom. I went to the door and saw that she was lying naked on my bed, trying to seduce me."

"No," I said emphatically. "Put your clothes on," and I left the room. It was quiet again, but I could hear her moving around. It sounded like she was opening and closing drawers. Let her, I thought. I'm not going in there. Before long, she came out dressed with her purse on her arm. She was angry and hurt.

I understood how she felt, but I wasn't going to encourage her to stay.

"Goodbye, Roxie. I am sorry, but it really is over," I said, looking her straight in the eye.

She said nothing and headed out the door. When she was gone, I went into my bedroom. I saw there were drawers left open that she had rifled through. She had taken everything she could find that she had given me including pictures. As I straightened up my room, I found a picture of us that she had missed. I tore it up. I was done. I was committed.

"Wow, you are going to have to refresh my memory on how Felicia came into your life now that I have all that background," Donald stated with a look of curiosity.

"We better save that for another day, Brother, or Tamara will be wondering if you are coming home."

"Yeah, you're right. It is getting late. It has been a good day, Mike. Thanks for sharing all of that with me. I certainly see God's hand on your life during that time," Donald acknowledged.

Mike finished his meal and walked Donald to his car. Walking back to the hospital room, Mike drew in a deep breath, smiled and said "Thank you, Lord. I know Your hand is still on us."

CHAPTER 17

Forgiveness Is Best

"I AM SO TIRED of being in the hospital," Mike voiced to the kids one day. "I wish I could just bring Mom home for a few days. She's doing so much better."

"Maybe you can, Dad. Why don't you ask her doctor?" suggested Mikey.

"Yeah, you kids will be out of school next week for Thanksgiving vacation. Maybe we can finally be home as a family. It would be so nice to be together for the holiday."

Mike spoke with the primary care doctor and he agreed that Felicia could go home for a short visit. "This is progress," Mike smiled to himself, "This is definitely progress. Thank You, Lord.

It was Thursday, November 24, 2005, Thanksgiving Day. It had been four months since the accident; a very hard four months.

Mike knew they still had a long way to go, but they were moving ahead and that's what counted.

Everyone was excited that Felicia could leave the hospital. The staff prepared Felicia for her outing. They wheeled her to the emergency exit where Mike parked long enough to get his wife and everything she would need packed into the SUV.

It was a quiet-yet-electrified drive to Newburgh to the home of Felicia's parents. It was not just Thanksgiving Day. It was reunion day. Relatives from both sides of the family were coming together to welcome Felicia home. They were thankful for much. Today was the first "normal" day for their family in months.

Mikey helped his dad lift Felicia into the wheelchair. They weren't sure just how much she understood, but it was good to be together anyway.

They were a spiritual family. They loved God. They especially wanted to show their gratitude to the Lord on this day. It was the family custom, handed down from her father's Caribbean roots, that the oldest male says the blessing. Mr. Stanley spoke with great confidence and great gratitude, thanking God for family and for saving Felicia's life and restoring her health, even to the point that she was able to celebrate the day with them. His voice faltered with emotion, as tears filled his eyes. They were a very thankful family.

They always celebrated Thanksgiving in a big way. The table was filled with the bounty of much hard work on the part of the women of the family. Mrs. Stanley prepared a plate of Felicia's favorites; turkey gravy over white rice and stuffing, seven-cheese macaroni, sweet potato pie and pineapple-coconut cake. They had to be careful what they gave her. Her food had to cut up small and the smoother the better to avoid choking. Felicia seemed to enjoy her first home cooked meal and Mrs. Stanley and Mike took turns sitting with her and feeding her. The family was just glad to have her in their presence.

After a full day of food, football and fellowship, Mike gathered his children and took his wife home. A strange feeling came over him. It seemed as surreal to be going home with Felicia as it had felt the night he got the call to come to the hospital. At least this surreal feeling brought positive thoughts rather than fear. Mike sensed that Felicia had enjoyed her day. He recognized that things were still very cloudy for her and it seemed she was more coherent sometimes than other times; almost slipping back into the trance temporarily and then more alert again. The doctor's had told him to expect it, so he wasn't concerned. This was normal, and he knew she would be all right.

They tucked Felicia in bed. Nadia and Avery crawled up on the bed, poking pillows behind their mother, under her arms and legs, doing everything they could think of to make her comfortable. Mikey sat on the edge of the bed, trying to keep order in his younger brother and sister's rowdy attempt to care for their mom. The children giggled with excitement. Mike watched from the door. A feeling of sweet gratitude came over him. It was so good to see Felicia in their home instead of in a hospital bed; so good to see his children happily playing with their mother just like they used to do. If he closed his eyes, he could believe it had never happened; for just a minute, he pretended.

Mike opened a large bag and turning it upside down, dumped more than a dozen little plastic medicine bottles on the bed.

Some were brown, some were clear, all had long words that were nearly impossible to pronounce. "Take two at bedtime"—"take one with meals", the instructions read. He picked up the list of medications the staff had written up for him to dispense. He slowly figured out which pills to give her and helped her with a glass of water. Swallowing the pills was still a challenge; sometimes causing coughing and choking but Mike had watched dozens upon dozens of times as nurses administered the meds so he easily mimicked their actions and the pills were swallowed without incident.

"I'll be back in a minute," Mike assured Felicia. "I need to see if the kids are in bed. It really doesn't sound like it," he laughed happily.

When he returned from the kids rooms, he found Felicia sleeping with one leg hanging off the side of the bed. Even though they had moved to her to center, she must have rolled or perhaps she was trying to get up, Mike thought.

"This isn't going to work," he said to himself. He moved Felicia, sitting her back in her chair so he could make a sleeping space on the floor. Scooting things around, Mike garnered enough room to squeeze the mattress, which he pulled off their bed, between the bulky furnishings. He made their bed on the floor and then got Felicia resettled. During the night, Mike realized he had forgotten to see to her personal needs. Lovingly, Mike cared for his wife as he would a baby. Settling back into bed for more rest, Mike had to face the reality that she still required too much care for him to handle alone. They had a two day pass. He hated the thought of taking her back to Northwest, but he knew he must.

❦

Over the next couple of weeks, Mike saw good changes in Felicia. "She is definitely more alert. She seems to be more aware of what is going on around her. She still has times when she slips back into what seems like a semi-conscious state, but it is just for short periods and is becoming more and more infrequent," Mike had explained to a friend who had not asked about Felicia for a while.

Thoughts were stirring in Mike's spirit. He kept thinking about something that had been said at Helen Hayes Hospital. "When your wife is better, you are welcome to bring her back here for more therapy. When she is more alert and responsive, we will be able to help her."

Maybe it's time, he thought, rolling over in bed. It seemed there was always so much to think about. Before the accident, Felicia had handled so many details of their lives. He was aware of it at the time. It's not that he took it for granted. Now, doing life one handed, he was even more appreciative of the difference she made. Should I move her back to Helen Hayes? It adds more than thirty minutes to my trip to see her. I always feel like I should be somewhere else, than where I am; taking care of something other than what I'm doing. What am I saying? That can't weigh in my decision. I will do whatever it takes to help Felicia get well. I will talk to the doctor about it tomorrow, he resolved, rolling over to a more comfortable position; satisfied, he was soon asleep.

This shouldn't be so difficult, Mike thought to himself. I should be able to take Felicia where ever I want for care. But, it didn't seem to be working out that way. He supposed it was a money issue. The hospitals have to have the beds occupied in order to have funds to operate. He had never thought about it being a competitive business, but he could now see that to a point, it was. When he had first asked about moving Felicia back to Helen Hayes, there was an apparent attempt to dissuade him. Then, when he pressed, procrastination was the tactic.

"What is it going to take to get Felicia moved back to Helen Hayes?" Mike asked, leaning on the counter at the nurse's station late one afternoon.

"Talk to the doctor about it tomorrow," the nurse suggested, showing little interest.

That does it, Mike resolved, walking back to Felicia's room. The next morning, Mike was at the hospital early to ensure he did not miss the doctor.

"I want my wife moved back to Helen Hayes, Doctor. I appreciate what the staff here has done for her, but now she needs to go back there for more therapy. That is what they suggested and that's what I want," he voiced, with what he thought sounded like false authority.

"Okay, that's what we'll do then," the doctor responded. "I'll make the arrangements to have her transferred back." With that, the doctor left the room. Mike was perplexed. When I asked nicely and expected cooperation, I was resisted. Did I really have to get tough to get action? I hate that. Oh, well, it is done, that's what matters I guess, he thought shaking his head.

On December 15, 2005, Felicia was readmitted to Helen Hayes Hospital. Now almost everything in her day revolved around therapy. The doctors were pleased with her progress, but were cautious as to the outcome since she was still not responding to voice commands. It was still unclear if there might be some cognitive damage or if the lack of response was still just a temporary condition.

Visit after visit, family and friends continued coming to Felicia's bedside. They talked to her, encouraged her, and told her they loved her. Mike was thankful to have so much loving support. He was also thankful to God that he continually got little signs of progress. The doctors were still willing to work with her, continuing the therapy disciplines.

The family had been fully focused on Felicia's care and recovery. Little thought had been given to the legal side of the matter, even though Mike had hired an attorney, as did the others who were involved in the accident. He knew the wheels of justice turned very slowly and so chose to leave it all in the attorney's hands. After much time had passed, a letter arrived advising that a court date had been set for their case. Mike planned to attend the hearing and asked Donald if he wanted to go with him.

Emotions ran high as the brother's anticipated what would happen, now that they knew the time for justice had arrived. On the day of court, Mike and Donald slid quietly into the courtroom and seated themselves on the left hand benches. They looked around the courtroom wondering who it was that had caused the accident that fateful night. It was not apparent who the offender was, except they knew it was a young man.

Donald spotted someone who fit the description he had in his head. The young man looked sad and very nervous. There were many cases on the docket that day; simple driving tickets, financial and domestic issues, and even some corporate matters. Finally, their case was announced. The young man Donald had pointed out to Mike, stood with his attorney. The attorney spoke on his client's behalf and asked the judge for a continuance based on extenuating circumstances. The judge granted the continuance and it was over.

What had been anticipated with a mixture of vengeful thoughts and erratic emotions; wanting justice yet feeling sad for the accused, uncertainty about just what they did want to happen, knowing punishment was in order, yet, also knowing it would change nothing, was now anti-climatic. It was back to waiting.

As they walked out of the courthouse, Mike felt a little let down on one hand, yet relieved on the other. "It is what it is," Mike told Donald. "I choose to forgive him, so however the court system decides to punish him doesn't really concern me. I don't want it to ruin his life, but I do pray he changes so he won't cause harm to anyone else."

"Forgiveness is best," Donald agreed, "but he does have to pay the consequences for his actions. There will be another day in court. His attorney can't put this off forever."

Spring was approaching. One day Mike wandered into Felicia's room as a matter of course. He sat down in the chair and spoke to Felicia as though she would respond, as was his habit. Suddenly a nurse rushed through the door and excitedly said, "Have you been told what happened?"

"No, what happened?" he asked, thinking he had missed some big news event. With a really big smile, the nurse began to tell him that without apparent stimulus, Felicia had spoken a few words that morning. "I couldn't understand what she was trying to say," she explained, "but it seemed like she was trying to tell me something. I tried to make out the words but couldn't figure them out; then I realized she wasn't speaking English!" She went on to explain that she went for help, asking other nurses to come to Felicia's room. "I was so excited," she said, "I told them, come quick, Felicia is talking. No, get someone who speaks Spanish. I think she is speaking Spanish."

"I know who will understand her," one of the nurses said, hurrying down the hall to ask her friend to come to Felicia's room.

She went on to explain to Mike that the Spanish-speaking nurse came immediately to her room. "She slowly approached the bedside and placing her hand on Felicia's arm, gently asked, '¿Qué te pasa? (What's the matter?) ¿Como te sientes? (How do you feel?)'" The nurse related every detail.

"Felicia answered 'Tengo dolores. Tengo dolores en mi cabeza.' (I have pain. I have pain in my head)." The words were slurred and slow coming, but the interpreter was able to piece together the syllables until she finally got the message. Then she smiled, "She says she has pain in her head." Several nurses had gathered around Felicia's bedside as word spread around the nurses' station and down the hall. There was great excitement as several among them had cared for Felicia on her first stay at Helen Hayes, and they realized how remarkable it was to hear her communicating. They knew how far she had come. They knew they were witnessing a miracle. Few of them had really expected Felicia to recover.

Mike laughed in relief. "Wow, that's great! I just knew she would be alright," Mike beamed. "And she spoke her first words in Spanish," he chuckled, almost to himself, knowing Felicia loved speaking the Latin language. He felt like dancing around the room. He felt like falling to his knees. "Thank you, Jesus," Mike almost shouted his relief, as suddenly he was so overwhelmed with gladness. It seemed almost impossible to express himself.

He sat beside her bed anticipating her next words. He listened throughout his visit for Felicia to say something more. He spoke with her hoping for a response, but none came. He was not disappointed. He was encouraged and peaceful. Thank you, Lord. It seems every time I get weary, you give me encouragement. He was confident Felicia had tried to communicate with them when she squeezed their hands, now he was even more assured that she was recovering. She had spoken a clear message to the nurses. Although it appeared to be an isolated incident for now, she was able to think, able to express herself. It may be a long road, Mike thought to himself, but with God on our side, we have a sure destination.

"Your mom is coming out of the coma," Mike reported to the kids and friends that were staying at their house. "She talked to the nurses today,"

"What did she say?" Mikey asked.

"She said she had pain in her head."

Mikey was disappointed in the response. He was hoping for something different. He didn't know what he wanted to hear; but not something that still showed trouble.

"I guess that makes sense," Avery said.

"Yes, it is a good sign. She was able to tell them what she needed. That is a huge step, kids. They gave her something for pain. It is a very good sign!" stated their father.

It was a time for celebration. Everyone had worked long and hard to bring Felicia back to health. Hers was now a success story. Even though she had a lengthy road ahead of her, this very real message came from an intact mind. The handwriting was on the wall: Felicia was back!

"Listen kids, the nurses would like for you to give them a little mini-concert. Would you do that? Just consider it a thank you for all the good care they are giving Mom."

"Shonya and Tatyana, you could sing with the kids too. Would you like to do that?"

"Yes, that is our thank you for welcoming us into your home," their parents added appreciatively.

Everyone agreed it would be fun. All the kids started talking about which songs they would sing. They had to choose songs their friends knew too. Mike left it to the kids to put their program together, hoping Mikey would take the lead. He did not want to push the children. If they were to have a ministry, it needed to come from within themselves.

The next visit was great fun for the kids and the staff. They sang a number of songs. Felicia had taught praise dancing at church with both adults and children. The kids knew the dance steps and performed them in the hallway much to the delight of their audience. Several patients were brought out of their rooms so they could enjoy the little show too. Mike stood off to the side, glad to see the joy they were bringing to the people, breaking the monotony of their day and taking their minds off their own problems for even a little while. This is what it is all about he smiled to himself.

CHAPTER 18

And You Need Closure

DAILY THERAPY CONTINUED. MIKE'S hopes were high. He sustained the hectic schedule, energized by the signs of progress. One Saturday Donald popped his head in the door of Felicia's room. "I have all afternoon, Mike. Today is the day for you to tell me about the courtship of Miss Felicia. I know most of that story, but it will be fun to hear it again and just maybe, Felicia will have something to say about it too," Donald laughed, thinking what a welcome interruption that would be.

The brothers took their seats and faced each other, sitting close to Felicia's bedside. "I'm not sure where to start," Mike stated. "You know we first met at IBM, but I guess it kind of started the day I was looking for someone to be a guest singer for the prison ministry at Beacon. I was searching for just the right person. I was talking to an IBM co-worker, Felicia's Aunt Mary.

"I know who could sing for you," she said, "my niece, Felicia Stanley. I'll give you her number. Give her a call and ask her."

"I had not seen Felicia for quite a long time. After she left IBM, a mutual friend had mentioned that she was working at a New York City hospital emergency room translating for Hispanic patients. That was the last I knew of her."

"I immediately called her. I already knew enough about Felicia to know she would do a great job for us. I was very pleased when she agreed to come to the prison and sing. She was such a nice girl and I knew she loved the Lord. I thought it would be fun to see her again."

Mike went on to tell Donald that he made arrangements to meet Felicia at the prison. He had escorted her into the room where they ministered and soon the services began. When it was time for the special music, Felicia sang, "His Eye is on the Sparrow" and "Faith That Conquers". "The inmates loved her. They gave her a standing ovation," Mike bragged.

Before Felicia left the prison, I told her I would like to see her as a friend, but that I needed to spend time with Prophet Motley who had also ministered at the prison that day. We spoke briefly about the prophet, Felicia acknowledging her mutual respect for him. She agreed to meet me sometime and gave me her address. She was still living at her parents' home and taking a train everyday to her job at the Mount Sinai Hospital.

I spent the next couple of hours with the prophet. What I heard was a shock, but a pleasant surprise to me. The prophet told me Felicia was to be my wife. I was in denial, and told the prophet, "No, that couldn't be." But, on the inside, I was yelling "Yes!"

When I had shared with a mutual acquaintance that Felicia was going to sing for me at the prison, the man warned me against her, saying she was crazy because she was so into God. To that man, Felicia was crazy but his words excited me all the more. I knew Felicia had been raised to be godly and I had prayed for that kind of wife.

Driving home that afternoon, I told God, "I am not going to tell Felicia what the prophet said. I know how you have dealt with me in the past. You have sent people in my path to confirm things for me and I am asking you to do that again."

Even though I had prayed for confirmation, I was too excited to wait patiently. That evening I drove to Felicia's home. When I arrived, Felicia was visiting with another man who obviously liked her. As I watched Felicia, it seemed light actually radiated from her. She is so beautiful I said to myself, inside and out.

After the other man left, I had my chance. After a brief visit, I asked Felicia if she liked to play racquetball. Felicia had always been athletic. She said it sounded like fun and readily agreed to meet me at the gym at 5 o'clock on the following Friday evening.

I was excited to meet with Felicia, but I still wanted to hear from God. I fasted, taking water only, from Saturday through Friday. I listened for a messenger from God. I didn't want to second guess God this time. My mistake with Roxie had been a hard lesson. I didn't want a repeat performance. I waited all week, but no one came.

Finally, it was Friday. I was disappointed that I did not get a confirmation, but knowing Felicia was a great person to have as a friend, I decided there was no harm in playing a game of racquetball.

After an hour and a half of game time, we went to the break room for a rest. As we sat at the table talking, Felicia seemed restless. She would start to say something then stop herself and make small talk. Finally, she said, "I need to tell you something. You'll think I'm crazy but I have things I need to tell you." She started by telling me her educational background, how her job was going, about different relationships she had been in.

"I could have gotten engaged many times," she confided, "but it just didn't seem right. I want a committed Christian husband. Those guys would go to church with me, but they weren't committed

to God. I have to tell you, I have not been able to sleep all week. Every night I have tossed and turned knowing God was talking to me."

I laughed to myself. Sounds like me, but at the same time, I thought it was a weird conversation. "Why is she telling me all of this?" I wondered. "Where is she going with this?"

Then I heard Felicia saying," Well, I'm not crazy, but the Holy Spirit has been telling me you will be my husband."

I know I had tears in my eyes, as I told Felicia what the prophet had said to me. I told her I had fasted all week waiting for confirmation but no one had come. Now I see that God is actually using you to give me the confirmation I had asked for, I told her. We both knew without a doubt that God had brought us together. I had my confirmation, but I knew I shouldn't propose too quickly.

However, I didn't abide by that wisdom very long. I just could not contain myself. After only two weeks, I went to Felicia's father and asked for her hand in marriage. Her father gave his blessing without hesitation. Even though, I was not well acquainted with the family, Mr. Stanley said he felt like I was a good man and Felicia seemed happy with me.

Mrs. Stanley did not see it the same way. She said, "We don't know you. Felicia doesn't know you. You need to give it some time. You don't need to be in a hurry. Besides if you wait, you can have a very nice wedding."

I could understand why Felicia's mother questioned the

match. I was quite a lot older than Felicia. I didn't fit the mold she had pictured as a husband for her daughter. She will come around I told myself. I would just need to be patient.

Felicia agreed with her parents not to rush into anything but she wanted to get married. Still, she did not want to go against her family's wishes and so we waited.

During that time, I would meet Felicia at the Beacon train station. I would take her gifts of roses and other nice small gifts. I always tried to surprise her with something. Sometimes, we would go to dinner. We had a nice courtship. It was a long one, but we enjoyed each other so much it was a special time.

Later, Felicia confided that she was attracted to me when we first met at IBM. She even had the thought that she would marry me but she never told anyone. She didn't want to do anything to encourage me because she didn't want me to think she was running after me. "God sure has His way of working it all out," Mike smiled, patting Felicia's leg as he reached for her from his chair at the foot of her bed.

"You may not know this either," Mike continued, "I don't exactly brag about it but one day, at my office, a co-worker was saying she was divorcing her husband due to suspected infidelity. She pulled her wedding ring off and asked if anyone wanted it. "Do you need a ring?" she asked me.

"Well, yes, I am going to buy an engagement ring soon," I admitted.

"You can have this one. Use it to buy a nice ring," she said, pressing the rejected symbol of matrimony into my hand.

I stood there looking at the ring. It was a nice stone and obviously had value. "Thanks," I said, "I will."

Sometime in the next few days, I took the ring to a jeweler and had it appraised. I had waited long enough. I had decided I was going to make our engagement official. Even though I had already proposed, I hadn't bought a ring yet. I was still waiting for her family's blessing. At that point, I wasn't sure I was going to get it, but I knew that eventually Felicia and I would be married.

I knew it was time. I sold the lady's ring to the jeweler for cash and used it to help pay for a very nice diamond engagement ring.

A nurse came into the room, interrupting the story. "I think I am going to stretch my legs a little," Donald said, "I'll be back in a few minutes.

The nurse finished her task quickly and Mike was again alone with his thoughts. He was transported back in time. He specifically remembered what happened as he slipped the sparkling engagement ring onto Felicia's finger. She looked into his eyes and said, "I will never leave you." Mike felt a huge lump in his throat. He knew this was his secret fear. He also knew he had never told her that. Being separated from his family at a young age planted a deep fear that he could never trust a permanent relationship. He had not seen a good example of a marriage relationship through his parents, he wasn't able to get a commitment from Roxie, and wasn't convinced that he could trust permanency with anyone.

Yet, he had a lasting relationship with his Heavenly Father. God had never let him down. He had always been there for him; even to the point of using Felicia herself to give him the confidence to propose marriage to her. "No," he smiled to himself as he embraced his fiancée, "I do not have to be concerned about being left, ever again."

Still the wedding date was delayed. For two years, Mike tried hard to prove himself to Felicia's family. One day, they were driving with one of Felicia's brothers. He said, "You guys never argue about anything."

"That's because we agree on everything," Felicia threw out the statement, with a cocky grin at Mike.

"We have all seen that," her brother replied.

After this long wait, Mike felt that he had become part of their family, at least to some degree. Felicia spoke with her parents and felt they finally trusted her decision; they would be married.

Donald returned to Felicia's room. "And that's about it," Mike said. "I gave her the ring and we waited until Felicia was comfortable to set the date."

"It was quite a wedding," stated Donald.

April 6, 1991, was to be their wedding day. Felicia and Mike had been putting away money towards the wedding expenses and making plans for a beautiful ceremony and celebration.

And a celebration it was. The ceremony was performed at Felicia's childhood church, Ebenezer Baptist Church in Newburgh, New York, where she had attended since she was eleven years old; the same church where her parents had been married.

Approximately 350 relatives and friends gazed at the radiant bride and the handsome groom and their fourteen attendants attired in peach colored dresses and black tuxedos. Mike and Felicia presented themselves before the Lord to take their holy vows knowing God had put them together and no one could ever separate them.

It was a huge social event. A catered reception was hosted at the Meadowbrook Lodge in New Windsor, New York. The day was a huge success and Mike and Felicia were ready to travel down the road ahead of them. They were so happy just to be together.

"But the devil tried to separate us," Mike acknowledged. "He tried to kill her, but he failed."

Mike knew Felicia would be whole and strong again soon. She was his helpmate. She was his soul mate. She was the one God had chosen for him as a wife.

That led him to think about something that had happened a few years after he and Felicia had married. He proceeded to tell Donald about what he considered to be a true miracle. He remembered that Donald knew a little bit about it, but he wanted to review the miracle in his own mind. He knew God had done so much for him. And he knew God wasn't through blessing him either.

For several years, he had had the recurring thought: was Roxie okay? He had had a six-year relationship with someone and he didn't even know what had happened to her. Did she finish school as she so desperately wanted to do? Was she happily married? Was she even alive? He didn't know. God knew he carried a concern about her. He wished he knew what had happened in her life.

He and Felicia had been blessed with two wonderful boys. Michael Anthony Cole was born in June, 1992, and Avery Daniel Cole in February, 1996. They had a great family, and great jobs. When they weren't at work or home with their family, the Coles could usually be found working at their church. They were devoted servants and loved the Word of God. Together they had arranged a notebook, <u>Sermons to Remember</u>, which they had printed, distributed to friends and family and sold to the public.

"One day," he told Donald, "I received a call for a large order of books. The woman who contacted me ordered 150 books, asking if they could be shipped to Long Island. I have family in Long Island," I had told her. "For that large of an order, I would be happy to bring them to you. I can visit relatives while I'm there."

The books were to be delivered on a Saturday. After I hung up, I heard a voice in my spirit. If you go to the Roosevelt district, pull up on the side of the street, wait until you are there to write your receipt for the books. When you finish writing the receipt, look up. Roxie will be walking by. That's a strange thought, I told myself. Now I know God gives us the desires of our heart. He knew I just wanted to know that she was all right. I didn't want to start anything with her. Just the opposite, I wanted closure. Then I forgot about it. I didn't take it serious.

On Saturday, I headed for Long Island. I had made arrangements to meet family members and looked forward to an enjoyable day with them. I would drop off the books to our customer and be on my way.

About halfway to Long Island, I again heard the voice. If you go to the Roosevelt district, pull over on the side of Fulton Street, wait until you are there to write your receipt for the books. When you finish writing the receipt, look up. Roxie will be walking by. Wow, that is such a strange thing to hear, but I will do it, I told myself. He didn't tell me what part of Fulton Street or what time

I should be there. I drove to Roosevelt, found Fulton Street and pulled over to a corner. I looked around, but didn't see anyone. I took out my receipt book and wrote the receipt out for the customer. When I had finished, I looked up and there was Roxie passing by my car. She immediately spotted me and called "Mike" just as I saw her and called out to her "Roxie".

I was stunned to see her there. I remember asking, "Why are you walking instead of driving?"

"I'm taking the bus to the hospital in the city where I work," she answered. She came around to the passenger side and slid into my car. We talked for a few minutes then she said, "You know, Mike, I really did want to marry you, but you weren't willing to wait for me."

"I waited for six years, Roxie. That was long enough. Besides, I'm married now. I have a nice wife and two little boys. It was just time to say goodbye."

"I never married," she said. "I never even seriously dated anyone else." She told me she had a good job and she was happy. She told me about her family. We talked so long that she missed her commuter bus.

"Can I take you to the bus station?" I asked her.

"Yes, that would be nice," she agreed. Before we parted, she gave me her telephone number. I did not give her mine. The Lord had given me all I needed. He showed me what I wanted to know…that she really was all right. I had closure.

As she walked away, I was amazed at the love of God. He had given me the desire of my heart. He had done it so supernaturally I could never doubt it. He didn't give a specific place or even the time to be there, yet our lives intersected again for just long enough to give me peace. You are amazing, Lord. You are so good to me. Thank You for loving me so—I prayed.

"I was so excited seeing God's hand on my life, I couldn't wait to get home and share the good news with Felicia. Well, you know the rest of the story," Mike laughed a little guiltily. "Felicia wasn't nearly as excited about the miracle as I was."

"Oh, I remember," Donald agreed. "Felicia was very upset with you. She believed that you weren't trying to start anything with Roxie but she did not understand why you needed closure. I remember her saying, "I have given you two babies, and you need closure with another woman. She had a point, I guess," Donald laughed. "It's a wonder she doesn't get up out that bed right now and tell us how she feels about it."

"Thank goodness, you were able to calm her down, Donald," Mike laughed. "She wouldn't listen to me. I guess it hurt her, but I didn't mean for it to. I just wanted to know Roxie was all right then I could put her out of mind completely. And it worked, but, the best part was seeing what God did for me. Felicia did see that. I guess it was just hard for her to understand because she had boyfriends before me and she wasn't concerned about them."

"Well, it makes a good story," Donald chuckled.

"And a good testimony," Mike added. "It reminds me of stories I have read in the Bible where God told people to go a certain place and do a certain thing and all the things he said came to pass. It was none of me and all of Him and that is what is so amazing and so exciting about it."

"Jesus is always doing great things for us. We just have to stay in tune enough to recognize it," Donald said thoughtfully as he picked Mike's Bible up from the window sill. He turned to Psalm 119, the word of God that the brothers spoke over Felicia routinely. She truly had sought God with her whole heart and always tried to walk in His ways, just as the verse in Psalms said. They could believe for the promises of God on her behalf, "Blessed are those who keep His testimonies, the verse said. They knew God was keeping Felicia and healing her.

"She is improving every day," Mike rehearsed with his brother. "And what the doctor said about her never being the same again…I don't have to accept that. But God said… that is my answer to that prognosis. I put my trust in Him that she will be restored. "'By his stripes, we are healed.'" Isaiah 53:5 (NKJV) "That is the report that I do believe," Mike said conclusively.

"And I agree with you," Donald smiled. "You know I have seen so many hopeless situations turn around in my work with the at-risk teens. People think they know things, yet often the outcome is different than they imagined. When we keep God in the equation, we can hope for better. There have been so many times, teachers and even parents have given up on kids at Binghamton High School yet many of those kids have turned their lives around. It wasn't hopeless at all. It's just that the people grew weary and quit on them. When someone believes in these kids, they are encouraged and that gives them the motivation to succeed. That's why I love my job. I don't quit and I get to see their successes."

"I don't remember. How did you end up in that kind of work?" Mike questioned.

"Well, I always knew that I wanted to get an education so I could make money. Growing up so poor the way we did, I knew I didn't want to spend my whole life that way, so I went to college and earned my computer science degree. But it didn't take very long to realize that kind of work wasn't for me. I am a people person as they say. I worked a number of jobs eventually continuing my education and getting my masters in education and counseling. In 1991, I took the job I have now at

Binghamton High, as at at-risk counselor and student advocate. It is very rewarding work. I know I make a difference."

"I'm sure you do," Mike agreed. "That's why Felicia likes teaching. She feels the same way about her job."

"That reminds me. I remember you saying that it was odd Felicia hadn't called you on your birthday. I know she tried because she called to ask if I knew where you were. She wanted to tell you 'Happy Birthday'. She knew I would be calling you, too, so she thought I might know what you were doing when she didn't get an answer on the home phone. But I hadn't tried to call yet. I remember that I took advantage of having her on the phone and reminded her she needed to be prayed up. I had told her before she left for Massachusetts of the spiritual challenges I had had while taking the same course of study last year. I asked her again that day, 'Are you prayed up?' I just felt in my spirit that it was very important for her to be strongly connected to God at that moment. Not that I thought anything like this would happen. I was just aware of the oppression I had felt there. She assured me she was and I am confident that is true."

"I am sure she was too," Mike agreed. "I know how Felicia's heart is toward God. She prayed daily."

CHAPTER 19

I'm Not Giving Up

MIKE CONTINUED TO PLAY the tape their children and the students and teachers from Newburgh had recorded. He wanted Felicia to hear it over and over. He also played a second recording of Mikey, Avery and Nadia singing to her. He tried to keep familiar voices constantly calling out to her.

He analyzed the kids' singing on the recordings. He knew enough about music to know they were good, but also, that there was room for improvement. He began praying for a way to give the kids voice lessons. "I don't know if it is in our budget, Lord, so I am asking You to make a way," he prayed. "If the children are going to have a music ministry, I want to do everything I can to help them excel."

The days passed quickly as Mike juggled his schedule between playing his roles as father, taxi-driver, chief cook and bottle

189

washer, IBM employee, and prayerful companion to his wife. He attempted to do his best with each responsibility. He couldn't help but wonder how it all would end.

One day as Mike was entering the lobby of Helen Hayes Hospital he saw a large crowd gathered, listening to a woman singing. He, too, listened. She had a very nice voice and seemed to be quite skilled.

Shortly after arriving at Felicia's room, he was standing in the hallway speaking with a nurse. The same lady that had been singing in the lobby came to Felicia's door.

"Hello," she said, addressing Mike. "I'm Dusty. I'm a friend of Felicia's."

"It's nice to meet you. I'm Mike Cole, Felicia's husband," he said introducing himself.

"Are you a teacher?" he asked, knowing most of Felicia's acquaintances were from school.

"Yes, but also we're both soccer moms," she answered jokingly. "I heard she was here and I wanted to stop by and check on her and see if there was any way I could be of help."

"Thanks for coming by. That is very kind of you."

"Actually, I'm here often. I sing to the patients. How is Felicia?" she asked, uncertain of her condition.

"Yes, I recognize you now. I was listening to you downstairs," Mike said.

They talked about Felicia's progress and about the accident. Mike told Dusty that he was still hopeful that she would make full recovery. "Even though it may look doubtful to the doctors, we walk by faith and not by sight. It has brought us this far. We can't give up hope now," he smiled.

"Yes, keep standing in faith," Dusty encouraged. She stepped into Felicia's room and stood by her bedside for a short time. Dusty was saddened to see Felicia. She knew her as a carefree, fun loving person, full of life. Would she ever be that way again? Dusty knew it had been quite a long time since the accident. She could only hope and pray for her friend.

"I need to go now," she said as she returned to the hallway. "I'll check in again soon. Let me know if there is anything I can do."

"Tell me about your singing," Mike queried, as his mind jumped at the possibilities.

"Well, I sing at various places, hospitals, nursing homes, ball games. You know, kind of where ever I'm asked."

"Do you ever give singing lessons?" he ventured.

"I have," she responded.

As they stood in the hallway, outside Felicia's room, Mike brought Dusty up to date on what was happening with the kids. He told her they too had been ministering in the hospital and that there seemed to be a call on their life. He related that they have ability, but that he felt they would benefit from professional training.

"I'd be happy to work with your children," Dusty agreed. Arrangements were made to meet for the first lesson. Mike was pleased. He knew it was a step in the right direction.

When Mike got home, he announced to the children "I have exciting news. A friend of your mother's has agreed to give you singing lessons. She'll start in a couple of days."

The kids were glad. They loved to sing and wanted to keep getting better. Music was one kind of lesson they knew they would enjoy.

But from the very first lesson, Mikey drew back. Dusty

leaned toward a country style that did not appeal to him. He had his own ideas about music and country wasn't on his list. Avery and Nadia, being younger, were not concerned about the style and gladly worked with Dusty even though they had been singing gospel and inspirational for the most part.

Mike didn't force Mikey to participate. If Mikey was serious about music, he would find another way to bring his skills up. Mikey was struggling enough with their situation. As his father, he didn't want to put any more pressure on him.

Dusty worked with the children for a season but then her schedule changed and she was no longer able to give lessons. Avery and Nadia had improved from her instruction and Mike was glad he had invested the time and money it had required.

The weeks flew by. Felicia continued to improve, but eventually hit a plateau. Mike had hoped to see more change in his wife by now, yet he refused to let go of hope.

The doctors told Mike they thought her body had responded physically to the therapy as much as it was going to. They didn't feel they could do anymore for her and recommended that he find a long-term care facility of his choice. This was discouraging, as it was obvious that even though they had been so hopeful once Felicia had communicated with them by first squeezing their hand and then eventually communicating verbally, she still wasn't ready for any kind of normal family life and from the doctor's reports, maybe she never would be.

Mike had to face the facts that it was time to move on. "Lord, we've come so far. What should I do?" he prayed. She was still very confused and had become irritable and combative if she was not able to do or have what she wanted. Yet she wasn't really able to communicate just what she did want. Mike recognized how frustrated Felicia must be feeling. The one who could always do whatever she set her mind to now could do very little. It was heart breaking for him to watch.

He was aware that there was a nursing home within minutes of their house. He shared the information with her doctor and it was agreed that Wingate at Ulster would be an appropriate facility for the care Felicia required. She could continue to get therapy and would be very close to the family as the facility was only a couple of blocks from home.

One of the first things Mike wanted to do now that his wife was back in their home area was take her to the dentist. Felicia's two front teeth had been broken off in the accident. Mike was excited to give Felicia her beautiful smile back.

The children were able to visit their mother regularly now that she was back in Highland. As they sang at her bedside, Mike realized they were getting better at singing together. When the nursing home staff would hear them singing they would wander into Felicia's room to listen. Often times, other staff and visitors would stand outside her room so they could hear the uplifting songs. There were many compliments and encouragements given to the children about their singing. Word spread and the children began receiving invitations to sing at other nursing homes. Mike was glad to take the children to minister, knowing they were blessing people who had few opportunities to go outside the facilities.

Spring was in full bloom and even though Felicia seemed to be more aware of the situation, she still was not totally coherent. It seemed she was sometimes more able to communicate than other times. She had had many hours of physical and occupational therapy, yet was still not able to do even the simplest tasks for herself. Her head, arms and hands shook as she attempted to do anything. Even holding a spoon was a strain for her. She could only function at a very menial level. Occasionally, she would voice a word or two. Sometimes it was understood, but more often, it was not.

It was Easter, 2006. Their church had asked for special music for Easter morning services. Mike had agreed that Nadia could sing if she wanted to. Nadia loved music and she loved to sing. She seemed to be a natural. She and the boys had grown up singing in church. How many five-year olds wanted to sing alone in front of a large crowd Mike asked himself. I wish Felicia could be here to listen to our little Nadia sing her first solo at our church. He beamed as he listened to his little daughter sing "Ten Thousand Angels" and then tears filled his eyes to the point he couldn't even see her as the crowd rose giving her a standing ovation. Thank you, God, for blessing this child with a tender heart and a huge voice. May she always sing for you. Thank you for our hoped for daughter who desires to sing your praises.

After a while, Mike noticed when he visited the nursing home that Felicia was always in her room. It seemed he never found her in therapy anymore.

"Have you stopped giving my wife therapy?" he asked one day.

"It's no longer helping her. There's no purpose in it. She has made as much progress as she's going to," the staff person retorted defensively.

"Then there is no reason for her to stay here, if that is your attitude," he said heatedly. "I'm taking her out of here. You may be giving up on her, but I am not!"

With that, Mike arranged to care for his wife at home. It was mid-May. It had been the best part of ten months since their lives had been turned upside down. Maybe, just maybe, this is the first step to turning it right side up again thought Mike, attempting to encourage himself.

Life was far from normal but at least they were home and they were together. Mike decided he would wing it and take care of Felicia by himself. If he had just a little help, he knew he could make it work. Felicia's mother, Sadie, had offered to help. If she can help me with the house and the kids, I can take care of Felicia he told himself. He was so tired of the whole hospital routine. All he wanted was to have things like they used to be. He knew he could get home health nursing care, but he didn't want it. He didn't want strangers in and out of his home all day and night. That would be like turning our home into a hospital, he told himself. I'm done with that. I'll do it myself. He was determined.

Sadie and Mr. Stanley came and they were a huge help. Sadie made sure the kids got to school on time, fixing breakfast, doing the laundry, running errands and keeping the house straight. Mike juggled his job and meeting Felicia's needs. But he soon came to realize, he was wearing himself out. Between keeping the medications dispensed timely, making sure she was bathed and changed regularly, taken to therapy sessions and all the other little things that were required by someone who was still basically helpless, he saw that he was slowly winding down.

He barely had time to be a father since he was playing full time nursemaid. After two weeks of a very intense schedule, he told Sadie and the children he thought he had better get help. He contacted the insurance company and they set up home health services.

Life was a little easier after that. Mike realized he had taken on too much and was glad he was again able to focus more on quality time with his family.

Periodically, Mike would come home from work and find dinner prepared and waiting for them on the stove; the table nicely set. He knew that a very dear lady had been there. Sister Anderson would come in like an angel of mercy. Usually it was a meal complete with fresh vegetables cooked to perfection, balanced with healthy meats and grains, as she liked teaching people about good nutrition.

He knew if he checked, clean clothes would be piled in neatly folded stacks on their beds; if he checked the bathrooms, they would be shiny and sweet smelling. "Bless you, Sister Anderson," would rise to his lips as he thanked God for her.

For the next six months, life settled down to a reasonable routine. Felicia's progress was slow, but she was able to be home and everything was going smoothly. She was still on so many medications Mike questioned if they were doing her more harm than good. He thought, perhaps her lack of alertness could be somewhat drug induced. Slowly he weaned her off one medication and then another.

After a time, he saw improvement. Taking her for a routine

visit, the doctor was pleased with her progress. He reviewed the medicines with Mike, verifying which ones she was still using. Mike had to confess that he stopped giving her a number of the prescribed medications. The doctor's only response was, "Keep doing what you're doing—she seems to be doing very well."

It seemed that after that, Felicia's recovery accelerated. Every day she seemed more like her old self, taking part in the things happening around her. Even though her speech was still slurred, her thoughts were clearer and over time, she was better able to communicate. They no longer had to guess at what she wanted. She no longer had the frustration of failing to express herself then lapsing into silent annoyance. Those days were behind them and everyone had a sense of relief and expectation for a brighter future.

The children had been singing together at churches and on request at some local nursing homes. They began getting request to perform at bigger venues on a regular basis, with invitations coming from farther and farther away from home. They packed everyone in the car, including Felicia, and made appearances, ministering song and words of encouragement.

One night, leaving a performance in Kingston, New York, Mikey told his mom and dad that someone had asked him what they called themselves. "I said, we are just the Cole family, but I was thinking, maybe we should have another name."

That's a good idea they all agreed. Everyone made suggestions. One person would like a name, but someone else would say no. Back and forth they went, coming up with different ideas. Then Nadia said, "I know, The Voices of Miracle." No, that one was shot down, too. Mikey tried hard to think of a name that hadn't already been used. Suddenly an idea popped into his head, "Voices of Glory".

"Now, that's a good name, brother," Avery said, offering Mikey a high five.

"I like that," Felicia said, nodding her head enthusiastically.

"It's agreed then. Right, everybody? Nadia?"

"Yes, Daddy, I like it too." Nadia's sweet voice came from the backseat.

"Voices of Glory" it is," Mike confirmed.

It seemed the children's music ministry was coming to pass. It hadn't specifically been planned, yet it seemed more and more that it was meant to be. One day, Mike said, "Felicia, do you remember the day we visited a different church when Avery was still a baby?" The pastor prophesied that our children would have a worldwide ministry.

"Yes, she stopped the service saying she needed to minister to us," Felicia recalled.

Mike smiled, "It is good to know you are able to remember things."

"Oh, I remember. She was the same one who told us Nadia was coming. It was hard for us to believe everything she said."

"Yes, it was, but we have Nadia so maybe this is the beginning of the rest of the prophecy," Mike said thoughtfully.

CHAPTER 20

Yet Another Trial

MIKE LAY IN BED next to his wife. He wasn't sure if Felicia was awake. He didn't want to move or speak in case she wasn't so he didn't share the thoughts that were coming to his mind. His birthday was coming up. It would be the two-year anniversary of the accident. They had come through so much in those two years. Yet their life had returned to a normal rhythm even though each day was still a challenge. The doctors had certainly been wrong about permanent brain damage. Felicia's mind was sharp. He remembered the sinking feeling he'd had when it was clear that she would live yet the doctors gave no hope that Felicia would have any cognitive ability. "Thank you, Lord, for healing her beyond the doctor's expectations," he sighed the prayer of gratitude. Limited motor skills and a little difficulty with speech were the only remaining results of the injuries. She couldn't walk even though she had had hours upon hours of physical therapy. Her head and hands were still shaky and she was unable to properly grasp things in her right hand. Even though she could grasp better with her left, it was awkward since she was a right-handed person. Mike knew it caused her a lot of frustration and made her even more dependent on him and the kids. Perhaps those things would change, too. No, not perhaps, they will change Mike corrected his thought.

They had prayed and believed that Felicia would be fully restored. However, God chose to do it, either through an instantaneous miracle or a healing process over time, they had faith that she would walk again. They knew it was God's will for her to be made whole. The Bible was clear on that. Just like in Matthew 8 when the leper went to Jesus and said, "Lord, if you are willing, you can make me clean…and the Lord said 'I will'". It was His will that the leper be cleansed and rid of the thing that kept him from having a full life. He rehearsed other verses that he knew like in James where it said that God is no respecter of persons, and in Malachi 3, that God never changes. He knew that God would do for Felicia what He had done for the leper. God hadn't changed His mind about wanting His people healed. Mike reached for his Bible and read Jesus' words in Matthew 9: 22… "Be of good cheer, daughter; your faith has made you well."

Mike's thoughts turned to his brother Joseph. Why had he not been healed? He did not know the answer to that question, but he knew faith was the key to healing just as it was the key to every promise of God, including salvation. It's all by faith. Mike understood that. "And without faith it is impossible to please God…," (Hebrews 11:6 NKJV) the words resounded in his mind.

He had been sitting at his desk at work when he got the call about Joseph. It was one of those pictures marked indelibly in his mind. When he answered the phone, he was pleased to learn it was Donald. He always liked hearing from family. Everyone was so busy they didn't get together very often. They visited briefly asking how each other was, and then Donald stated the reason for his call.

"Mike, I have been talking to Joseph. He told me he has leukemia," Donald said, with tangible regret in his voice in having to pass on this weighty news. Mike knew Joseph had been in the hospital but had heard that it was just fatigue. This new report was totally unexpected. Donald went on to say that Joseph had requested that each of them be tested to see if anyone would be a match as a bone marrow donor. "It's just a matter of a simple blood test," stated Donald.

"Mike, are you there?" He asked sensing the silence.

"Yes, I'm here. Yes, of course, I will be tested. Whatever it takes to help him," he responded. Mike took the news hard. "I thought we were done with hospitals," he reflected.

"I'll let you know what to do when I have more details," Donald offered. "I just wanted to let you know what was going on. I'll call you later when we get it set up. Are you going to be alright?"

"Sure, and you're right. We will get through this together, just like always," Mike said, trying to sound a little more cheerful. "Thanks for calling. I guess I need to give Joseph a call."

As Mike hung up the phone, he felt overwhelmed. He prayed someone would be a match, but he couldn't help but hope that he would not have to be the donor. "How can I do anymore?" Mike posed the question. He had all he could do with giving Felicia the time and attention she needed, taking her to therapy sessions and doctors appointments, taking the kids to performances, cooking and keeping house not to mention working a full time job. "How can I possibly do it?" he again questioned himself. Mike realized there was no use trying to rearrange his schedule in his mind. He didn't even know yet if he was a candidate. He rested with that thought and returned to the work on his desk.

At Sloan Kettering, Mike visited Joseph in his hospital room before going to the lab to give blood for the donor testing.

"Somebody will be a match," Mike had encouraged his brother. "With seven possibilities, I think our odds are pretty good of getting this done and having you back to work quickly."

"I think so," Joseph agreed rather solemnly. Mike realized that since Joseph was a doctor, it was hard for him to stay positive. He knew too much.

A few days later, Donald called Mike at work again. "Congratulations, you're the donor," Donald announced jokingly, trying to keep the situation light. Donald was sensitive to the pressure Mike was already under without adding this to his load. "You're it, because you are the only match," Donald continued.

There was an uncomfortable silence. "That's good. We can make it work," Mike replied as his mind grasped the reality that he had no choice. "What do I need to do?" he asked.

"As I understand it, they will schedule the transplant and you will give the bone marrow on the same day. It is supposed to be a simple procedure. Joseph can tell you more about it."

"Yeah, I'm sure he can. I will call him later," Mike responded.

It was frightening to think about being a bone marrow donor.

He assumed it would involve some sort of surgical procedure. He assumed it would be painful. *I will have to take more time off work, too,* he reasoned. With that, he got up from his desk and made his way to the human resources department. He would find out what he needed to do, and then he would talk to his manager.

Again, a letter arrived from the attorney's office. Once more, the court date was set for the sentencing of the man who caused the accident.

It was 2007. It seemed an eternity ago since that dreadful night that changed their lives forever. He had made adjustments. Felicia had made adjustments. Their lives had gone on even though there was little resemblance to what it had been in the past. The children had to make adjustments too, but for the most part, they were growing into their new circumstances with seemingly little awareness of the changes.

What appeared to be a series of small, innocent decisions had resulted in major life-altering circumstances. Yet, what was done, was done. The outcome of the legal matters wasn't going to reverse Felicia's condition. They had received some compensation from the insurance companies, which helped pay the astronomic medical bills. He knew the man who was driving under the influence of alcohol had to take responsibility for his actions, yet he recognized that wanting him to take responsibility and dictating punishment out of revenge were two different things. He wasn't sure that he even wanted to go back to the courtroom. The circumstances were irreversible in man's hands. Only God could make things right. He would pray about what to do.

Later that day, Mike phoned Donald to tell him another court date was scheduled. "I'm not so sure I even want to go,"

Mike told him. "I have so much going on and it won't make any difference if I'm there or not. There was a time I wanted him to be punished for what he had done, but I had to let that go. It wasn't good for me to dwell on such thoughts. As I told you last time we went to court, I chose to forgive him. I've had to keep forgiving him because some days it was easier than others. Now, I just want to move on."

Mike continued giving Donald reasons for not going. "And I don't want to stir up all that old emotion again. Felicia and I prayed together and put it behind us. Whatever the judge decides is fine with us. We prayed he be shown mercy."

"You're right," Donald agreed, "and you'll find out later what happened."

"Yes, I guess we need to know or we would always wonder what had happened to him. Thanks, Donald."

Mike and Felicia got a report from their attorney. The accused pled guilty to a single count of involuntary manslaughter by wanton and reckless conduct, operating to endanger, speeding and a marked lanes violation.

For that, he was sentenced to two and half years in a local jail and community service. Mike received the news with little reaction. "Thanks for telling me," he replied calmly. "God is the vindicator. We relinquished it all into His hands. We didn't want him to suffer. Whatever God wants is what we want. We're glad it's over," Mike added.

"It doesn't look like we will be getting much of a settlement from the accident after all the fees are paid," Mike stated as he laid aside a letter from their attorney.

"It's a good thing other people are willing to help us. The teachers fund is such a blessing," Mike shared with Felicia as he reviewed a bank statement from a special account that had been established to help the Cole family after the accident. "And there are other smaller deposits that are impossible to determine where they came from. I wish we knew, so we could give them a proper thank you. People have been so generous to help us. God knows we have needed the help with all the medical bills. But thanks to them we are able to stay current on everything," he concluded.

"To God be the glory. He is our provider," Felicia added.

"Yes, I am sure He has touched the hearts of many people to be His hands reaching out to us," Mike agreed, feeling comforted.

The scheduled day for Joseph's bone marrow transplant arrived quickly. Mike drove himself to the hospital. He checked in, and was directed to the surgical suite where the procedure was to be performed. He was nervous. Even though it had been explained to him, it was still intimidating. He was told to remove his shirt and then to sit in a chair. He watched as a doctor and the nurses busied themselves with the necessary preparations. The doctor then sterilized the area on his upper arm and administered the anesthesia. While waiting for it to take effect, Mike surveyed the tray of strange looking surgical tools. He closed his eyes. I think I can handle this better if I don't watch, he told himself. Then he began praying, "I can do all things through Christ who strengthens me." (Philippians 4:13, NKJV)

After a while, he felt the doctor touch his arm. He stiffened, feeling the invasive pressure of the aspiration needle, but kept his eyes closed, repeating the verse over and over.

"You are doing well," the doctor encouraged. "This won't take very long."

Mike tried to stay relaxed. He didn't want to jerk or do anything to cause the procedure to fail. For Joseph's sake, this will work and that makes it all worth it, he encouraged himself. He prayed for Joseph, for him to win his battle, for everything to be right for his brother again.

Before long, the doctor announced that he was done. Mike opened his eyes in relief. He tried not to look at anything but the faces of the people in the room. He didn't want to remember anything that would haunt him. He focused on the people and managed a smile, getting smiles in return. You need to lie down and give yourself some recovery time the doctor advised. He then repeated the instructions for the post-surgical care that Mike would require, warning him that he would feel fatigued due the trauma to his system.

Mike was relieved it was over. Anything he had ahead of him would be a piece of cake. He rested and even napped a little, then walked around the hospital to be sure he had enough strength to drive home safely. That wasn't so bad he told himself as he left the hospital. Toni, Joseph's wife, took him out to dinner as a thank you. Life had gone on as usual after that. The family was hopeful the bone marrow transplant would save Joseph's life. Toni was expecting their third child. Sadly, Joseph did not win his battle against cancer, but he did live long enough to see his new son.

CHAPTER 21

Harsh Memories

IT WAS JOSEPH'S FUNERAL that brought most of the siblings back together for the first time in years. Through the family grapevine, Mike later learned some of his sister Mary's story. When he and Donald were sent to the Susquehanna Valley home, they lost contact with her and years had passed not knowing anything about her life.

Several years later, he saw Mary one more time. The occasion was her wedding. She had met Marvin, her husband-to-be, at college. They had made plans to marry after graduation. Mary wanted to be married in a church, but the only one she was familiar with was the small chapel at the Wayside Home for Girls where she had attended chapel while a student there. Wayside had been good to her; helping her to make her way through college. Because of that, she was comfortable asking if she could be married in their chapel. A Salvation Army Brigadier performed the ceremony with her social worker and a staff worker from Wayside who had befriended her, acting as her attendants. It was a small affair with only a handful of family members attending. After that, Mike had lost contact with her again.

Gerard and Mary had reconnected at Joseph's funeral and their relationship started to be renewed. One day, Gerard told Mike about a telephone conversation between he and Mary when she had shared some painful memories with him. She had filled in some of the lost history between ages fifteen when the family was separated, and age twenty-two when she married. She also shared some of her successes that Gerard was glad to hear about.

"You will be pleased to know about some good things that Mary shared with me," Gerard continued. She has done so well in her career that in 2000, she was given the Directorship of the Title I Reading Program for Cleveland Heights; that's pretty impressive," Gerard added with a big smile. Also, and I'm not sure I understand everything about it, but it sounds like she already had a track record of success. She was the first master's candidate at the University of Toledo to be the primary instructor of a college class, teaching aspiring teachers when she was only 22 years old. That's impressive too!"

"Yes, I would say it is. I am very proud of Mary. She has overcome so much," Mike stated with a shake of his head as he thought of how all of them had prevailed over what seemed like impossible odds. "We have much to be grateful for," Mike added.

"It is to her credit and the help of the Lord that her life has turned out the way it has based on some of the stories she told me," Gerard continued, sharing what he had learned of Mary's early years.

"Yes, sadly, she hadn't had an easy way to go either," Mike interjected.

To this day, nobody knows why, but the staff at the Mineola shelter did not even attempt to place her in foster care. Nothing would have made Mary happier than to have a home with a mother who knew how to love her. Her heart yearned for a mother's love, but it was never to be realized.

Instead, she was sent to the Wayside Home for Girls, a facility for delinquent girls in Valley Stream, New York, operated by the Salvation Army. Things had gone from bad to worse for her. She had done nothing to deserve punishment, but she received the same disciplinary actions and had to follow the same strict rules as the troublemakers. She was not a troublemaker. She certainly had had trouble at home, but she was not the cause of it. She had never been in trouble with the law nor had she caused problems at school. In fact, she loved school. It was a safe haven for her and she quickly reasoned that people who were educated seemed to be happy. Early in life, she decided she wanted to be a teacher, even playing school at home with her brothers and sisters when it was peaceful enough to be able to play. She was always the teacher. She would be a teacher when she grew up and then she would be happy, too, she told herself.

She resented her situation at Wayside. She was withdrawn and didn't have any interest in making friends with the other girls.

"You think you're special," they chided her.

"I am," she retorted. "I'm not like you. I shouldn't be here." Mary knew it was true, but it only further alienated her from the others.

She attended classes on the Wayside campus and continued to excel in her schoolwork. She veiled herself in a world where books were her only friends. They were her escape from the harsh realities of her life. Through the stories, she could live a *normal life* vicariously. She could travel around the world. She could be anyone she wanted to be. She had a hunger for knowledge and books were an attempt to fill the huge void in her life.

The school at Wayside was basically vocational training and Mary had bigger dreams. She asked if she could go to a different school where she could take college preparatory classes. They agreed she could go to public school but only after she had completed a full school term at Wayside. She had to prove herself. Her family had moved so many times during her early school years, eight times by the ninth grade, causing her to miss so many days of school. It was thought best to hold her back when she was in the fifth grade. She was already a year older than most kids would be when they graduated. She reasoned, if she could take her sophomore and junior classes at the same time, she could leave Wayside earlier. She got the staff to agree and kept very busy doing double school work every day finishing two years work during one school term. She was seventeen and ready to start her senior year of high school.

The Wayside Home was in the Valley Stream Central High School district, and even though it was an all-white school still fighting integration, that was where Mary was sent for her senior year. Scholastically she did very well, but she had a huge struggle socially as the only black student. Very few were even polite to her so Mary kept to herself. However, her art teacher treated her kindly, inviting her to her home. Finally, she found someone who was not prejudiced. When she was introduced to the teacher's husband, it was evident why she had compassion toward Mary. Her white teacher was married to a black man. Mary was grateful for the nice time she had in their home.

Why are people so different, she asked herself? It was confusing and troubling, yet she was grateful for every thoughtful gesture shown to her.

One day in gym class, the girls were playing softball. When she was reaching to the floor to catch a rolling ball, a girl standing next to her called her *"Nigger"* and viciously stomped on Mary's hand with her cleat.

Mary lost it. The pain was excruciating. Anger rose up in her and she retaliated against her attacker; against the prejudice. She got even. She had suffered rejection, dirty looks and crude remarks. She didn't have to take it anymore. By the time it was over, the other girl was in worse shape than Mary. They were separated and sent home. Mary was shocked by her own reaction to the girl's brutality. She had never been a fighter. She did everything she could to keep peace even though it had cost her much.

The next day, Mary and her social worker from Wayside were summoned to the principal's office. As she waited, she felt so defeated. She had worked so hard. Now because of this mean girl, she would be sent back to the Wayside school. She would not be able to go to college and become a teacher. Tears ran down her cheeks as disappointment rose up in her.

The white girl and her father arrived just as the principal took his seat. The girl had worn short shorts to show the bruises on her legs in addition to the other bruises she had. At first, everything was calm. Then Mary heard the principal saying that she was an exemplary student and that it was his daughter's fault. He said Mary had never caused a problem and that he did not intend to suspend her or punish her in any way. The girl's father became very angry and started yelling at the principal, but he stood firm. Obviously there had been witnesses on Mary's behalf and they and the principal had had the courage to stand up for what was right; courage to stand for truth. Mary told Gerard that this kindness and fairness shown to her by the principal was life changing for her. She was not slow to recognize the goodness in him and was determined not to cause him to regret his decision. She would graduate without any more trouble.

When she was eighteen, just like Mike, she was told she could no longer live at the Wayside Home and would have to find a way to fend for herself. But unlike him, she had done well in school. She spoke up and said, "That's all right. I am going to go to college anyway. I want to be a teacher."

"If you want to go to college we may be able to arrange help for you," they offered. Mary chose to go to Anna Maria College for her freshman year. Due to the abusive experience with her older brother, Mary was more comfortable in an all girl environment. Anna Maria College in Massachusetts was not co-ed so it was a good choice for her. Wayside School for Girls paid for her first year's tuition including room and board and some spending money.

Unfortunately, she was again to suffer the ignorance of prejudice. When her dorm roommate's parents found out their daughter had a black roommate, they insisted she be reassigned. It wasn't hard to imagine what her first year of college would be like when it started out on that same hurtful note. But Mary stuck it out with the plan to switch to a state college the next year. Dealing with racial prejudice was even more painful than having to face her feelings of anger toward the male species caused by her older brother. She chose facing her fears over dealing with the pain of racism.

For her sophomore year, she transferred to Brockport State College. She kept her grades up and received scholarships for all three years, graduating Magna Cum Laude. She was able to do secretarial and research work for some of the professors, earning spending money to supplement what was provided to her by Wayside. She had to work hard. This favor and support did not come to her just because she was a college student, but because she applied herself and purposed to succeed. "What an accomplishment," Mike smiled. "Mary and I have a lot in common. I'm not the only one who had to work hard."

Then Gerard remembered another part of her story. One day while living at the Mineola shelter, Mary left without permission. She made her way back to the house where they had been living the day the child welfare people came and separated their family. She said she didn't know why she went there. She knew her family wasn't there. The house was vacant. It looked as abandoned as she felt. She slowly made her way back to the shelter. When she arrived, unbeknownst to her the police were there waiting for her. The manager of the shelter had called them to take her away. He did not want to have to deal with a runaway. He called her into his office to tell her and they had a lengthy conversation. Mary related that she did not know what she said to him to cause him to change his mind except perhaps he recognized how very sad she was. He dismissed her and told the police they could leave; Mary would be staying.

Shortly after that, he invited her to his home for the weekend. He had seven children of his own. Mary recalled that his wife was very kind to her. She spent many weekends with the family during the months she was living at the shelter. Soon after she started staying with his family on weekends, he told her of his intent to send her away with the police when she had run away from the shelter. I realized if I turned you over to the police, I would be making the biggest mistake of my career he had confessed.

After she graduated from college, Mary went to the Mineola shelter to visit her friend. She wanted him to know that his decision to allow her to stay at the shelter coupled with the compassion he and his family had shown was a life-altering course for her. She had met her goal to become a teacher and he had played a large role in it. For that, she was very grateful to him, and she told him so.

Mike thought about his sister Mary, how they still were not in contact much. They lived so far apart, Mary in Ohio, he in New York. "I'm fond of Mary," Mike smiled, "she's my big sister. Maybe someday we will be able to spend more time together."

CHAPTER 22

Time For Voice Lessons

ANOTHER FRIEND OF FELICIA'S, Cheryl, had been faithful to visit Felicia every Tuesday while she was at Helen Hayes. While Felicia was staying in the nursing home, Cheryl and her family continued the visits to her dear friend. Once Felicia was home, they saw no reason to stop their weekly visits. She knew it was good for Felicia to have friends around her and to have something to look forward to while she was still so limited on what she could do. While visiting their home, Cheryl started helping with meals and other small household tasks. She was a great help, lifting some of the load from Mike's shoulders.

One day, she asked if there was anything else she could do. Mike and Felicia knew that she too had musical ability. She worked with the choir at their church.

"Could you give the kids voice lessons?" Mike asked hopefully.

"Well, yes, I can do that," she agreed enthusiastically. "That would be a lot of fun." After that, Cheryl balanced her time between cooking meals in the evenings, and visiting with Felicia, then going downstairs, and working with the kids on their music. In just a short time, she found out she was expecting and could no longer keep up with the schedule.

With the instruction they had received, the kids really came up in their ability. It seemed right to continue lessons, but they didn't know anyone else to ask. Mike and Felicia again prayed for just the right person to instruct the children in voice.

One day, he and Felicia went to their bank to handle a business transaction. Mike was pushing Felicia in the wheelchair. As they were leaving the bank, they heard a voice call from behind them, "Felicia, Felicia, is that you?" The lady then said, "Oh, it was you. I've known for two years a black teacher who taught at Poughkeepsie was hurt in an accident, but I couldn't figure out who it was. I didn't know it was you."

She cried for Felicia. She felt so bad for her. Felicia was glad to see her old friend. It had been several years since they had talked. Ms. Consuelo Hill was a dear friend from Felicia's childhood. She was Felicia's music teacher when she was still a student at Gidney Avenue Academy, her elementary school. They exchanged addresses, finding out that they lived only about a mile apart. Ms. Hill told them she would come to their house for a visit. Felicia was so excited and looked forward to the visit, but with busy schedules, time passed and they did not hear from her.

Mike knew Felicia wanted to see her friend and that a visit would be good for her. They did not have a telephone number for Ms. Hill, but he knew how to find her house. He drove to her neighborhood, but had trouble finding the right house number.

He parked the car and asked a gentleman that was painting the outside of a house, did he know where Sister Hill lived. "This is it," he replied.

"Do you know when she will be home," Mike asked.

"Not until later tonight, but I will let her know you were here," he offered.

Due to conflicting schedules, it took two more trips to Ms. Hill's house before Mike was able to catch her at home.

Knocking on her door, she finally answered. "Ms. Hill, I have something I want to ask you," Mike started. "I want you to come to our house and see Felicia and meet our family. Our children are invited to sing at churches and nursing homes. I feel they need singing lessons. Would you please come to my house and meet them? I want you to hear them sing. "

Ms. Hill agreed that she would come right over. Mike was excited as he drove home. Maybe it was not a chance meeting that they had ran into Ms. Hill at the bank. She is a music teacher. Perhaps if she hears the children sing, she will agree to give them voice lessons, he pondered.

Very shortly, after Mike got back to his house, there was a knock at the door. Opening the front door, Mike welcomed Ms. Hill to their home. She and Felicia had a good visit, catching up on mutual friends and lost years. Mike then introduced each of the children to her.

"Ms. Hill, I would like for the children to sing for you. Would that be alright?" Mike asked.

"Surely, do sing," she encouraged.

The kids stood together and began singing "I'm Walking in Authority". As the children sang, Ms. Hill started crying. She was deeply moved by their sweet spirits, and the genuineness of their presentation.

Mike asked, "Would you give the children singing lessons?"

"Yes, I will," she quickly agreed, reaching in her purse for a tissue.

The next week, Ms. Hill showed up at the Cole house, her arms full of books, a tape recorder, and everything else she needed to instruct the children.

"Call me Aunt Connie," Ms. Hill instructed. "We're going to be spending a lot of time together." They worked on how to warm up, how to breathe properly and to sing from their diaphragm, how to hit high notes, and much more. Since the lessons were given after school, often times she would be invited to stay and have dinner with the family.

"The children are good students," Aunt Connie told Mike and Felicia one evening. "They are doing very well."

"I can hear the improvement myself," Mike agreed. "Thank you so much for all you are doing for them."

"Yes," Felicia joined in. "Thank you. Now they must practice, practice, practice." This brought a good laugh around the table.

It seemed that was the main word in the family vocabulary and one the kids were already getting tired of hearing. But they knew they had to work hard to be a success. They were starting to look beyond singing at churches with all the requests they were getting and wondering just what God had planned for them.

Felicia had come so far in just over two years. It was approaching fall, 2007. The teacher in her wanted to go back to school. She wanted to return to her job as a bilingual biology teacher.

She knew she still had physical challenges but her mind was ready to pick up her teaching mantle. She had prayed for a miracle so that she could walk again and she believed whole-heartedly for full restoration. She believed she was ready.

"Mike, I have been speaking with the school. I want to go back to work. It will be so great to see all of my friends and to get back into the groove. Teacher orientation is next week. Can you take me?"

Mike knew about earlier calls his wife had made to Pough-keepsie High School. He responded "Sure," without hesitation. He always wanted to encourage Felicia but his thoughts were flying. He knew her mind was sharp but there were still several physical handicaps to her being able to function independently.

Felicia knew her husband well. Even though he had quickly agreed to take her, she was able to read his face and knew to offer additional information to help him see the possibility of her returning to work.

"I think they will offer me a teacher's aide to handle the things I am not ready to do. I can do my lesson plans and teach the class; an aide can fill in the gaps," she said with confidence.

"Do you think they will give you an aide? That would really help," he responded.

"Yes, that isn't usually a problem when there is an obvious need," she stated knowingly.

The day of orientation arrived. It was a happy morning for Felicia. She had her life back. Their house was buzzing with high-spirited activity as they prepared for the day she had waited for so long. The kids still had a few more days of vacation but the teachers always had to report early to prepare.

At the meeting, Felicia was surrounded by friends and co-workers welcoming her back, and celebrating her recovery from the accident. As the meeting was called to order, she concentrated on the instructions to be sure she understood any changes that may have taken place in her absence. She was not yet able to hold a pen to write so she really needed to focus. She was grateful when they passed around handouts with much of the same information that the speaker was giving.

"I can do this," she assured herself as the meeting came to an end.

Mike had stayed close by, knowing that after orientation Felicia was to meet with the department head and school principal. The school staff required Felicia to demonstrate just how well she would be able to perform in the classroom. They scheduled a day for an observation class, where the school staff would monitor Felicia.

Earlier in the month, they had given Felicia a specific biology topic for her lesson plan. The school had offered the use of any resource that would help her. In the lesson plan, she had included the use of an overhead projector. She had worked hard to prepare it. Her mother, Sadie, had been a great help in making the transparencies for her overhead presentation.

On the drive home after the orientation meeting, Felicia said, "I understand that I am going to have to prove myself but I'm not worried. With just a little help I can do what I have always done."

Mike gave her a reassuring smile. He loved the fact that Felicia always approached things with a positive attitude. It was a demonstration of faith. It was the right way to live.

In just a few days, Mike and Felicia rose early to get ready for her big day. Nearing Poughkeepsie High School, Felicia asked, "Pray for me, Mike. I want to do well." She did not deny that her hands were shaky and her speech still somewhat unclear. She knew she could not do it without God's help.

Mike pulled into a handicapped space in the school parking lot. He took Felicia's hand, gave her a sweet smile and prayed for her success, her peace and for God's will to be done. He recognized they were at a crossroads. He hoped for a good outcome.

"Thank you, Mike," Felicia voiced after he closed his prayer. "Thank you for always being there for me. I know I would not be doing this, if it weren't for you. I know I would not be where I am if you had not been faithful to pray for me and to care for me."

Mike squeezed her hand, and then leaned over and kissed her cheek. "Ready?" he asked.

"Ready," she grinned.

Mike wheeled Felicia into the classroom. It felt like home. She looked around her, appreciating the familiar atmosphere: the wall posters, the lab, the student desks, the teacher's desk, the chalkboard. She was so happy. In her usual organized manner, Felicia laid her lesson plan and other necessary items on her desk. Mike helped.

The staff had set up the overhead projector for her use. She studied the switches and quickly recalled how to turn it on. She reached for the switch but was not able to press the toggle until she had made several attempts due to the lack of control of her extremities. Her head shook too, but not a lot.

She sat quietly, thinking. She would not be deterred. Her few moments of reflection were quickly interrupted by the arrival of the teacher who was the department head, followed through the door by the school principal and the school super-intendant. She was surprised to see the superintendant. She had not realized the he would be present for her observation class. She told herself she did not need to be nervous.

"Good morning," she smiled in her customary friendly manner. Each of them greeted her, and then readily took seats in the back of the room, knowing that it would soon be time for the bell to ring.

Students began wandering into the classroom, saying hi to "Mrs. Cole", some standing at her desk to speak with her, others giving her a quick wave or nod of their head, and taking their seats.

Before class began, another teacher came to the classroom to be of assistance to Felicia. Mike, also, was at the front of the room, ready to help Felicia on a more personal level, if the need arose.

The bell rang. Smiling, Felicia introduced herself to the class and immediately went into teaching mode. First, she took attendance, attempting to pronounce each student's name clear-ly. She introduced the topic of the day's lesson. Sometimes she repeated herself, sensitive to the expressions on the student's faces, realizing she had not made herself understood. It was frustrating, but she was not about to give up so easily. Everyone seemed to be more than willing to make it easy for her.

It was going rather slowly and Felicia recognized that she was more nervous than she had anticipated. She ran her finger down the page to again find her place but her hand shook, mak-ing it difficult.

When the appropriate time came, Felicia reached for the first sheet to place on the projector. She fumbled a little but managed to lay the transparency on the glass. The other teacher quickly observed Felicia's difficulty and straightened the sheet so it displayed correctly on the screen.

Felicia worked her way through the lesson. At one point, picking up a few transparencies in an attempt to sort them, in order to review a point, they slipped out her hand, and scooted across the classroom floor. A student sitting on the front row was quick to pick them up and lay them on the desk before her. It was frustrating to Felicia. She knew she was wasting time. She knew she was not giving a concise presentation. She could only hope her auditors would give her grace. She was teaching an English speaking class, not a Spanish speaking one, so she knew the staff would be able to evaluate every word and action. It was obvious that class time was almost gone and she had not shown all of the transparencies, but she was confident that they knew she was a good teacher and would offer her old teaching position to her. She noticed the kids were reaching for their backpacks, preparing to go to their next class. Soon, the bell rang. She had not completed the lesson.

She attempted to explain herself as the staff stood at the front of the classroom, but decided to say no more. It was done. It was what it was, Felicia told herself. They encouraged her in regard to her progress, and said they would be in touch, and left the room.

Felicia packed up her paperwork. Mike let her try to do it by herself. If this was going to happen, she would need to do as much for herself as possible. The attending teacher stood in the hallway just outside of the door.

"How will your family get along financially if Felicia isn't able to come back yet?" she asked with concern.

"I'm not sure," Mike answered.

"Do you think they will offer her a job?" he questioned.

"I really don't know," she responded. "I hope so."

It was quiet in the car on the way home. Felicia had told Mike that they knew she was a good teacher and with more help from an aide, she was sure she would be teaching again.

"We'll know soon," Mike said, trying not to sound doubtful. After that first exchange, there wasn't anything else to say.

They waited for a response from the school. It was slow in coming. Felicia didn't understand why it was taking so long. She was so ready to go to school each day, just as she had for years. She wanted to teach.

Almost two weeks had passed since Felicia's observation class. "When are they going to call me?" she had voiced. School was well under way. If she was going to teach this semester, they needed to give her the go-ahead.

Finally, the call came. They were being asked to come to the district administration office to discuss Felicia's job application. Felicia was excited. They hadn't said she was hired, but they hadn't said she wasn't.

Felicia went to the appointment in high anticipation. Unfortunately, the outcome was not what she wanted. They stated that they did not feel she was ready to take on the responsibility of a classroom. The same people that were in the observation class were in attendance as well as a representative from the teachers' union. The spokesperson said they felt she needed more time to recover and would be happy to reconsider her for a position at a later date.

Felicia maintained her composure. She was so disappointed.

She wasn't really prepared for their denial but Mike saw the logic in their decision. They discussed the possibility of the extension of her benefits and the meeting was dismissed. They expressed their regret but tried to encourage her at the same time. There was nothing to do. Mike took his disappointed wife home.

One evening after work, Mike gathered the mail from the mailbox. He thumbed through the pile of medical bills, and other letters. As he entered the kitchen, he noticed the school district logo on one of the envelopes. He saw that Felicia was sitting at the table talking to the kids. Mike hesitated thinking he should know what it said before giving it to her, but then handed Felicia the letter. He watched anxiously as she tore at the seal, finally pulling the letter out. She slowly unfolded it and read. The tears running down her cheeks, told Mike the contents without her reading it aloud. Felicia handed the letter to her husband without saying a word. Mike read it silently. The letter only confirmed the decision to not offer Felicia a job at that time and advised of a meeting time to further discuss her future benefits with the administration staff and the teachers' union representative. They had requested that Felicia bring her written resignation to the next meeting. In closing, it said, that the teachers' union representative would be present to work out the details of disability guidelines and health insurance for her family.

He laid the letter on the table and said, "I'm sorry, Hon. I don't want you to take this too hard."

But she did; Felicia was extremely disappointed. Even though she already knew she would not be teaching that semester, the letter had just reopened the wound. "I'm a teacher inside and out. It is who I am. I don't want to resign. I am still a good teacher even if my hands do shake, even if I can't walk yet," she responded as tears raced down her cheeks.

"We probably tried too soon," Mike offered. "You will get another chance. We can try again later," he encouraged.

Felicia stared at the floor. She stared at her feet placed on the wheelchair footrests. There was an unnatural silence. Mike put his finger to his lips to signal the children not to speak.

"Maybe I did try too soon," Felicia finally acknowledged with sadness in her voice. "But I want to do it. I am going to try again. Next time, I will be able to do it. Next time they will hire me," she said through a stifled sob.

Over the next several months, the kids kept very busy between school, frequent performances and voice lessons. Christmas came and went. Invitations came from every direction; from civic groups, for Martin Luther King Day, even an appearance before the mayor of Newburgh, New York. It seemed every week they were headed in one direction or another. Ms. Hill had even scheduled them in the 2008 National Gospel Choir Competition sponsored by the Black Music Caucus of New York. They were not only getting voice lessons but were learning performance and competition techniques.

It was the spring of 2008. It was early morning and Mike and Felicia were still in their room preparing for the day. It had been almost three years since the accident and Felicia was getting restless.

"Mike, I want to go back to school."

"You want to what?" Mike answered in disbelief. "How can you do that?"

"I don't know, but I want to try," was her answer. Mike knew she was serious. He smiled inside. This was the Felicia, he had always known. He would not discourage her even though it seemed impossible. Running through Mike's mind were the thoughts—she can't walk, she can't even hold a pencil. How can she possibly go to class?

"Well, check it out. Let's see what we can put together," Mike returned. "First you need to call the school and see what they say."

Later that morning Felicia called Massachusetts College of Liberal Arts, her almost alma mater, and identified herself. "Do you remember me, Pat?" Felicia asked. Pat had worked in the administrative office at the time Felicia was attending in 2005.

Pat's response was immediate "Yes. Wow! This is Felicia? Yes, I remember you. You were in that terrible accident. How are you?"

"I am fine," Felicia replied with enthusiasm. "I'm ready to finish the classes and get my degree so I can work as a principal." Felicia had to repeat herself often to be understood but she did not care. She wanted to return to school and she wasn't going to let a little thing like a speech impediment stop her.

"I can't believe you want to go back to school. I am so excited for you! I will do whatever I can to help you come back to school," Pat committed with enthusiasm.

Felicia and Pat visited for a long time; Felicia answering many questions about all she had been through, her progress, the family and many other things. Hanging up the phone, Felicia turned to Mike with a big grin and said, "They are willing for me to come back."

"Really? Do they know you are still in a wheelchair? Do they know you can't write? How is it going to be possible?" he questioned.

"Yes, they know," she insisted. "We will just have to figure out a way to make it happen. I want to finish school. You know, Mike, what I start, I finish." She was resolute.

"Yes, we will figure it out," Mike grinned. He knew going back to school would be a good motivation for his wife to continue progressing. Mentally Felicia was on top of things. It seemed her only holdbacks now were physical. She still did not speak clearly, even though she knew exactly what she wanted to say; and that, too, was slowly improving. If I can be her arms and her legs maybe we can make this work, he thought, but I sure don't know how.

CHAPTER 23

VOG Boot Camp

"AUNT CONNIE, CAN YOU stay for dinner with us tonight? Felicia has something to tell you," invited Mike.

She had become like one of the family. As they settled around the table, curiosity had gotten the best of her. "What is your news, Felicia?" Aunt Connie asked.

"I am going to go back to school to finish earning my administration degree," Felicia smiled, delighted.

Connie gave Felicia a big smile, saying, "I am so happy you feel you are ready to go back." Being a teacher, Connie fully understood Felicia's desire and goals. "Let me know if there is anything I can do to help you," she offered.

"I am really surprised they will let her go back since she is still in the wheelchair and she can't write." Mike interjected.

"How is that going to work?" Aunt Connie asked.

"Felicia says that she can do it if I will go with her. But how can I do that? I have to be here with the children," Mike stated.

"If I did go, I figure I could push her from class to class and if she could dictate her papers, I could type them for her. But I can't leave. It's a full two-week course and I just don't see how we can do it. I don't have anyone who can stay with the kids for that long."

"I can," Aunt Connie immediately offered.

"Could you really do that?" he asked, hesitantly.

"I would be happy to," Aunt Connie declared.

"Are you sure?" Mike questioned, "That's a lot for us to ask of you."

"Certainly, I'm sure. It'll be fun. We can continue the voice lessons and maybe even get in a little more practice," she teased, looking at the kids. "If it is only for two weeks, I can handle that easily."

"That's great," Mike said, "Thank you so much. I have always supported Felicia in whatever she wanted to do, but I just didn't see how I was going to be able to pull this one off."

"You gotta do what you gotta do," Felicia grinned. The family knew those were her famous last words. How many times had they heard her say it?

"I'm glad I was able to have dinner with you tonight," Aunt Connie said. "I have some news myself."

Everybody's ears perked up in anticipation knowing it was going to be good news.

"I have spoken with Columbia University. They have invited Voices of Glory to be guest performers at the Omega Psi Phi Talent Contest at Columbia University this year and Mikey can compete if he wants to.

"How does that sound?" she asked teasingly.

"It sounds like a great opportunity to me," Mike responded.

Felicia nodded her head in agreement and the kids laughed with excitement. Aunt Connie had set up some great venues for them and they knew this one would be just as good.

"What do you think they should sing?" asked Felicia. Consuelo Hill had been working with the kids for several months now and had worked on a number of songs for performance.

"How about the song I wrote," Aunt Connie suggested meekly, "It's About Christ."

"Yes," Felicia nodded her head with enthusiasm. "That will be our thank you for all you're doing for us," Felicia said, smiling at her old friend.

Felicia and Mike made their preparations to head back to Massachusetts. Mike asked for vacation time at work, but as usual, IBM went above and beyond and allowed him to work satellite via his laptop computer instead of using his vacation time.

"Felicia, guess what?" Mike said, "They told me at work to save my vacation days for family time and just work from Massachusetts. Isn't that great?" Felicia gave Mike a big smile. She was pleased that Mike was able to help her without it causing any pressure on him.

"Teamwork," she beamed.

Felicia couldn't wait to tell her friend, Sonia Brown, she was going back to school at MCLA in North Adams. She thought about calling her, but she wanted to see her face when she told her. On Sunday, Felicia pushed to get to church early so she would have time to talk to Sonia before service. She couldn't wait any longer. Mike obliged her and got to church earlier than normal, wheeling her into the sanctuary to await Sonia's arrival.

Felicia did not have to wait long to share her exciting news. As soon as Sonia stepped through the sanctuary doors, Felicia raised her arm in a wave to get her friend's attention.

"Guess what I'm going to do, Sonia?" Felicia began. She was all smiles and went on talking without giving Sonia time to respond. "I'm going back to school," Felicia squealed her delight.

"That's great," Sonia replied with guarded enthusiasm. "Are you sure you're ready?" she questioned, knowing her own hesitation. Rapidly thoughts flew through Sonia's mind. She had known she should return also but had had a difficult time pushing herself to do it. It wouldn't be easy to go back to Massachusetts and relive so many devastating memories. She had called the school in hopes that they would tell her it was too late to register for summer classes but, in fact, it was not, so she enrolled in spite of her feelings. When she had decided to return to school, she had called Alleen-Josephs Clark to see if she had any desire to finish the course. Alleen had dealt with the same emotional roadblocks, knowing she needed to return but had not wanted to go for all the same reasons as Sonia. Sonia found it curious that three years seemed to be key for their emotional healing and to gain the capacity to face it all again. Now here was Felicia on the same timetable.

Sonia reached down and gave her friend a hug. "Me, too," Sonia announced. This brought another squeal from Felicia.

"This makes it even better," Felicia grinned.

"Alleen is going back, too," Sonia shared.

"Wow, we will all be principals," Felicia laughed, nodding her head in delight.

Mike initiated a call to the admissions office of Massachusetts College of Liberal Arts asking for special consideration. "Would it be possible for me to stay with my wife in the dorm even though I'm not a student? I need to be there to help her, if she is going to go back to school," Mike explained.

"I don't know if that will be possible," the clerk said, "but I will ask for you."

"Thank you, and also would you see if Ms. Alleen Josephs-Clarke, Ms. Sonia Brown and us could be in the same area of the dorm. I have given this a lot of thought and I think it would be good for the girls to be together."

"I'll see if that could be arranged, too," the clerk agreed, with kindness in her voice.

In just a few days, a call came back advising room assignments were finalized. With a cheery voice, the clerk advised that Mike's requests had been approved. Mike was allowed to stay with his wife in the dorm room and the three friends were booked on the same dorm floor. Maybe this *will* work out, Mike thought.

Mike packed up his office and home laptops—just in case one of them failed, he would have a back up. He took a printer for his work and Felicia's assignments. He packed enough clothes for two weeks so they would not have to drive home and made sure the kids had everything they would need during their absence. All packed and ready to go, Mike and Felicia took off on a new adventure.

"When this is done, it will be closure for you," Mike said. Felicia nodded her head in agreement. It was exciting to go back on one hand, but a bit overwhelming at the same time.

She knew she would have to work hard and it wouldn't come as easy to her as it had in the past. She really had very little use of her hands. She didn't know what it would be like to tell someone else her thoughts and expect them to get it down on paper. So, she was very thankful for a husband that was willing to try for her sake.

When they checked in, one of the administrators told Mike that there was some concern that going back to school together would be a highly emotional experience for the ladies and that it may cause difficulties for them. Their fears have no basis, Mike reasoned. These were three strong ladies. I will just keep that thought to myself, no use in planting bad seeds he told himself.

The first day of class Sonia and Alleen took charge, protectively seating Felicia between the two of them. Subconsciously they had set themselves up as her defenders. It seemed they were given a lot of strange looks. They supposed the students weren't used to seeing a wheelchair in the classroom. Admittedly, Felicia did not look capable of completing the course, let alone being able to function as a school principal. But the other students did not know their friend. They did not know the tenacity of this one who from the outside looked like damaged goods, but on the inside was a lion with all the bite and all the roar that completing this course and doing the work would demand.

The instructor noticed the curiosity and underlying tension in the classroom. At the appropriate time, she shared with the class. She explained that three years ago these same ladies were students at the college with the same goals in mind as many of them. She told what she knew of the accident, confirming with Sonia, Alleen and Felicia the details she was uncertain about.

The climate of the room began to change as the other students gained an understanding of how remarkable it was that these three teachers were even in the classroom. There was a new appreciation for their perseverance to complete their goals. There was a fresh dynamic. Camaraderie developed as some of the students offered to help in any way they could.

Alleen, being medically trained, instructed the male classmates on the best way to move Felicia from her wheelchair to a student desk, which Felicia always preferred. She hated sitting in the wheelchair and being 'the odd man out'. It became a routine that as soon as Felicia arrived at class, the guys would be by her side to expedite the transport from the chair that held her captive, to the student desk which freed her spirit through the sheer familiarity of it.

They had known returning to school would be challenging, but they had not expected it to effect the other students and even the staff the way it obviously had. The instructor had handled the situation in such a sensitive and insightful way, setting up priceless interaction between the students and Felicia, Sonia, and Alleen. The students asked many questions, allowing the ladies to minister to them in ways that could have only been orchestrated by God. It was surprising to all of them—the level of intimacy that developed in their relationships with the other students. The three friends knew they were a testimony to God's love.

This summer session would go down in history as remarkable for many of the college staff. The students were inspired; the younger ones getting an up close and personal look of how fragile life could be while they all learned that overcoming obstacles could simply be a matter of determination.

And so, the return to school was an amazing experience. The three girlfriends went to class together, they ate together, and they laughed together. They helped each other in every way they could. If there was a computer or printer problem, they shared equipment. They encouraged each other, schooled each other, and studied together, making sure they all made it through this time. Mike did all he could to be accessible to them, but remained on the fringes allowing the seasoned teachers to do what they did so well.

However, one day Felicia was having difficulty. It just wasn't a good day for her physically. Mike stepped out in the hallway and caught Sonia and Alleen crying. He questioned them, not understanding what was wrong. He came to find out there was nothing wrong with them. They were just feeling bad for Felicia. They knew what a powerhouse she was. Seeing her now, so dependent on everyone else was painful for them to watch. They had been injured too; but nothing like Felicia had suffered, and they grieved for their friend. Perhaps the staff had been right to some degree Mike had to admit.

In the meantime, at home, Aunt Connie and the kids were having a great time together. From the beginning, she put the rules in place.

"This is VOG Boot Camp," Aunt Connie announced as soon as their parents had pulled out of the driveway.

"VOG Boot Camp? What's that?" Avery asked with a little fear in his voice. Mikey was looking at her like he wasn't sure he wanted to know.

"That sounds funny," Nadia laughed.

"Here's what we are going to do," she went on. "We are going to have chores to do and when they are done, *then* you can play. Everybody is going to pick up after themselves. But, we'll have fun too. You can choose special meals that you want to have and you can help fix them.

"I want pizza sauce on spaghetti, and ice cream," Nadia piped up.

"We'll have to talk about that one," Aunt Connie laughed, "and speaking of that, we'll be working on table manners, too… and voice lessons, and practice of course."

The kids looked at each other unsure what their parents had gotten them into, but the days went by quickly. It was summer and there was plenty of time to be outdoors with their friends. Aunt Connie was lenient with sweet treats and the kids were having a good time with their new friend.

"If this is boot camp, I won't mind joining the army," Avery joked one night at dinner. That brought a laugh around the table, especially from Aunt Connie.

"I have some good news for you," Aunt Connie said. "Your parents called today. One of the teachers from the college asked if you would come to the campus and give them a concert. Your dad asked if I would drive you to Massachusetts so they could see you and you could sing for the teachers. I told him, I can do that, just tell me how and where," Ms. Hill told them. There were smiles all around the table. Their parents had been gone for almost a week. It would be fun to take a road trip to see Mom and Dad.

The kids were a hit at the college. Every time they performed, it seemed they did a little better. Of course, having their coach there helped them to do their very best. The teacher behind the concert idea arranged for rooms at a top rated hotel for all of them. The kids thought they were living the high life. Mike and Felicia were just happy to be together with their family, enjoying life at least a little more like it used to be.

When the two weeks were over, Mike was amazed and so pleased with his wife. Even with all of the challenges, she managed to earn an A in each of her three classes.

At their graduation ceremonies, Mike was pleasantly surprised when his name was called out to come to the platform and receive an honorary degree for the remarkable support he had given Felicia in fulfilling her goal.

That step completed, she had only to complete her internship when the 2008 fall school session started. How amazing that after everything that happened, Felicia was still able to accomplish her goal. Mike thanked God for His grace and mercy that had seen them through so great an endeavor.

Arrangements were made at Temple Hill Academy. Felicia was to work as the vice principal for her internship for twelve weeks. Everyday Mike got up early, preparing breakfast, and getting Felicia and the kids ready for school, so that he could be at work on time and to get Felicia where she needed to be. Mike took Felicia to her parents' house each day. Felicia's father was working as a custodian at the school so it worked out well for them to take Felicia to her job. She worked through the semester, getting full credit for the internship, qualifying her for the position of school principal; the goal that she had set three and half years before.

When the internship was over, the school issued a letter of acknowledge to Felicia's parents, commending them for the help they provided to ensure that their daughter succeed in her efforts.

CHAPTER 24

Aretha, Bojangles and the Jackson Five

IT WAS SPRING AGAIN. Felicia looked at her children in amazement. When did they get so big? So much time had passed. Much of it had passed without her full awareness. Nadia was only five when the accident happened. Now she was eight and half, about the age Avery was at the time of the accident and Mikey had gone from a young teenager to a young man. Tears slid down Felicia's cheeks as her mother's heart felt the pain of knowing how much of her children's young lives she had missed. She couldn't let herself think about all the things she had not been able to do with them or for them. She caught her breath and choked on it making a coughing sound that caused her family to turn and see if she was all right. She turned her face away from them so they didn't see her tears. She pulled herself together and thanked God that she was alive. She thanked

Him for saving her life. She thanked Him that she was with them now. She thanked Him that she was home and not lying in a hospital bed, still in a coma. She knew there was much for which to be thankful. Her family was doing well. She would not live with "if only's". She would keep a grateful heart. She turned back and faced her family with a big smile.

"I love you," she said.

"We love you too, Mom," they answered in chorus, having no idea about all she had been thinking about.

Just before it was time to go to Columbia for the talent show, Mike learned about another contest, Amateur Night at the Apollo in New York City.

That night around the dining room table, Mike asked the kids, "How about going to another competition? The old Apollo Theatre in New York still has talent shows. They are actually having one the night before we go to Columbia University. Would you like to go to that one too?"

He explained to the kids about the Apollo Theatre and all it had meant to the black entertainment world. The family agreed it would be a fun thing to do. Even if they didn't win the talent show, just going to the Apollo would be a fun outing, they all agreed. So, they made their plans to go, and in just a few days, it was time for the contests.

"Is everybody ready? We need to leave right now if we're going to make it in time for the tryouts," Mike called out. He was helping Felicia into the wheelchair. It took a lot of time to get ready to go somewhere, but it was getting easier all the time. Still, they had a two-hour drive ahead of them without complications or stops.

This was a new direction. If they did well at the Apollo, their lives could be changed forever. For the past two years, Voices of Glory had been on a steady schedule of four or five performances at various venues and competitions each month. But this was different. The Apollo Theatre was famous for giving black performers their big break; did they dare dream?

They had talked about expanding their ministry, but weren't sure where to start. When they first heard about the tryout at the Apollo, Mike and Felicia talked together about whether they should be entering the children into contests. They reasoned that there were benefits in taking advantage of every opportunity to perform. It would give them training in voice, and stage presence and build their self confidence. It seemed to be the right direction in preparing them for a successful gospel ministry.

"Should we step out and see just what they can do?" Mike asked Felicia. He knew they should consider it very carefully. The children seemed to have a real knack for performing. So many people had encouraged them, yet were they really ready for the possibilities this door could open?

Felicia in her usual, nothing-is-too-big-to-try attitude, readily said, "Let's go for it! Nothing ventured, nothing gained."

Mike pondered her statement seriously. If they were good enough to qualify for the amateur show, then maybe they should be given the chance. If they didn't make it, they could continue to minister at churches. But if there was something bigger ahead of them, it didn't seem right not to give them every opportunity.

Since the last round table discussion, with all in agreement to go for it, things had moved very quickly. Driving to New York City was an experience all its own as everyone was at the height of enthusiasm and expectation.

"Tell us about The Apollo Theatre again," Avery cajoled his father.

"Well, it's an icon of African-American culture. Big name performers got their start there: comedians, band leaders, singers, and dancers," Mike explained. "Have any of you heard of Sammy Davis Jr., Duke Ellington, Bojangles Robinson or 'Moms' Mabley? How about James Brown, Al Green or Aretha Franklin?" knowing they would be more familiar with the three of them.

"Or maybe you've heard of the Jackson Five," Felicia teased.

"Oh, come on Mom, everybody's heard of them," Mikey laughed, responding to Felicia's joke.

"Well, they all got started at the Apollo Theatre, so if you get to perform there, you'll be in good company," Mike said with renewed excitement.

"What did you say about the Tree of Hope last night," Avery asked.

"You remember, Avery. It's part of a tree they called the lucky wishing tree. A long time ago, back in the 1930's, musicians and actors would hang around the tree on the street they called 'The Boulevard of Dreams'. They thought the tree would bring them good luck in their careers. Many of them performed at the old Lafayette Theatre before amateur night was moved to the Apollo. It's just superstition that rubbing the tree would bring them good luck but it is fun to be a part of a long tradition of black performers. Eventually the tree had to be cut down. They put a section of it in the Apollo to keep up that tradition. So rub away, son." Mike answered proudly.

"I am going to rub and rub and rub the Tree of Hope," said Avery." If Michael Jackson rubbed it, I am going to, too!"

"We should all rub it," Nadia popped in.

"Yeah, just think of all the famous people that have rubbed that piece of the Tree of Hope. I'll be able to say I rubbed it too, before I'm famous," Avery laughed with confidence.

"Before *we* are famous you mean, don't you, Bro?" chided Mikey as he reached across Nadia's head and playfully punched his younger brother's shoulder.

"Oh, yeah, I mean *us*," Avery answered a little sheepishly. There were big grins all around and in every heart… high hopes.

Once in the city, Mike maneuvered the car through the traffic. Although he had driven around New York City many times, visiting in Manhattan, Brooklyn and Queens, he was unfamiliar with the Harlem area around the theatre.

I'll just plug the address into the GPS and we'll find it with no problem," Mike stated, asking Felicia for the exact address. Felicia had been to the Apollo before, but it was a brand new experience for the rest of them.

Locating the theatre, Mike dropped Felicia and the children as close to the entrance as possible and then circled the neighborhood searching for a parking place.

"Ah, ha…there's one," Mike smiled to himself saying, "only three blocks away, not bad."

As Mike stepped out of the car, there were several people passing by obviously with destinations in mind. But one woman was approaching very slowly and deliberately, looking his way. As he started walking away she spoke to him, but he didn't really hear what she said. However, he couldn't help but notice the way she was dressed. Low cut blouse, short skirt and what do they call them he asked himself, spike heels; too friendly, he thought. He didn't have to hear her words to get her message. There was a dark blue police van sitting on the side of the street. "Is this a setup?" Mike wondered. She hollered something after him. Hurrying away, Mike was aware of the harshness in her voice. "Not me," Mike chuckled under his breath as he made his way to a restaurant to get sandwiches for his family.

There were people everywhere. Mike spotted Felicia and the kids just a few people from the back of the line. With both hands full, he delivered the deli sandwiches and orange juice. As he joined them, he leaned down and kissed Felicia on her forehead. "What's that for?" Felicia asked with a shy smile noticing Mike looked a little flushed. "I'll tell you later," Mike answered with a wry expression. She had thought he was flush just because he had been hurrying; now she wasn't so sure.

Having regained his composure, Mike listened as everyone around them was talking at once. He heard someone say the line of competitors ran for blocks ahead of them. It was going to be a long wait for their turn to compete for a chance to perform for a sophisticated New York City audience, but just being in the theatre would be a treat for all of them.

As they stood in the midst of the crowd, introductions were made and they visited with those next in line as they nervously checked out their competition. Some of the more confident performers were sharing a bit of their act with others in line.

As time passed and the Cole children began to relax and started playing around too; humming, and snapping their fingers to the rhythm they were creating. Mike told the kids to go ahead and sing. Song rang out as the crowd gathered around them and they let their voices rise. It soon became apparent to several people that this was a class-act, even though the children were young and amateur performers. A woman and her son were very impressed and readily told them they should try out for America's Got Talent tomorrow.

"What's America's Got Talent?" Mikey asked.

The woman simply answered, "It's a TV show."

Her son quizzed, "Haven't you ever heard of it, it's been on for three years."

"No," the kids shook their heads. Mike and Felicia were listening with great interest, looking at each other with a knowing that they were in the right place at the right time. To try out for a TV show was more than they had imagined.

"Is it like American Idol?" asked Mikey.

"Sort of, but groups can perform, and there are no age restrictions. There are all sorts of acts. Some of them are pretty weird, but there are a lot of really talented people on it too. It's fun to watch. You guys really should check it out," the young man encouraged them. "Just go the Javits Center tomorrow and try out."

"Wow, that's just what I've always wanted to do—be on TV," squealed Nadia, grinning from ear to ear.

Her brothers looked at her, shaking their heads embarrassed by their little sister's naïve excitement.

"You never know," the woman responded. "You kids are really good. By the way, what do you called yourselves?"

All three answered in harmony, "Voices of Glory."

"Wow, you even sound good talking together," she laughed.

It was an unusually cold day for April. Mike was chastising himself for not seeing to it that they were dressed warmer. The line ahead of them was still very long. It was going to be a cold wait if he didn't do something.

"Here, boys. Go down the street to that store," he said pointing toward a likely looking sign, "and see if they have hats and gloves." He handed what he thought should be enough money to Mikey and sent them on their way. Soon they were back with black hats and gloves for themselves and pink ones for Nadia. "They have scarves too, Dad. Can we go back and buy scarves? It would be so much warmer."

"Yes, do," he quickly decided. "It's not a good time to get chilled; right before two talent contests."

"Can I go with them?" Nadia, pleaded. "Yes, you can," he gave his permission. Normally Mike kept a tight rein on his children, but though they were in the city, he felt comfortable about letting her go in her brothers' care.

When the children returned, Felicia gave Mike their secret sign. It was time to find a restroom. Mike looked around for the closest possibility. There was a funeral home just a few doors down. He grabbed the handles of the wheelchair moving toward the funeral home doors. Conveniently, there was a ramp so wheeling her in was easy, but much to his surprise as they pushed the door open, the vestibule was full of people. Mike flushed with embarrassment as he realized he was crashing a funeral. People smiled and greeted them with questioning looks and queries as to their relationship to the deceased. Smiling back, but avoiding the questions, he asked where there was a restroom for his wife. A funeral home attendant graciously answered, directing them to an elevator to the second floor. Felicia got the giggles in the elevator asking, "Mike, how do you manage to get us in these predicaments?" "I don't know," Mike laughed. "It was easy enough to get in, but how are we going to get out of here without being found out?"

The ride back to the first floor wasn't as much fun as the ride up just thinking about what might happen. When the elevator doors opened, Mike pushed Felicia's wheelchair back among the crowd, working his way toward the front door. Someone who had not seen them come in, but was watching them leave said, "Wait, we are getting ready to go the cemetery." Mike answered, "That's okay, go ahead. We won't be able to go the cemetery with you."

"Quick thinking, Mike," laughed Felicia as they turned off the ramp onto the sidewalk. "I'll think twice about where to take you from now on," Mike said, shaking his head and feeling a little deceptive.

CHAPTER 25

Amateur Night At The Apollo

LOOKING AROUND FOR THE kids, they realized the line had moved a long way forward in their absence. Soon they were in sight of the entry door. Anticipation was high as they watched people exit the building and walk past them. Some had laughter in their eyes, while others had long, sad faces, their eyes brimming with tears.

Voices of Glory were confident, hopeful and excited. Mike wheeled Felicia up a ramp and maneuvered his way to the registration desk. Mikey completed a form giving their names, address, ages and contact information.

"They said you kids should wait in the balcony," Mike instructed.

Taking Nadia by the hand and keeping his eye on Avery, Mikey followed the line to the balcony. From there they could see the famous stage. Avery spotted the Tree of Hope. He couldn't wait for his fingers to feel the smoothness of the wood, worn down by time and many hands. The kids were in awe of everything. Their eyes took in all the sights; the beautiful décor with the red seats, the elegant gold trim on the walls, the ornate balconies, and the glowing chandeliers. Their hearts beat swiftly with excitement and anticipation. They marveled at each new vision, each new discovery.

Finally, it was their turn. Their name, Voices of Glory, was called out among a group of five other competitors and they were sent into an audition room. One at a time, each group performed their acts. Mike and Felicia were allowed in the audition room along with other family members and friends to watch the performances.

Voices of Glory were called to the mock stage. They sang God Bless America, a cappella. It was obvious to Mike and Felicia that the judges were pleased, but nothing was said and the rest of the groups and individuals took their turn at the eliminations. At the end, a spokesperson thanked all of the performers and advised they would be getting in touch with all of them soon. The room quickly emptied. As Mike was helping Felicia from a chair into the wheelchair, one of the judges approached them.

"Come back on June 3rd—you're in," she told them. She asked about Felicia, wondering why she was in the wheelchair. They briefly explained about the accident.

"The children have beautiful voices. Will they be available for Amateur Night at the Apollo?" she asked.

They were speechless. They assumed they would have to wait for a telephone call just like everyone else. She had let the cat out of the bag.

"We will still call you with confirmation." It was all they could do to hide their grins and giggles.

They took the elevator to the lobby of the theatre. Their attention was drawn to the pictures of many famous people. It was luxurious and fascinating. There was so much to look at, but best of all, they were coming back to be on that famous stage themselves.

It was still light when they left the theatre. Daylight savings time was in effect and with the bright city lights, it seemed as midday rather than late evening. "We need to get something to eat before we start home," Mike said, thinking aloud. Moving toward the car, he had another thought. "Children, what do you think about America's Got Talent?" Do you want to try out for that, too?" Things were moving so fast. Now they had a chance to compete in three different contests. They were still talking about it when they reached their car; piling in, everyone was talking at once.

Mikey was unsure. "They said tryouts were tomorrow. Can we do two contests in one day?

"Let's go for it and see what happens," Avery said, putting in his two-cents worth. Felicia's head was nodding in absolute agreement.

"Yeah, it would be fun," Nadia squealed with excitement.

"We better check some things out before we decide," Mike reasoned, "but Nadia's right, it would be fun to try. Where did they say it was, Mikey? We can't waste any time getting lost tomorrow."

"I don't remember. I don't think it's too far."

They drove around the city, looking at marquees thinking it would be well advertised and easy to spot. They couldn't find a thing. "Why don't you call Aunt Joy? She keeps up on things like that." Felicia suggested. But calling Aunt Joy turned out to be a dead end too.

"We better head home," Mike finally decided. "Maybe we can find something on the internet."

"What should we sing for the America's Got Talent contest?" asked Avery.

They talked about the different possibilities. Even though they were full of excitement about the near future and dreams of the distant future, it soon got quieter and quieter in the car until everyone but Mike was asleep.

An hour later, pulling into the driveway in front of his house, he pushed the gearshift into park, switched off the key and leaned his head back against the seat. He had been fighting sleep for the past twenty miles and now all he wanted to do was close his eyes. About an hour later, he jerked awake realizing they hadn't gone into the house. Now with naps behind them, their excitement was revived.

"Let's find out where this contest is," Mikey suggested, crawling out of the car, and gathering up his things from the car seat.

Nadia was the first one to the computer and was already doing an internet search when the others entered the room. She was good on the computer for a little kid and was doing her best but confessed, "Daddy, I can't find it."

"Look up New York, America's Got Talent," Mike instructed. Immediately Javits Center popped up.

"Found it. Javits Center, New York City," she announced proudly, knowing she had heard the name somewhere before.

"It says it's on West 34th Street," Mikey said, looking over Nadia's shoulder.

"No wonder we didn't find it," Mike laughed, shaking his

head. "We were miles from there." Mike studied the map to be sure he would know where he was going.

Stepping away from the computer, he commanded, "Everybody, get to bed. We have a very big day tomorrow. Morning is going to come all too soon."

"Yes, too soon," Felicia agreed. Nobody argued. It was good to go to bed and dream sweet dreams of winning talent contests and maybe even having glamorous careers.

Mike and Felicia prayed for wisdom in directing their children, and thanked God for the amazing opportunities and favor that seemed to be in their new path.

CHAPTER 26

It's The Right Thing To Do

"GOOD MORNING. GOOD MORNING, boys," Mike announced with plenty of volume and an attempt to sound alert and enthused. "We need to rise and shine. You are going to try out for America's Got Talent today," he reminded them.

"Now, hurry and get ready. You can get a little more sleep in the car," Mike said to encourage them. Of course, that was a given, Mike smiled to himself. Their kids were like babies when it came to sleeping in the car. You almost couldn't keep them awake. As soon as the car starts, and the wheels are rolling, all three of them are out like a light. That will be a good thing this morning Mike had to admit. It had been a short night and they had a big exciting day ahead of them with the talent contest at Columbia University and the tryouts.

Mike had wheeled Felicia into Nadia's room so she could help awaken what they knew would be a very sleepy little girl.

When he was confident the boys were awake, he returned to Nadia's room to check on his girls.

Mikey swung his long legs off the bed and stood up stretching with a big smile on his face. This is too good to be true. "We're actually going to the city to try out for a television show," he laughed. "Wow, Avery, can you believe it? America's Got Talent. This is huge, Bro!"

Avery was sitting on the edge of his bed, his elbows resting on his knees, his chin cupped in his hands. He was sleepy but excited.

"You can shower first, I just want to sit here a minute and dream about being on TV," Avery yawned and grinned at the same time.

"Good. That was my plan, too," Mikey laughed as he grabbed a clean pair of jeans from the closet.

"Everybody into the car," Mike hollered, to be sure he had everyone's attention. "I'm taking Mom out now."

"Be sure to get everything you need," he reminded them as he opened the back door. He wasn't really sure what they would need. He didn't know what to expect out of this day anymore than his children did. All he knew was they were being led down a path that he could not have imagined ten years ago. It seemed this was another step in the fulfillment of the prophecy about the children having a ministry. Mike and Felicia were excited and in awe.

"Can you believe we are doing this Felicia?" Mike asked his wife.

"I believe," she answered.

That said it all, Mike reflected. Felicia had always been a

believer, not just in her Savior, not just in a loving Father, but she believed in the goodness of life. Felicia believed in the value of effort. She believed in doing and then reaping the reward of that effort. Felicia believed in their family to do good things.

The drive to New York City went quickly. Mike and Felicia had decided it would be best to go to the Javits Center first to determine what they needed to do for the tryouts. They didn't have to be at Columbia University until noon so getting an early start allowed them to get organized. The kids slept until Felicia announced that they were approaching the George Washington Bridge, signaling it was time to wake up.

They arrived at Javits Center, found street parking and stepped out of the car. They were surprised by the early morning chill and dampness still in the air. They walked hastily toward their destination. The wind blew hard against them as they walked down the street. Finally arriving after walking several blocks, they hurried inside to get out of the cold. Taking an elevator down to the lower floor, they were fascinated by the huge number of people that had gathered. There were people everywhere. TV cameras were already filming. People were cheering and clapping as different groups of performers came into the spotlight. There were people inside a ribbon barrier and people outside of it. Later they figured out that part of the crowd was just there to be in on the excitement and watch, while the ones inside the barrier were actually going to participate.

They spotted the registration tables and made their way through the crowd to get in line. As they worked their way closer to the table, Mike could see there were many different forms to be completed. He gathered them up and moved the family to an empty table. There were no chairs available, so they knelt beside the table using it for a writing surface. Each participant had a separate form to complete asking for personal data and experience, plus there were parental authorization forms and even more permission forms in case they were chosen to be on TV. Mike handed each of the children a form to complete in order to speed up the process. Even Nadia filled in her own personal data as much as she was able.

As they worked on the forms, a conversation was overheard. One girl was hesitating, unsure if she really wanted to tryout. She said she was too nervous and scared and afraid she wouldn't do well. She didn't want to be embarrassed.

"I'm glad you kids have had lots of chances to perform and good training from Aunt Connie," Mike said. "That will make it easier for you." Felicia nodded her head in agreement, as she watched her children.

"I'll be nervous, but I still want to do it," Avery responded.

"Yeah, we'll just do it scared," Mikey laughed.

When the forms were done, Mike walked back to the registration table and asked for advice on what to do. "Our children were already scheduled for the talent contest at Columbia University today when we heard about this tryout," Mike shared with a lady sitting at the registration table. "The waiting line for auditioning is too long for us to get through in time," he said. "What do you suggest?"

"Just be back before seven," she warned in response to his question. "Since you're already registered, all you'll need to do is get in line when you return," she smiled. "Good luck at Columbia."

Mike breathed a sigh of relief. He returned to where the family was gathered. The kids were very excited and ready to get in line. They had talked to other contestants while Mike was at the registration table and were in high gear to get on with it.

"Let's get in line," Nadia proposed, moving in that direction.

"No, come back, Nadia. We have to go to Columbia first. We don't have time to wait in line or we will be late." Mike explained. Looks of disappointment appeared on all their faces.

"We might miss our chance," Avery voiced his concern, looking at the long line of people. "They may pick everyone they want before we get back.

"We made a commitment to Columbia University. It wouldn't be right not to do what we said we would do. You can't ignore that just because you have a better opportunity. It will be all right. The lady said we just had to be back before seven," Mike advised.

"It's the right thing to do," Felicia instructed her children. Felicia's speech had improved greatly. Even though she didn't talk a lot, she wanted to plant good seeds into her children's lives whenever she had the chance. She gave her children a look that they were very familiar with. It said, "Listen to me. I know what I'm talking about."

"You're right," Mikey said, "and Aunt Connie would be very upset with us if we were a no show."

"That's the truth," Felicia agreed, nodding her head vigorously. She had known Connie for a lifetime and knew what she expected. She had fed so much into Voices of Glory, it was only right to expect much from them.

CHAPTER 27

On To The Next Round

ARRIVING AT COLUMBIA UNIVERSITY, they found a parking place, and then walked around the campus trying to find out where they needed to be. They asked people for directions and soon found the right building. They moved their car to a more convenient parking place and were finally ready to compete in the contest.

Mike, Felicia and Nadia found seats in the large auditorium. Mikey and Avery were directed to the contestant room to register. For Mikey, it was the second time to compete at the Columbia University contest. The first time he sang "Ole Man River" and took second place so he planned to compete with the same song. It was Avery's first time to compete and he had chosen to sing "The Lord's Prayer". They were again asked to be guest performers. Nadia was too young to compete, but joined her brothers when Voices of Glory were called on stage to present their special guest song.

The family enjoyed the talent show watching each contestant giving their best effort in the competition. They were impressed with the level of talent of so many people and enjoyed the entertainment of all of the different types of music and dancing. As the boys names came up, they took their turn to compete against their peers.

It was a great day and they regretted having to cut it short by leaving Columbia before the competition ended, but they needed to in order to be back at Javits Center in time. It was getting late. They quietly exited the auditorium and hurried to the car.

When they arrived back, they had no trouble finding a parking place. The street was practically empty. Javits Center looked like a ghost town in comparison to their departure. The auditorium was a wasteland of plastic bottles and chip bags, but deserted by people. A different woman was sitting at the registration table and Mike had to explain to her that they were already registered and had come back to audition.

"You're lucky," she said. "I was just getting ready to shut down."

"Come along with me," she said hurriedly.

She led them to the waiting room where there were only about fifty or sixty people remaining. She said to take a seat and someone would let them know what to do next. Soon the AGT staff divided everyone in the room by their performance category; singers, instrumentalists, dancers, et cetera lined up for their auditions.

When their turn finally came, they sang "Holy, Holy, Holy". Their voices rang out in perfect harmony. Their intensity and sincerity was palatable. The producers seemed pleased but nothing was said. They watched until the last audition was completed.

The producers dismissed the group, giving instructions on what to expect next. The crowd slowly dispersed. Avery went after Felicia's wheelchair in preparation to leave.

One of the producers approached Mike saying the children had done very well but that a song like "Holy, Holy, Holy" while beautiful, would not necessarily be received by their television audience.

"I would like to suggest you sing a different song for us," he related. "Can you stay a little while longer and do another audition?" he asked. "I want someone to meet you."

They readily agreed. Mike and Felicia were awestruck. They had dismissed almost everyone else and were giving them special attention. "What was going on?" they asked each other.

Mike told the children what the man had said. Most of the songs they had trained on were for their gospel ministry. "They want you to sing another song for them. Which one do you think?" Mike asked his children.

"How about "God Bless America?" Mikey suggested.

"Yes," Mike agreed. "That is a good choice."

Voices of Glory and two other groups were asked to wait in the hall. As they waited, they talked with the other contestants who were also getting another chance to sell themselves to the producers. They quickly connected with two sisters, Monica and Nia. The girls performed both a duet and solos in the competition. Monica had an operatic style while Nia was all about rhythm and blues. Excitement was running high. They quickly got acquainted, sharing all of the excitement of the day.

Things were moving very fast. Again, the producers approached the kids and they were taken aside for photo shots.

They were beginning to feel like celebrities already. They were then escorted to another audition room. As they walked along, the promoters asked their names. The kids introduced themselves and then Mike introduced himself and Felicia. One of the gentlemen asked what had caused Felicia to be in the wheelchair and Mike explained about the accident. He went on to say the children started singing together at church and then at their mother's bedside in hopes of bringing her out of the coma. Knowing the children's talent, it was a surprise to the producers to hear of such a humble beginning.

Voices of Glory again took their places in front of the America's Got Talent producers. Mikey took the lead in an attempt to get each of them singing the same note. He started to sing but Nadia said, "No," and sang a different note. Mikey persisted and went forward, singing the same note as before. Nadia and Avery joined in, but it was soon obvious it wasn't working and they stopped singing. This false start was embarrassing and frustrating, but quickly Nadia began singing again, starting them off in e-flat. Now they were on track and a song rang out that couldn't help but evoke strong patriotism and pull on the listener's heartstrings. They sang it beautifully and with passion.

"Wow, you guys are great," said the producer who was hearing them for the first time. Addressing Mikey, he asked, "What happened there? It sounded like you should have listened to your little sister." Mikey stood there with egg on his face having to admit to a big time television producer that he had been wrong and his younger sister by seven years had been right.

He was wise enough to admit his error and answered, "Yes, Sir," albeit a little sheepishly.

"Well, you are definitely going on to the next round," the producer responded.

They were told they needed to come back on Thursday. Mike was hesitant. It would mean the kids would miss another day of school and that didn't seem like a good idea. "They have already missed school today. We can bring them back next weekend though," Mike offered.

"They need to be here on Thursday for the competition at the Manhattan Center," he persisted. "They are good. I think they have a pretty good chance."

"What do you think, Felicia?" Mike asked. Felicia just shrugged her shoulders. She wasn't sure either.

"Okay, I guess we will be here," Mike agreed, realizing that was the way it worked. It was too late to turn back now. This may be their big break and they can make up their schoolwork, he reasoned.

They were sent to the travel room for instructions on the next step in the competition. Monica and Nia were there when they arrived. They visited with their new friends, exchanged phone numbers and agreed they would see each other at the Manhattan Center on Thursday.

It was late before they were back in the car and on the way home. For once, even though the kids were tired from their demanding day, they were too excited to sleep.

"Let's call Aunt Connie," Avery suggested.

"Good idea," agreed Mike and Felicia at the same time. Mikey grabbed the phone and dialed the number.

"Hello, Aunt Connie," Mikey started as she answered. "You'll never guess what we did today," he said nearly laughing into the phone.

"Oh yes. How did it go at Columbia?" she asked, assuming she knew what he was talking about. "Did you win?"

"We got a great response, but we have something else to tell you. We don't know how we did because we had to leave to try out for America's Got Talent and we were chosen. We get to go to the next round and be on television."

Mikey moved the phone away from his head a full foot. Aunt Connie was screaming so loud it hurt his ears. She was so excited she couldn't even talk. Only scream. Finally, she calmed enough to listen. "Tell me about it, tell me everything," she commanded, now ready to hear all the details between her shouts of joy.

"On Thursday we will be performing at the Manhattan Center. They are giving us ten complimentary guest tickets for our friends and family. We want you to be there," Mikey said confidently, knowing one of the tickets would be hers. "We're going to email them our guest list. All you need to do is give them your name at the door and you'll be admitted."

"Great. This is just so great, and congratulations. You kids have worked so hard. I should know," Aunt Connie laughed. "Now let me talk to your mom, please."

Mikey handed the phone to Felicia. "Here Mom, Aunt Connie wants to talk to you." As Felicia put the phone to her ear, she could hear Connie already talking, saying how proud she was of Voices of Glory. They talked several minutes, laughing, crying and repeating how excited they were.

"Your turn, Avery," Felicia said, handing the phone to the back seat. They all took their turn talking to Aunt Connie, ending with Mike. With each new conversation, Connie's excitement would rise again. It was so rewarding for her to know that her students had done so well in their performance. She just knew they were going to be the stars of the show.

"Wow, I am so thrilled," she said, choking and laughing and crying at the same time. "I'll talk to you tomorrow, Mike. I have to tell everyone," she said, her excitement heightening again revealed by intermittent squeals of delight.

"No. No, Connie. Are you still there?" Mike called into the phone.

"Yes, I'm here," she answered, sensing concern in his voice.

"Don't tell anyone or the kids could be disqualified. We'll explain more tomorrow. Just don't say anything."

"Okay, I won't. I probably won't sleep either," she laughed again.

"Who else are we going to invite?" Avery asked.

"Oh, yeah," Mike responded, handing the phone to his wife to call her family. Felicia called her parents to give them the good news. It was decided Felicia's brothers, Brian, Richard and a friend would attend.

"How about the Falco's?" Mikey asked.

"Yes," Mike and Felicia agreed. Mikey placed the call to the Falco's and their excitement overflowed through the phone. They were cautioned to keep it a secret, which just added to the fun.

"That's ten," Mikey announced.

"Friends and family will be cheering you on from the audience. How great is that?" Mike declared, smiling in the rear view mirror at his children even though it was too dark for them to see him.

CHAPTER 28

Calm Down Little Sister

THE NEXT DAY, IT was difficult for the kids to concentrate at school. They had to keep their exciting news to themselves. America's Got Talent had made it very clear that telling the outcome of the tryouts would be considered a breach of contract and they could be disqualified from participating. The network wanted to maintain the element of surprise for the actual live airing of the acts.

When Mike checked his email that morning, he found a transmission from America's Got Talent with a large attachment. He printed the file. There was a pile of papers an inch thick: it was the legal document that he'd been told about. Mike stacked the papers on the dining room table to review that evening when he returned home.

The day went by quickly with so much to think about and do in preparation for their return trip to the city on Thursday. After work, Mike and Felicia read over the legal document.

"We better get some help on this," Mike told Felicia. "I'm going to take these papers next door." They had the good fortune to be friends with their neighbor who was an attorney. He gladly reviewed the contract and congratulated the Coles on their success.

Relieved to have that off their plates, they made final preparations for their big day. Again, they were caught up in surreal circumstances. They were exhilarated and they were grateful.

Mike reminded the kids that their talent and success was a gift from God and that without Him they could do nothing, but with Him everything was possible. "We must keep all of this in perspective. We must stay humble and remember we are serving God or the devil will sneak in and cause us to get big heads and eventually steal our joy. God is faithful to take care of us. We want to be faithful to give Him thanks for all He is doing for us." With that, Mike asked his family to bow their heads for prayer. Again, he thanked God for all the blessings in their lives.

"We serve a good and loving God," he said at the end of his prayer. "Now it's lights out. We have to get up early in the morning." The kids hugged Felicia and Mike, said good night and went to their rooms. Sleep came quickly, but it was full of dreams of the past few days and a bright future.

Recalling their conversation from not too many days before, Mike teasingly asked Felicia if she thought national television was "big enough to go for". She just laughed in response. Was it just by chance that they had learned about the tryouts for a TV show they'd never even heard of just hours before they needed to sign up? Was it just by chance that they were already scheduled to be in New York City that day? "Where will this one take us?" Mike asked rhetorically, knowing neither of them could possibly have the answers.

When they arrived at the Manhattan Center, they received instructions on where to wait until it was their time to be on stage. They were given a performance number and directed to the waiting area.

It was a long time until their number would be called. They were free to look around and enjoy themselves during the wait. They took the elevator to the second floor. As they stepped out of the elevator, they heard voices and followed the sounds to the balcony. They realized they were watching the elimination process of one of their competitors.

A virtual shock went through their bodies as they heard the buzzer for the first time. Hearing about the buzzer at try-outs, they had been quick to check out the show online when they got back home. The buzzer meant elimination by each of the judges. When the judge had heard or seen enough, they hit their button, causing a loud obnoxious buzz to vibrate through the ears of the very disappointed contestant. Three strikes and you're out.

They had also learned that sometimes acts that weren't all that good still got through the eliminations to add interest and intrigue to the show. So even if you didn't get the buzzer, it didn't mean the judges liked you.

Mikey wasn't really nervous about being on stage until he heard the buzzer. It unnerved him. He did not want to hear that buzzer while they were performing. He hoped he wouldn't.

"I hate that buzzer," Mikey confessed.

"I don't like it either," Nadia answered "but I guess that's how it works."

"Of course, nobody likes the buzzer, but I don't think we will hear it anyway," Avery said, looking to his brother and sister for agreement.

They returned to the main floor to wait. Box lunches were being distributed to all of the participants. They got in line for lunch, visited with the people closest to them—everyone sharing their stories, and their excitement.

After lunch, one of the producers approached them and said they wanted Voices of Glory to do an interview with Nick Cannon. Nadia got a big, funny grin on her face, and then leaned forward on her chair, grabbing her stomach.

"What's the matter with you," Avery asked.

"I think I'm going to puke. I love Nick Cannon. He's so cute," she squealed as all of her adolescent admiration bubbled out of her.

"You're going to puke because you love him," Avery taunted his younger sister.

"No, I'll be so nervous. I can't believe I get to meet him," she answered, still feeling shaken.

"Calm down, little sister," Mikey laughed.

"Yeah, please, calm down," Avery said, taking her by the shoulders giving her a light shake in fun.

One of the producers for America's Got Talent approached Mike and Felicia, requesting an interview with them, also. Mike was not excited about the idea because he could not see himself being on camera, but he put his reservations aside knowing it was important to the kid's success for their story to be told. She asked many questions about their circumstances, showing sincere interest and concern for Felicia's plight and getting the background on the kids, their history and performance experience.

Mike found it hard to answer so many direct questions. Tears came to his eyes as he attempted to explain the severity of Felicia's injuries, the days of not knowing if she would live, turning into months of not knowing if she would regain consciousness and having to face the fact that even if she did live, she may never be able to be a wife to him again. Mike was surprised by his own reaction. He thought he had gotten beyond the emotion. Nevertheless, Felicia was sitting beside him now, in her right mind, and able to communicate. Their children were in an amazing place, preparing to audition for national television. What more could he ask?

He looked at the producer and smiled. "Would you like to meet the children?" Mike offered when she appeared to have asked all of her questions. They were standing off to the side not able to hear what was being said, but came quickly as Mike signaled to them.

Introductions were made and the kids shared their excitement over the remarkable turn of events that had brought them to America's Got Talent.

"You will enjoy your interview with Nick Cannon," the lady producer affirmed. The kids readily agreed, Nadia beaming with flushed cheeks.

The producer excused herself and the Cole family again was left to wait for the next step in the process. It was going to be a long day, but they were energized by the electric atmosphere created by everyone's excitement. They talked to other contestants, practiced playful handshakes to entertain themselves, and tried to control their nervousness.

Nadia looked up and spotted Nick and the camera crew as they were walking across the huge waiting area. The crew, having a picture of the kids for reference, was searching for Voices of Glory. Suddenly, they were spotted and Nick and the others made a beeline for them.

Nadia was so excited and nervous she literally froze after taking a seat across from Nick Cannon. He opened the interview by asking the name of their act. Mikey responded to each of Nick's questions, saying they were just regular kids who loved to sing so much they would go wherever they were asked to perform. He talked about how important family was to all of them. Avery shared that singing together had helped them get through the tough times.

Nick asked the kids for their reactions to certain events that had led up to that point. They had a good visit and Nadia was finally starting to relax. At the close of the interview, Nick said, "Your parents definitely did a phenomenal job and I know that they are proud of you guys and I'm rooting for you guys, and I wish you nothing but success."

"Thank you," each of the children responded with big smiles.

"Oh, yeah and before you leave, my sister has a huge crush on you," Mikey announced. Nick just smiled at Nadia.

Nadia glared at her brother. "Are you serious, Michael? Are you serious? What have you done? You just told Nick Cannon I had a crush on him." Her little brown cheeks glowed with embarrassment.

Nick watched this sibling exchange with great humor. Turning to Nadia, he said, "It's okay, I'm just a person—just like you."

He then told the kids it was a huge blessing to talk to them. They thanked him again and said they had had fun talking with him, too.

As Nick walked away, Nadia gave Mikey the evil eye as only she could do; that look that always made her brothers laugh.

"I can't believe you did that," she said again.

Mikey and Avery were laughing and not taking her seriously, as they punched each other, enjoying the joke Mikey had pulled on their little sister.

As the afternoon passed, they found a quiet place to talk as a family. They reminisced a little about what had brought them to this place. They talked about their love for music and how they had first sang together at church. They talked about the fun they had had at the Falcon and all of the people who had inspired them musically.

Mikey said, "I have always loved music, but while we were staying with the Falcos, I learned a lot about different styles. Tony introduced me the songs of Jimmy Hendrix and Sam Cook and a lot of other guys. It was neat to go to concerts with him."

"I liked talking to the musicians and helping them set up to play at the Falcon," Avery added. "I like the technical side of it, working with all of the instruments and speakers and everything."

"It was fun." Nadia added. She loved anything to do with music. Music just seemed to be in her. The time spent with the Falcos only reinforced the musical foundation that had already been laid.

"Yes, I believe they were a great influence on all of you." Mike stated.

They watched for their guests to arrive. They were glad Aunt Connie, the Falcos, and Felicia's brothers would be there to cheer them on. Everyone else in the audience would be strangers.

The theatre was full of excited guests awaiting the first elimination round. Spirits were high. The emcee engaged the audience through wit and conversation and joke telling. They opened the stage to anyone who would like to perform just for the fun of it. Aunt Connie was so keyed up with anticipation for her students; she was one of the first to volunteer to take the stage. These unscheduled amateur acts kept the audience entertained in the pre-show time. Aunt Connie sang an old favorite and got a good round of applause.

"It was a lot of fun," she told the Cole family later. The kids thought it was great that Aunt Connie had had a chance to show off her talent too.

Anxiety was building as it got closer to time for them to perform. A member of the America's Got Talent staff approached them, saying it was time to go backstage. Felicia's wheelchair was too wide to go up the narrow stairway. It was decided they needed to go outdoors and come in through the rear entrance. They then carried her in the wheelchair up the stairway and onto the backstage. Mike was pleased and impressed at the kindness and accommodations given to Felicia in an effort to be sure she was included.

Once there, the excitement level skyrocketed and the butterflies in the kids' stomachs took flight. They were in awe as they saw all that was going on behind the scenes. They spotted the monitors and watched the act that was currently being judged on stage.

One of the stage crew handed each of the kids a microphone and instructed them on where to stand.

"I'm scared," Nadia confessed.

Avery looked down at the microphone in his hand. "You can do the talking, Mikey. I'm too nervous," he said, smiling shyly.

"That's okay. I'll talk," Mikey agreed, appearing unusually calm for the circumstances. His stage time had served him well. Being the oldest he had had a lot of practice introducing Voices of Glory, first at the hospital, then at nursing homes and churches, at competitions and prestigious venues. This was the third time they had been on stage in as many days so he was feeling pretty confident.

"Let's get the note right," Mikey instructed and began humming. Nadia joined in, attempting to match him. The two of them did it several times, insuring that they had it right. Mikey wasn't going to risk having a problem like they had at tryouts. He wasn't going to embarrass himself again. Avery listened, knowing he would catch the right note once they started singing.

Nick Cannon asked, "Are you ready?"

"Yeah, we're ready," they answered with nervous excitement. Anticipation accelerated as Voices of Glory stood ready. The boys were dressed in traditional navy blue suits, and blue ties with silver stripes that matched Nadia's dress. Her dress was designed with a navy velvet bodice and silver-blue taffeta skirt.

Mike and Felicia watched from a close distance. They too were nervous, but so happy to see their children getting ready to compete on national television. They were confident they would do well. Their voices and talent were a gift from God. He would see them through.

They were given the signal to take the stage. As they walked out, the audience cheered. As instructed, they lined up with Nadia in the middle.

Piers Morgan was the first to speak. "Okay, who are you guys?" he asked.

Michael answered, "We are Voices of Glory. I'm Michael, this is Nadia, and that's Avery. We come from Highland, New York.

"Great," Piers responded. Again, the crowd clapped their approval.

"Are you brothers and sister, or…?" Piers questioned.

"Yes, we are," Michael answered.

"You are?…okay."

Sharon Osborne asked, "Can I just ask how old you all are?" pointing to them with a big smile.

Michael started to answer saying, "I'm sixteen," pointing to Avery, "my little…"

Nadia started to speak, but Avery seemed to get his stage nerve and spoke over her, "I'm thirteen," he smiled.

Quickly, Nadia joined in, "I'm nine." This brought a chuckle and smiles from the judges as they saw the younger members of the trio interrupt their appointed spokesman.

"What are you going to sing for us today?" Piers asked.

Mikey responded, "God Bless America. We want to dedicate this to all of America."

"Great, great," Piers agreed.

"What was your inspiration if you don't mind my asking?"Piers asked.

"About three years ago, my mom got in a head on collision caused by a drunk driver. We started singing by her bedside just to comfort her and try to see if she would respond because at the time, she was in a coma and she stayed in the coma for eight months. From that time on, we just started singing to her and singing to all the other people in the hospital and it just went on from there."

David Hasselhoff started clapping along with the audience. Sharon gave them a look of motherly admiration. The crowd continued to cheer until they were interrupted by another question from Piers.

The kids were humbled by the response they were getting. Nadia and Avery looking toward the floor and out to the audience with serious expressions obviously sobered by the telling of their own ordeal.

"Do you mind me," hesitating, Piers asked, "do you mind me asking what happened to your mother?"

"Well, my mother is yet alive and she is right back…backstage," Michael answered, gesturing toward the curtain.

The crowd went wild erupting in joyous applause. This time clapping came from Sharon as a hidden camera revealed the backstage scene of Felicia in her wheelchair, seated beside Nick Cannon, with Mike their father standing behind them. Felicia looked radiant as she waved and smiled to the audience and judges; her grateful smile expressing that indeed she was alive and well. Again, the audience's display of support for Voices of Glory was only interrupted by Piers leaning into his microphone and saying, "Wow, what a story. Alright, you guys, whenever you're ready," he instructed.

The judges readied themselves, waiting to see just what these three kids from Highland, New York, had to offer.

The kid's turned from side to side, making eye contact with each other, Michael snapping his fingers and counting to get their timing exact.

As the first phrase was sung in beautiful harmony, David Hassselhof raised his hands as if gesturing, "Just listen to you," and the crowd stood to their feet in honor of their country and the magnificent performance of this well-cherished patriotic song. By the end of the song, the judges, too, had risen to their feet and were clapping for this young trio.

David gave a double thumbs up, crying out "Yeah, yeah," as Piers, Sharon and the audience continued in rowdy applause and unrestrained heartfelt cheering. As everyone took their seats, the camera caught Sharon Osborne wiping tears from her cheeks. There were sweet smiles on the faces of Avery, Nadia and Michael as they enjoyed the obvious delight of their audience.

In natural response, and totally unrehearsed, Michael stepped behind his younger brother and sister, placing a hand on each of their shoulders in a protective stance portraying a precious picture of love and unity for the entire world to see.

The judges were obviously pleased with their performance as they sat in awe of this highly emotional performance.

David said, "I think you should just go around to hospitals and make people walk." That caused laughter and applause from the audience, but also touched the children; their natural response was laughter and grins as they too pictured the wonderful vision.

Piers was the first to speak with heartfelt sincerity. "Well, let me tell you, God bless you three. You are the pride of America tonight. That is one of the best vocal performances we have heard thus far."

"Yeah," David Hasselhoff declared giving his sure agreement. "Your mother's proud of you today. Wow!",he added as the camera swept to an elated Felicia, nodding in agreement.

"That was beautiful. Fantastic," David said, seeking the right words to express his enthusiasm.

"Fantastic," he repeated. "This is what this show is about. America has got talent!" he called out with conviction, slapping his hand on the table.

Piers deferred to Sharon, but as she began to speak, the unexpected happened as the audience started chanting, "We want Mom. We want Mom." Sharon turned toward the audience, focusing her attention to hear just what they were saying. "We want Mom."

Piers readily got the point and played into the audience's hands as he, in agreement announced, "Yes, let's see your mom. Let's see your mom." The crowd couldn't get enough of Voices of Glory as they again left their seats as they yelled and applauded their excitement.

Nick Cannon pressed a microphone into Felicia's hand. Mike pushed his wife onto the stage, to join their children in front of the judges. Felicia bowed from her wheelchair and released her magical smile.

"So Mom, Mom, let me ask you," Piers called over the noisy crowd, "you must feel incredibly proud of your children tonight."

Felicia held up the microphone in response, "Very proud," she said slowly, through her pretty smile.

"Yes. Sharon?" Piers deferred to her a second time for a response.

"Don't quite know what to say," came forward as she choked on her tears..."just, just an amazing family. You must be so proud to have such great children and they must be so proud to have you as their mom." Felicia quietly nodded her head in agreement.

"So let me also say this," Piers interjected. This is a talent competition…all right…so as incredibly powerful although the story is…that is not what we are here to judge. We are here to judge you on your ability as performers so I listened very carefully to your singing. That was one of the best singing performances we've had. By the time you put your miracle working together with the singing, you've got a pretty hot act here. Thank you so much."

"David, yes or no?" Piers asked.

David responded with "Absolutely. Yes."

"Sharon?" Piers questioned her for her vote.

"Oh, it's just my pleasure to say yes."

"And it's my great pleasure to say that you three are going through to the next round," Piers added, making it official that Voices of Glory would continue to compete.

Sharon Osborne was obviously been deeply touched by the family and their story and Piers and David both reached out to her with tender pats as she wiped more tears from her eyes. As the family left the stage, David Hasselhoff continued to display his support by raising his arm and again giving them another thumbs up as the audience clapped with abandon.

Emotion ran high as America was represented by its finest in these three young siblings showing honor to their country, their family and their God. Theirs was a story of triumph in a triumphant country; a tribute to God who no doubt had smiled on this gathering of people on such a special night. It was a moment caught in history that would be remembered by all who had the privilege to be in the audience that night. There was barely a dry eye.

Back stage, Nick Cannon spoke directly to Felicia saying, "Probably one of the most beautiful stories I've ever heard. You should be extremely proud of your children and regardless of what happens; God knows there was something powerful here tonight."

The children rallied around Felicia's wheelchair, her sons leaning over each shoulder, little Nadia leaning across her mother's lap, all embracing with tears of joy.

Later, Sharon and Piers were caught on camera, off stage. Piers stated, "That was the most powerful thing I've ever seen in the past three years.

CHAPTER 29

Pinch Me

BACK HOME, IT WAS hard to settle into a routine. The kids returned to school, but couldn't tell their good news to anyone. There was almost two months of school left and they would have to see their friends everyday and still keep their most exciting secret. Anticipation was high knowing all that was ahead of them; traveling, competing, making new friends, and best of all, actually being on television. They seemed to be walking slow motion through a fairytale.

Finally, school was over for the summer. On June 23rd, Mikey's seventeenth birthday, America's Got Talent aired their first show of the 2009 season. They had a huge combined viewing and birthday party. Over sixty family members and friends gathered in their living room to watch Voices of Glory compete on national television. It was a night of joy, laughter and tears. A night of celebration that none of them would ever forget. At the end of the evening, they announced that they were to fly to Las

Vegas in July and again face possible elimination, but in their hearts, they just knew they would go to the top.

Over the next couple of weeks, Mike received emails from the staff of America's Got Talent with further instructions regarding the competition in Las Vegas. He responded with acknowledgements that they were still in the game, worked through their process, received plane tickets, and organized all the details to be sure they were where they were supposed to be when they were supposed to be there.

Finally, it was time to go. Voices of Glory boarded an airplane at Stewart Airport in Newburgh, New York, making a connecting flight for Las Vegas from Philadelphia. The airplane was a small commuter so the turbulence was noticeable. This wasn't their first flight. The kids had flown to Florida with their aunts and uncles four years ago when Felicia was first in the hospital. Nadia was only five at the time, so even though she had flown before, she was nervous, and uncertain what to expect. She kept close to Avery for security, as he seemed to know what to do.

While in the small airport restaurant, the kids caught some people's attention that recognized them from an America's Got Talent TV advertisement for the upcoming show. The cashier was so excited to meet the family that she paid for their meal. Voices of Glory sang a thank you song in appreciation.

"Pinch me," Mikey said as they took their seats aboard the plane departing from Philadelphia. "I can't believe this is happening."

"I can," answered Nadia, feeling more relaxed after their short flight from Newburgh. "This is fun."

"Do you really want me to pinch you?" Avery asked,

knowing he better not start something with his big brother, especially not on an airplane.

The kids had practiced many hours since that first night of elimination at America's Got Talent. The judges had been very kind and complimentary of their performance, but they knew they had to measure up to be able to stay in the competition. They felt they were ready for what lay ahead.

As they exited the plane in Las Vegas, they immediately spied the shuttle bus with America's Got Talent plastered on the windows. One of the AGT staff members was standing outside the bus with the show logo on a large sign. They had received written instructions telling them to board a shuttle bus that would take them to a small local airport.

When everyone was off the bus, they were advised that parents and non-contestants were to wait in one area—the contestants were sent to another. There was a large tent with folding chairs set up in rows. Off to the sides, drinks were provided for the friends and family while they waited. It was warm and close with so many people in the friends and family tent.

It was hard not to feel edgy when their future was on the line. Would this be the end of the road or just the beginning? Mike and Felicia quietly discussed the possibilities realizing that their children's future rested in someone else's hands instead of their own. We'll just keep on trusting, they concluded as they each held a cool drink in one hand, and with the other, a tender grasp.

The contestants gathered in a large hangar. They found out approximately two hundred acts had been flown to Vegas, but only half of them would remain for the next elimination. They had been given an envelope with instructions on how to locate their designated section. They were confident they weren't going to be eliminated as they were placed in the same line as the Texas Tenors and G Force. They knew they both had great acts, but again had a long wait for the suspenseful announcement of their fate.

The judges arrived in a private jet. Sharon, Piers and David took the stage and explained what would happen next. There was a lot of tension as it was announced that many of the performers who had been flown to Vegas had in fact already been eliminated and were instructed to re-board the buses back to the airport only to return home; their short lived stardom—already over.

As the day progressed, the performers were weeded out. They held their breath listening for their name to be announced as part of the performers who would remain in Las Vegas for another chance to be critiqued by the judges.

As time passed, the crowd in the parents' tent dwindled with each additional elimination. Mike and Felicia waited to hear news from their children. Finally, as more and more performers came away from the competitor's tent, they couldn't stand it any longer and Mike began asking about Voices of Glory.

"They are still in there," was the response he received.

At last the threesome appeared. They had made the Top 100 cut. Again, they were moving on to the next level of competition. Immediately, along with the other chosen performers they were given celebrity treatment. They were seated in a limo for a photo shoot. There was much cheering and laughing as the contestants interacted with the judges and the AGT staff. However, they were disappointed to learn they didn't get to enjoy the fun of riding to the hotel in the limo. Since there was alcohol in the limo and they were under age, they had to take the not-so-alluring shuttle bus to the Palms Hotel.

Once they arrived at the hotel, their excitement was reignited as they took in the glitz and glamour of the massive interior.

They checked into the hotel and went to their rooms. Excitement ran high, but there really wasn't much to do but wait for the scheduled events. Felicia had family living in the area so they arranged for the relatives to meet them at the Palms for a visit. They spent time hanging out with other contestants and getting better acquainted with the different groups. They went to see a movie to help pass the time. They hung out with G-Force, a three-girl band from Cleveland, and Hairo Torres, a break-dancer.

Some of the hotel conference rooms were made available for the groups to hang out in. They helped pass the time by singing together. Sometimes with seriousness and dedication, other times just clowning around and teasing each other.

The hotel was busy with the America's Got Talent crew and contestants, not to mention the regular hotel business. There was lots of activity, but the wheels seemed to be turning very slowly. A couple of days passed and still they were uncertain where they stood. There was an occasional hint dropped by the AGT staff indicating they were in a good place, but no official announcements had been made. They knew there would be another cut before leaving Las Vegas. They didn't know if they would make it.

They had been in Vegas for five days. When it seemed nothing was going on, at last, they were called into a conference room in groups. The judges analyzed their acts, questioned different contestants about their performances, and made suggestions on how to improve. They announced that only a certain number of acts would remain in Vegas. The atmosphere was serious and heavy. No one wanted the contest to be over for them at this stage. Then when everyone was nervous and uncertain of their chances, the announcements were made. The judges had been playing with their heads, being dramatic, bringing them low before announcing the good news. They heard their name announced. Voices of Glory were still in the race.

They were on the go again. Down a back hallway, they went for more picture taking and more interviews. Avery spotted a sign on a door that said, "Winners— Voices of Glory". With a big grin on his face, Avery questioned an AGT staff member, "What's that?" The staff member appeared surprised, but quickly said, "Oh, that's just a joke."

It seemed strange, but they laughed it off. "Oh, okay," Avery grinned thinking he had inside information. Mikey just gave his younger brother a shrug. They had made it to the Top 40; that was good enough for now.

Once home from Las Vegas, they had to dig their heels in and practice even more. They had risen above the majority of the competitors. It was a pretty easy choice for the judges for the first part of the competition, but things were changing. Voices of Glory were now competing against only talented acts. They were coming down to the best of the best. The smaller numbers meant they really had to shine to stay qualified.

Excitement ran high as they prepared for their second performance. They knew they would go through the wardrobe department for costume choices, but more importantly, they needed to choose just the right song.

Aunt Connie was quick to help with options for their next

song selection. They focused on "Wind Beneath My Wings", and "You'll Never Walk Alone" as songs they could perform well the next time they were called upon.

The television producers referred the top contestants to people in the industry who could be of benefit in developing their performances. It was decided that the family would fly to Los Angeles and meet with Nigel Wright, a very talented music director. He assisted them in their choice of songs and arranging the music to best enhance their singing ability. He suggested "The Greatest Love of All" and "Anytime You Need a Friend". They settled on "You'll Never Walked Alone". Nigel Wright reviewed the musical arrangement to make sure it would bring them to the next level.

The family stayed at the Universal Studios Hotel. They attended meetings arranged by AGT. The new vocal instruction could take them to a completely different level. It could move them from amateur to professional if they had what it took.

It was hard work. It was intense. To give the kids some down time, they took a little break and toured the area. They checked out Universal Studios City Walk, window-shopped and enjoyed being outdoors in the fresh California air. Out of the corner of their eyes, they watched to see if just maybe they would spot a famous Hollywood actor or diva. The fun was over. Soon they were on a plane back to New York, but they would be returning to California for the next step in the competition.

Mike attempted to reach Aunt Connie to help them hone their skills for the final eliminations. He learned the reason he was unable to contact her was that she was caring for her mother out of state. What should they do? They knew they had to do something. They had to keep pushing forward. Marva Clark, a close acquaintance was a superior pianist even performing at the White House. Perhaps they could call on her for assistance. Marva agreed and everyone buckled down for practices that would bring them to their highest possible level of performance. Marva assisted them in choosing songs that were best suited to all of their voices.

Summer was passing quickly. They rehearsed almost daily. "You'll Never Walk Alone" was not an easy song, but they had worked hard to get it right. They would give it their best. They packed their bags for the California sun and another flight to Los Angeles.

They were on their own this time. They took a shuttle to the hotel. After they were settled in to their rooms, they checked in with America's Got Talent, getting their appointments for wardrobe and interviews. The producers made a film clip of the VOG talking about themselves and their act.

Michael told America's Got Talent, "We believe in ourselves as a family and we are going to take it all the way."

Nadia chipped in saying, "We want to make our mom the proudest mom in America." They were confident, but humble. They were having fun and they intended to win.

Next, it was time for wardrobe. White suits were chosen for Michael and Avery, and a long white dress for Nadia. The accent colors for the shirts and ties were gold tones and the sash on Nadia's dress, bronze. How elegant they looked as they made their stage appearance and began singing "You'll Never Walk Alone".

They sang their hearts out. Nadia seemed to take ownership of the song. The composure and concentration of this nine-year old child was remarkable and did not go unnoticed. When the last notes were sung and the crowd roared with applause, Nick Cannon stepped forward on the stage and said, "Voices of Glory. The presence is in the building. Powerful performance—great job."

"Mr. Hasselhoff," Nick passed to David.

"Now that's what this show's about," he again tells the children. "Thank you. I mean the talent tonight I said was weird, wacky and wild. It was terrible. You guys are fantastic. Thank you for being on this show. And you're nine years old, and you guys have got the right attitude. Absolutely terrific tonight. Thank you."

"Mr. Morgan," Nick addressed Piers.

"I thought it was a bit shaky at first." The crowd booed Piers. "Shakier than the first time we saw you. Love the suits though, love the suits. And what we discovered tonight is that you have a star in your midst guys and it's your little sister. Because when it was a bit shaky in the start, I was worried for where this song was going to go. It's a big song. I needed somebody to step forward and take that song. You, young lady took that song—really good."

"Right," Sharon spoke up. "Nadia, I think tonight was your night, Nadia. Definitely, just, I mean, just, I just adore you. I'm all...I can't come up with the right words to say. But it really, you are just very special, you're very pure, you're very special, and Nadia let me tell you—this was your night. Congratulations."

Nick addressed Voices of Glory and asked, "I mean, how do you guys feel about your performance?"

Michael answered confidently... "I...I have to say that I agree with, uh, Mr. Piers when he said that it was a bit shaky in parts but uh, all in all, I think we finished it off all right and I think we can continue to do better and better as the show progresses. And if you vote us to the next round you can look forward to a greater performance." Again, the audience burst into applause.

The votes came in and Voices of Glory were still showing as a favorite. They would be competing again. The family flew back to New York to go through the processes of choosing yet another song—then of course, practice.

CHAPTER 30

A Night Of Vindication

L. A. HAD BEEN another whirlwind experience, and it wouldn't be long before they would be returning again. They had already competed twice: first the tryouts, then performance number one. Now on to preparation for competition number three: another song to choose, another song to perfect. Competition was getting more and more intense as the voters eliminated act after act. They had to be good. They had to be very good.

They worked on different songs, trying to decide which would be best for all three of them. It was great that the judges thought so highly of Nadia's talent, but they were a family. Voices of Glory were a trio, and as a family, their desire was to continue performing together. The boys were talented, too, and Mike and Felicia weren't going to allow them to be left out just because Nadia had a unique gift. It would be one for all and all for one.

They chose to sing "Anytime You Need a Friend". Practice

makes perfect and practice they did. The kids were determined to be the best they could be. They now had a following. They didn't want to let their fans down.

It didn't seem right to go back to California for another performance without Felicia, Mike thought as he read yet another email from America's Got Talent. They always received confirmation of their flight information by email and Mike was surprised to see the additional note indicating that AGT would be providing only four plane tickets, not five.

America's Got Talent's policy required that any contestant under the age of eighteen be chaperoned by an adult. That had not been an issue because Mike and Felicia always wanted to be with their kids during the trips and the performances. It was just a given that they would go as a family. Now there was a wrench in the plan.

He pondered the situation. He hated to tell Felicia. She had had so many disappointments. Yet, he knew there was no way she could act as the chaperone. He would have to be the one.

Even if he paid for Felicia's ticket himself, it was unlikely she could be scheduled on the same plane and there was no way she could go alone. Mike hesitantly shared the contents of the email with his wife. She sat with her head downcast for several moments.

"Are you okay?" he cautiously ventured.

"Yes," she choked out. "It's not a problem," she added attempting to minimize her disappointment. Betraying tears spilled down her cheeks.

"That's not fair," said Avery.

"Yeah, it's not fair," echoed Michael and then Nadia.

"I'm sorry, Felicia," Mike frowned. "I don't want you to miss out on this." She had missed so much of their children's lives in the past four years. The kids were right. It wasn't fair.

"It's okay," Felicia quickly told them, in an effort to keep her family from feeling too bad about the situation. "I can stay with my parents and watch you on television. Mom and Dad will like that. We have been so busy I haven't seen them very much lately."

"It doesn't seem right but I guess we don't have any choice," Mike stated. Regretfully, it was decided. They called Felicia's parents to be sure it would work for them and made the necessary arrangements. They had to be back in Los Angeles in just a couple of days.

"If they make it through this round, you will be with us next time," Mike assured Felicia, knowing there would be one more show after this one. "Even if we have to pay for it ourselves," he added.

"Thanks, Mike, that does make me feel a little better," Felicia admitted.

Settling Felicia in with her family, Mike, Michael, Avery and Nadia headed for the airport for yet another step to try to win the America's Got Talent contest.

Arriving in L.A., Mike and the kids settled into the familiar routine. Practice was priority; rest mandatory.

They knew the ropes. Wardrobe would coordinate their costumes. The wardrobe staff knew their measurements, what size clothing they wore and their shoe sizes. The wardrobe specialist would sketch his thoughts onto paper so everybody had the same vision. They discussed color preferences as well. Once that step was completed, the staff members went shopping to find pre-made clothing that was designed as near as possible to their vision. Next, the purchased clothing was dispatched to the alterations department for fitting. The end result—handsomely coordinated outfits for the trio.

Time passed quickly and it was performance night again. The producers had designed the stage with a huge white double stairway on either side for that week's show. Michael descended the stairs from one side, Avery from the other. They were dressed in navy blue buttoned vests with silky silver shirts and ties. Avery opened the song, with Michael joining in on the second verse.

The curtain opened and Nadia dressed in an elegant blue dress with a long silvery underskirt, joined her brothers in the beautiful chorus.

They sang their chosen song. They sang it with conviction and purpose. They sang it with heart. At the end, they got their reward with words of praise from the host and from the judges. It wasn't an easy performance for Avery. Fires were burning out of control in areas surrounding Los Angeles and the smoke and residual debris caused an allergic reaction. He developed a sinus infection, giving his voice an uncharacteristic nasal tone. They prayed Avery would be able to sing well enough to get through the round. They couldn't let this minor setback stop them and send them back to New York prematurely. At the end of the song, Nick Cannon came onto the stage saying, "Voices of Glory—Wonderful. Wonderful, wonderful job."

Nick deferred to David Hasselhoff for his opinion. David charmingly addressed the kids saying, "You know, you guys could just bring the world together. You are so sweet, and you're so good, and you are so honest. And that's what entertaining is about…it's just going out and moving people with song and telling the story and bringing the world together and boy you guys do it beautifully. Congratulations."

There was no doubt throughout the contest that David was a fan and on their side. Again no buzzer, just three thumbs up and three yeses! They still had a shot at first place!

Piers told the children, "What I like about you is what you stand for." He said, "You are polite, and well dressed. I like that you are tight with your family. You're impressive, and more importantly, you've got talent," he stated, ending his comments.

Felicia had taken it all in twenty eight hundred miles away as her eyes were fixed on her parent's television set from the first second of the program. Mike had called her many times over the past few days. She was aware of Avery's health issue and had prayed he would be able to perform with excellence. It was difficult not to be there with her family but her joy overflowed as she listened to the wonderful comments made by the judges. She was so pleased with her children. It was a bittersweet time as her mother's heart ached to be with her family, but her face revealed the happiest of smiles as the children's grandparents celebrated their success with Felicia. It wasn't long before the telephone ran and Felicia had the opportunity to congratulate each of her children individually.

"I'll call you tomorrow," Mike promised after rehearsing all that happened in the last hour in his excitement. Felicia was glad to relive it too. It made her feel more a part of this special night. They had a lively conversation, exuberant over the outcome and having every confidence in their children to give their all for the final show.

"I wish I was there with you." Felicia said regretfully.

"I wish you were too," Mike answered. "I wish you were too.

Mike sat in the lounge waiting for the children to change from their costumes after the show was over.

"Hi, Mike," an AGT staff member greeted him, a second staff member nodding her head in acknowledgement.

"We've been talking and think it would be best for you to just stay in California until the final night. We, also, would like for Felicia to be here. Do you think that would be possible?"

"I don't know. I know she wants to be," he grinned, "but I don't see how we could do it. She needs my help." he hesitated.

"Well, see what you can work out and let us know. We will do everything we can to help. We will make arrangements with the airline if she can get to the airport. We would really like to have her here," he reiterated.

The Stanley's were surprised when the telephone rang. It was late in New York and the phone alarmed them but readily found out it was Mike with good news. Before he spoke with Felicia, he explained the situation to his in-laws. He wanted to be sure that they could take her to the airport before he told Felicia. He didn't want her to have another disappointment. Mrs. Stanley handed Felicia the telephone.

"Mike wants to speak with you again," she smiled. Felicia squealed with delight when Mike gave her the news.

"I'm so glad, Mike. I can't wait to see you and to be there with all of you."

"We will have to work out all of the details tomorrow but I wanted to let you know right away. I will call you tomorrow once I know more," he confirmed.

"I love you, Mike."

"I love you, too," he responded.

The plans came together easily. Felicia's parents took her to Stewart Airport in Newburgh. America's Got Talent had made arrangements for the airline staff to assist Felicia on boarding and making the connecting flight in Philadelphia and then to de-board in Los Angeles. She was able to transfer from the wheelchair to the airplane seat by herself, so the trip was basically uneventful.

The AGT van chauffeured Mike to LAX to meet Felicia. Felicia arrived first and waited for Mike at the appointed location.

"You made it," he grinned, relieved that there was no apparent problem.

"You gotta do, what you gotta do," she laughed, reaching for his hand.

During the next several days, the kids concentrated on their music. They already knew what their next song would be. They would sing Whitney Houston's "Greatest Love of All."

Practice and rest. They were so close, they didn't want to risk losing to illness or injury.

When asked what they would do with the million dollars if they won, without hesitation Michael responded, "First, we will tithe to our church and then our dad will divide up the rest of the money between us."

Before the whole world, the true character of this family shone through as an astonished audience heard a seventeen-year old boy allow God and his parents their rightful places. He did not speak of flashy cars and expensive clothes, but instead he stood on the solid ground on which he had been raised. It was a testimony to the integrity and conviction of Voices of Glory that had been displayed throughout the competition.

As the day of their final performance arrived, they were fired up and ready to shine. They had made it to the Top 10. Wardrobe had done an outstanding job. Nadia was to wear a lavender taffeta dress with a wide beribboned waistband. The guys were to wear black dress slacks, white shirts, black vests and orchid jackets with matching ties, and orchid boutonnieres to match the flower prettily pinned at Nadia's side. Sharp. Sharp. Sharp. Everyone was pleased with the choices. They were number eight on the list of performers; a great spot to have, as they knew some people would be tuning in late. Being first or even second could increase the possibilities of their performance being missed by the television audience, resulting in fewer votes.

However, for whatever reason, one of the producers wanted to change the wardrobe, picking a pink dress for Nadia. That left the boys without costume. A quick suggestion was made for them to wear black dress slacks and pink shirts—no jackets. That translated into—no pizzazz for the boys. It was apparent that Nadia had become a favorite and there were those who were trying to give her preferential treatment, acting as though the boys were not an important part of the act.

This upset Mike and Felicia. Since they had some input into the costuming and how the kids were handled, they stood up for the boys saying, "No, let the kids wear what the wardrobe department had already designed." They got their way and the costumes remained as planned.

Was this a mistake? It wasn't long and Voices of Glory were moved to the first performance spot, not a coveted place to be. Mike wondered if that was a warning or even a disciplinary action. He could only hope that it would not affect their performance or the final outcome.

Indeed, their last performance was a great success. The kids gave it their best and the crowd responded with the same enthusiasm as each time before. Again, they received a standing ovation, not just from the audience, but from the judges too. David Hasselfhoff gave his usual two thumbs up, twirling his arm in the air with an enthusiastic shout—"Wow!"

Nick charged onto the stage and announced, "Living up to their name—Voices of Glory!"

As the evening ended, the final votes were in. Voices of Glory would hold fifth place in their final competition. It was a ranking of honor.

For the first time in the history of America's Got Talent, because of the audience reaction to a heart-warming story and their overwhelming demand to see Felicia Cole, the judges chose to showcase the family of the contestants on stage, giving national exposure to the story behind the act.

Then again, for the first time in the history of the show, the judges chose not to use their Judges Choice vote. They just couldn't decide between Voices of Glory and the Fab Five. It was decided that both groups would be allowed to go through to the semi-finals. Voices of Glory realized they could have been cut after the quarter-finals, yet the extraordinary happened, an exception was made and they had another chance to woo the judges. By the end of semi-finals, the Voices of Glory were still standing, still being voted as favorites. Voices of Glory purposed to honor God and God had honored them just as His word says, "I will honor those who honor me..." (I Samuel 2:30, NCV)

Their final performance really was their best performance. They got better each time just as Michael so graciously spoke when critiqued by Piers after a less-than-perfect performance of "You'll Never Walk Alone".

They had begun their journey with an attitude of "it would be fun to go to the tryouts" and ended it, six months later, with national notoriety. They could hold their heads up high knowing they had been true to themselves. Their fame had skyrocketed and the kids from Highland, New York, who had a heart for God and country, now held worldwide recognition. They had proven themselves as professionals; winning the hearts of many, from the judges sitting before them, to their live audiences, to fans all around the world.

They now had a clear picture of who they were as Voices of Glory; three kids with a bright future in the music industry—still serving God with big smiles and big hearts for all. In spite of the destructive accident, God's purpose for their lives would not be stopped. They were now ready to fulfill the destiny that had been prophesied over them in that small church in New York over ten years earlier, before Nadia was even conceived. The destiny of a global ministry had been introduced through what seemed like a by-chance experience with America's Got Talent. Yet the family knew it was not by chance, but, indeed, by the very hand of God.

Mike, Felicia, Donald, Tamara, and Gerard were in the audience in Los Angeles that night. The other five Cole siblings, grandparents, cousins, aunts and uncles on both sides of the family, were glued to their television screens; whether physically present or there in spirit, they were there in support of Michael, Nadia, and Avery. They were there in support of Felicia and Mike who had fought the good fight of faith and won.

What could have ended in a story of defeat, generational poverty and lack, addiction, violence and abuse, instead ends with success. When Michael, Avery, and Nadia stood on the stage that final night, they stood for their entire family.

The final night was victory night for all eleven of Cybald and Jan Cole's children and their children. They all knew in their hearts they had not taken the easy route of giving up, but all of them had met the challenges of life head on and were now reaping the reward. Perhaps their rough start in life made them even more determined to succeed. It is remarkable that from the roots of sorrow and heartache came careers as doctor, police officer, nurse, corporate workers, real estate agent, a youth advocate for high school students, military service men, teachers, and responsible parents with strong families. Their story culminated in a glorious outcome and they were all a part of the success of Voices of Glory.

For some, their thoughts went to their sister and brothers who were not there to enjoy the excitement. They thought of Warrie Cole, a young woman with much promise sadly taken from them when she was still so young, and of Dr. Joseph Cole, a strong family man who had proven nothing was impossible to overcome. They also thought of Christian, who despite the mayhem of his younger life, served his country honorably, taking his earthly resting place in Arlington Cemetery.

It was victory night for Felicia, Mike, Michael, Avery, and Nadia, not as winners of a contest, but as victors over the tribulations of this world. It was a night of vindication against all the sorrow, all the pain, all the prejudice, all the suffering that this world can inflict. It was a night of triumph as the third generation of this humble, God-fearing American family, stood in a better place, not for the sake of fame, but for the sake of righteousness. Regardless of ranking, they had prevailed.

It was a night for the Lord Jesus. "No weapon formed against you shall prosper, and every tongue which rises against you in judgment You shall condemn. This is the heritage of the servants of the LORD, And their righteousness is from Me, Says the LORD". (Isaiah 54:17, NKJV)

Bringing You Current

FAST FORWARD FOUR YEARS and you will find Voices of Glory performing their own show six days a week in Branson, Missouri, the Live Entertainment Capital of the World. Obviously, this did not happen overnight. They still had challenges to overcome before they were to enjoy the success they have today.

After America's Got Talent, the buzz didn't quiet down. Voices of Glory were now on the fast track. They were invited to sing at a New York Knicks game at Madison Square Garden on Martin Luther King Day in 2010. The crowd stood as the pure voices of Michael, Avery and Nadia Cole sang the national anthem a cappella with all their hearts. Quoting the manager of Madison Square Garden, Michelle Harris, "Voices of Glory are an excellent group of young talent. With their beautiful harmony, they were one of our top anthem performers this season. They are young professionals with a strong work ethic and family values, and they were just lovely to work with. Voices of Glory were the perfect act to help us celebrate the legacy of Dr. Martin Luther King Jr."

Voices of Glory was thrilled again as the huge New York Knicks audience gave standing ovation to the trio as they sang, "The Greatest Love of All".

They have appeared in Jet magazine and Gospel Today. They were excited to see their names in print, while reading about the AGT contest in People magazine that featured a tribute to Michael Jackson. They were invited to present a program at the NAACP local chapter in Newburgh, New York.

During a conversation with an employee at the IBM credit union, Mike was given the name of someone experienced in the music industry. They arranged a dinner meeting at Sylvia's Soulfood in Harlem. Through that contact, came the very exciting invitation to open for the GMA Dove Awards in 2010 at the Grand Old Opry. Suddenly, it seemed they had a full calendar.

Early in 2010, Felicia's mother received a letter from a promoter from Chicago. The promoter had somehow through hints in media releases tracked her down, finding her home address. Mrs. Stanley passed the letter on to Felicia and thus the ball started rolling on a series of events that had both hills and valleys.

The letter indicated that a talent promoter was interested in booking them for their own show in Branson, Missouri. They would be the headliner and she had other vocal groups booked to act as openers and relief acts for them. It was important to Voices of Glory that they continued to minister and not be tied solely to an entertainment venue. They recognized that their achievements were from Jesus Christ and they would not compromise their ministry for worldly success.

The Coles were not familiar with Branson, unaware that it was a tourist destination, featuring live entertainment of all kinds. They obviously were thrilled with the recognition of their musical ability and the thought of having their own show, but where in the world was Branson? There were subsequent telephone meetings with the Coles including Uncle Gerard Cole, acting as their manager, and it was now time to decide the next step on their career path.

After one such telephone meeting, they went online to see just what Branson was all about. In reviewing websites, they saw some of what they had been told. They learned of the shows on the strip, seeing names of popular entertainers who performed there, the honor that everyone paid to God and country and to military veterans and service men and women. They beheld the beautiful backdrop of Table Rock Lake, the trout fishing in the Taneycomo, the wonderful hills and valleys of the Ozarks. Their interest was piqued and they decided to trek to the Ozark Mountains, a twenty-hour drive from their home in New York, and see for themselves just what their opportunities were. As they drove down Highway 65 south of Springfield, Missouri, they were delighted with the signs announcing the stars and shows of Branson, and no doubt seeing themselves on one of those huge billboards.

Arriving in Branson late in the evening, they checked into a nice hotel for a good night's rest after their long journey. The next day they met the promoter for lunch, were given a tour of Branson, the surrounding lakes area, and last but not least, the Branson Meadows theatre where they were to perform.

That evening, they were invited to the promoter's home, a

very elaborate residence for dinner. Everything was very nice. Good food and fellowship were lavished on them. They were introduced to a liaison they would be working with, a very sweet lady and her husband. Part of the evening was spent in a business meeting, determining the finite details of the contract. However, as the evening passed, something seemed amiss. Mike and Gerard Cole went outdoors to talk. Something just didn't seem right, yet they couldn't put their finger on it and so continued as agreed. Starting their sentences almost in unison, the brothers said, "I hope this isn't a scam."

The VIP treatment continued, the promoter showing them the best of Branson. They went to the Legends show, an act featuring impersonations of legendary performers such as Elvis, Aretha Franklin, the Blues Brothers, and many others, paying tribute to their fabulous careers. Some of the audience recognized Voices of Glory from America's Got Talent and were excited to see them there. The promoter had let management know that Voices of Glory were in the audience, and as it was announced, they received a standing ovation.

While alone, Voices of Glory were discussing whether the offer was for real. Avery told his parents about a conversation he had with the promoter's young daughter. "I told her, you have a really nice house here and she said…yeah, but Daddy says we can't stay very long because we can't afford it." Soon after that, they learned the promoter had the luxurious home rented on only a short-term lease.

Gerard, acting as their manager, requested reimbursement for their travel expenses as agreed. The promoter stalled but finally came up with a check. She told them she hadn't had time to get a company check but she gave them a personal one for their travel expenses, alleviating some of their doubt. She also instructed the liaison to contact Big Mama's, a coffee house, in Springfield, Missouri, and arrange for Voices of Glory to sing there. The audience was small but they were glad to perform as a way to let people know they would be moving to the area.

By mid-March of 2010, Mike had taken the leap of faith asking for leave from his job with IBM, packed up their belongings, leased out their home, and headed for a new life in the Branson hills, and a big boost to the career of Voices of Glory. Even though Michael was just one and half months from his high school graduation, he knew the sacrifice of moving would be worth it all. Uncle Gerard too, left his real estate business and made a fulltime commitment to Voices of Glory as their manager. Felicia, Avery and Nadia were sad to leave their friends and family but were very excited about their new adventure.

Driving back to Branson, excitement ran high. They contacted a publicist to schedule them for other venues in the Midwest during their free time. They did everything they could think of to promote themselves and to raise awareness that Voices of Glory was available to perform.

Once in Branson, they rented a nice condominium to be their home base. They worked with the promoter and liaison, but things were moving slowly. The promoter kept stalling, both in getting them into the theatre and in paying them on their contract, always coming up with additional paperwork which needed to be handled.

In the meantime, Voices of Glory were working on their first CD. Mike and Felicia had made another trip to New York to finalize business arrangements. The days were passing quickly and it would soon be time to leave for the Dove Awards. Mike and Felicia would be meeting Gerard, Michael, Avery and Nadia in Nashville.

While at a Branson recording studio, working on their CD, Gerard and the children decided to take a break and go to a local department store to have their measurements taken for their new performance clothing. Gerard was talking to another customer while waiting for assistance. Yet another customer overheard their conversation. A man approached him, took out his wallet and handed him a card. "Did you just mention Voices of Glory?" he asked. Gerard read the name on the man's business card—Jim Bakker. Mr. Bakker said, "My wife and I are not star struck by many, but we are star stuck by Voices of Glory. My wife is in the dressing room and would really like to meet them."

The kids were standing off to the side and hearing what was being said, joined the group and were introduced to Mr. Bakker. "My wife would really like to meet you but she is trying on clothes right now," Mr. Bakker explained as he led them to the fitting room area. Gerard started calling out to her, "Lori Bakker, someone is out here to meet you."

Hurrying to dress, Lori came out. There was much excitement among them as Lori took the kids under her wing. Voices of Glory had already been invited to be guests on the Jim Bakker Show but had not yet scheduled.

Gerard knew who Jim Bakker was. He knew his name from the past. After meeting the Bakkers in person, he meditated on his thoughts from many years ago. Sometime in the early 80's, he and his brother Mike had made plans to do something together. Mike had said he needed to go to the post office and mail a letter before he was free to go with Gerard.

"What's so important?" Gerard had questioned. Mike told him he was sending a donation to PTL.

"Just give it to me if you don't want it," Gerard had joked, not understanding why his brother would send money to a preacher. Gerard was stunned as he pondered that all those years ago in New York, Mike had planted a seed in faith to Jim Bakker's ministry and now, thirty years later, it seemed God was giving him a harvest. Little did either Mike or Jim Bakker have any idea that someday they would both be living in Branson, Missouri, and have such a unique reason to be acquainted. God had truly brought things full circle, Gerard realized.

Voices of Glory departed for Nashville and the Dove Awards with things still not settled in Branson. While they were on the road, Gerard received a phone call from the liaison telling him, the promoter had fired her. Because the liaison had worked in the industry for a number of years, she was suspicious about the way things were going. After being fired, she investigated the promoter, and found in a simple Google search, that the promoter had fraud charges filed against her.

With this news out, everything had blown up in the promoter's face. Some of the performers who were to be included in the Branson Meadows show still trusted her but several including Voices of Glory believed what the liaison was saying, the proof being in print. In the interim, for whatever reason, the Branson Meadows cancelled the contract.

The Coles confronted the promoter. It was obvious she was still trying to put things together but they had lost their confidence in her. Seated in a meeting room in a Branson hotel, Gerard acted as their spokesman, addressed the promoter sternly. "This is Mike. This is Felicia. This is Michael. This is Avery, and this is Nadia. This is our family. Now! You tell us right now! Is this deal for real?" Again she assured them," Yes, it is for real." Wanting it to be real, they could only hope she was telling the truth.

They left the meeting with the decision to make a written demand for the money owed to them per the contract. Gerard hand-delivered the demand letter. "You are going to be a rich man," she told him.

"No, it is for the family," he responded, not liking her demeanor.

"The check will be ready on Friday," she assured him. Friday came and was passing fast with no word from the promoter. Finally, Gerard called her and found out she was on her way back to Chicago. She told him the investor had backed out. She said she was so upset about it that her husband was afraid she was going to hurt herself. Gerard hung up the phone knowing it was over. There was nothing to do but sue her and that seemed fruitless.

Was she that distraught or was this just a ploy to get out of the mess she had created? Was there ever an investor? As their manager, but from an even more hurtful position, as their uncle, he had the most painful task of telling Voices of Glory that they had been scammed. There would be no Branson show.

Mike and Felicia had been praying about what to do. They prayed together. They prayed with the children and with Gerard. They wanted to make the right decision. They had to regroup. Did they have any choice but to stay in Branson based on their living situation? Their New York home had been rented out and a year's lease was signed on the condo. Also, was the fact the children were already attending Branson schools. They spent the next couple of weeks becoming better acquainted with Branson. They went to some shows to meet fellow performers and learned more about the dynamics of Branson as an entertainment center.

The kids liked school and everyone seemed to like being in Branson. They scheduled an appearance on the Jim Bakker Show, singing several gospel songs. They discussed their time on national television with America's Got Talent. Mr. Bakker was excited learning Michael had just graduated from high school and offered him a place in the Master's Media program.

"Perhaps God wants us to be here," Mike discussed with his family. "Even if we got here through what seems like fraud, your mom and I remembered a prophecy spoken over Mikey. A prophet from New York had said he was going to be awarded a scholarship from somewhere southwest," he reminded the kids. "And that has happened with Jim Bakker offering the scholarship in the media program. It seems a perfect fit for your budding musical career," he said, smiling at their children.

Yes, Branson seemed to be the right place for them, at least for a while. They were in one accord. They trusted they were in God's will. With that decided, they came to peace with the disappointment of not having their own show as promised. Some of the other performers, who had been brought to Branson at the same time, wanted them to join a class action suit against the promoter but they chose not to. However, Gerard made a verbal complaint with the Illinois State Attorney General's office against the promoter in the interest of other entertainers not being caught in the same trap.

They learned that the Texas Tenors, a group that had performed with them on America's Got Talent were performing at the Branson Starlight Theatre. They went to the show to support their fellow contestants. While there, they met a lady by the name of Sandy who recognized them from AGT. She already knew a little of their difficulties in Branson. She indicated she had some connections with the theatres and said she may be able to offer some help.

She introduced them to Barbara Fairchild and arrangements were made for Voices of Glory to sing at her diner on Shepherd of the Hills Boulevard two nights a week. Ms. Fairchild was very gracious and generous to them, not asking for any of the proceeds from their show, in an attempt to let them know that what had happened to them was not the way things were in Branson. She hoped they would not lose heart.

Through their new found relationship with Barbara Fairchild, they met her cousins, Buster and Julie Prine, who were in the process of opening a Christian nightclub, The Night Light, next door to Barbara's diner. The Night Light's plan was to create a gathering place, giving a venue to performers in Branson who did not have a theatre in which to perform. The doors had not yet opened. In fact, Voices of Glory jumped in helping with renovation of the space, painting walls, helping lay the floor, and lending a hand wherever needed.

On July 1, 2010, Voices of Glory opened as the Night Light's first and featured act. It was a small modest stage, a small modest beginning for the young siblings with high hopes for a music career. It can be said that over the next two years that Voices of Glory paid their dues. It was a time of honing their performance skills, refining their act and developing as entertainers. They continued to travel to local churches, branching out to neighboring states and returning to New York for special performances.

Voices of Glory had caught the interest and earned the admiration of many in the music industry. The list of their accomplishments is remarkable for the short time they have been performing. They were guests on Bobby Jones Gospel, with television appearances also on ABC, NBC, FOX, TCT AND TBN. Voices of Glory were featured guests on television with Dino Kartsonakis, Victim to Victory with Brian Arnold, and a Fox Network Family News Special on Mother's Day.

In 2010, they performed a featured act at the ICM (Inspirational County Music) Awards. They won the 2011 SGM Scoops Diamond Award for "Favorite Up Rising Southern Gospel Group". and were nominated for the 2011 ICM Youth in Music Award. They were thrilled to be award presenters at the Schermerhorn Symphony Center for the ICM Awards in 2011. They were honored that several of their songs from their first CD made it to the Dove Award ballot in 2012.

In the fall 2011, they were excited to be chosen as one of a group of performers invited to participate in the annual Christmas festival in Germany, Weihnacht Zauber, being invited again for Christmas, 2012. While in Germany, they continued their ministry outreach by singing at a children's hospital and socials for local nursing homes.

They appeared as special guests performers at TBN'S Holyland in Orlando, Florida, and made a personal appearance on TBN's Praise the Lord, hosted by Carman. These are just a few of the many honors and performances of Voices of Glory since that fateful night on America's Got Talent. While all of this was going on, they were loyal to their commitment at the Night Light whenever they were in town.

One evening while attending an American Idol Finalist Show at the Andy Williams Theatre in Branson, they saw Pete Peterkin, a contestant with them on America's Got Talent in 2009. He was acting as host for the American Idol Finalist Show.

After the performances and autograph signing by the American Idol finalists, Pete Peterkin introduced Voices of Glory to the contestants as well as others still in the lobby area. He said, "You should hear these kids sing." Readily they sang "Put Your Records On" and "Mercy".

One of the participants in the American Idol Finalist Show told the kids, "You've got to meet, Janna. She's a vocal arranger and coach." They were introduced to many people that night making several new connections.

That was the beginning of great relationships between Voices of Glory and some members of Andy Williams' staff.

One day, shortly after that Gerard received a call asking if it would be all right to give his number to Andy Williams' management.

What a question! They were walking on clouds. Soon they were contacted and told that Andy Williams would love for the kids to be part of his annual Christmas show if they would be interested. Gerard chuckles as he relates the story that he jokingly responded, "Let me think about it a couple of seconds... okay... yes!" They set a time to meet. The staff asked them to put together a packet including their bio, their CD's, and pictures. They prepared a professional packet and included a personal greeting card to Mr. Andy Williams thanking him for the opportunity and wishing him good health.

At a later meeting, they were told that one of the last professional decisions made by Andy, just four days before he died, was hand picking the entertainers for the Andy Williams 2012 Christmas Show. Voices of Glory was among that small handful of entertainers.

"We are honored," was the response of all of Voices of Glory family members.

With much hard work ahead of them, Michael, Avery and Nadia practiced daily. It meant long hours and lots of instruction but they were living their dream. Finally, their big day came, November 1, 2012, opening night at the Andy Williams Moon River Theatre. It was exciting. It was fun. It was exhausting.

Mike and Felicia were at every rehearsal, every show. The goodness of God was indescribable. They had come so far. From the days of singing in their little church, to the months spent at the hospital, the nursing home, and running back and forth to rehab, to being brought to Branson seemingly by mistake to now seeing their children perform on stage with true professionals to now being given such an incredible opportunity was astounding. They could be nothing but thankful to an amazing God who had given them an amazing life. They were performing before crowds of one to two thousand people a night. They were loved. They were applauded; often receiving standing ovations. Often times, they would board the tour buses before the show to welcome their guests. After the show, they would exit the stage with the other performers and greet their audience, giving hugs and autographs as requested. They were truly a hit!

One evening, after a show, Mike was approached by a lady who introduced herself as Lena Hughes, the mother of the Hughes Brothers, who have a highly successful show on the Branson strip, "It.". She asked him if they had a place to perform after the Christmas show was over and told him they would be interested in talking to them about a show at their theatre.

Voices of Glory still had an afternoon show at the Night Light and Mike invited Mrs. Hughes to attend, saying they could speak after the performance. Within the next few days, Mrs. Hughes and Jason Hughes, the director of their family show, watched Voices of Glory sing an array of songs, starting the wheels turning towards a big jump in their career.

Voices of Glory were still in negotiations with the Hughes Brothers when it was time to leave for Germany for the 2012 Weihnacht Zauber. That was okay with Mike, Felicia, Gerard and the kids as they had much to pray about and needed the time to be sure they made the right decisions. Should they tie themselves down with scheduled performances? Would it possibly cause them to miss greater opportunities?

However, by the time they returned from Germany, they were at peace that they were on the right track. They would continue to minister through their show at the Hughes Brothers Theatre which would include several gospel songs, and their testimony which would keep them true to their calling. Because they had a set schedule, they could continue to travel regionally, ministering at churches and civic events.

The year was off to an exciting start. Their name again gained national attention when the Billy Graham Evangelistic Association honored them by requesting an interview for a feature article.

Once the contract was signed, Michael, Avery, and Nadia jumped in with both feet to create a show worthy of their talent and keeping with the excellence customary to the Hughes Brothers Theatre.

It was up to Voices of Glory to put together their band. The kids stepped up to the challenge, themselves conducting interviews with local musicians, with Mom, Dad and Uncle Gerard listening and evaluating from the sidelines. They chose a band director and with his help selected the other members of their four-man band. They hired a vocal arranger, a scriptwriter and a choreographer, as they wanted dance to be part of their high-energy show. The Hughes family provided the rest of the production team.

What a great team, it was. They practiced twelve to fifteen hours a day. They had to learn new songs, taking vocal tips from their instructor, incorporating them into the arrangements, co-ordinating it all with the band. They had fun learning the dance steps, making sure their timing was perfect. Sound, lighting, video, costume, music, voice; it had to all come together. Opening night was fast approaching.

March 18, 2013—their landmark date. Three years after they first came to Branson, they had their own show. They had stuck it out in Branson, while all of the others had thrown their hands up and left town. They stood in faith, trusting there was a reason they had come half way across the country.

They would be performing at what used to be the Roy Clark Celebrity Theatre...now the Hughes Brothers Celebrity Theatre. Some of the biggest names in country music had stood on the stage they could now claim as theirs. Celebrities Lee Greenwood, Loretta Lynn, Tony Orlando, Tammy Wynette, The Gatlin Brothers, Ricky Skaggs, Boxcar Willie, Pat Boone, Mel Tillis, Conway Twitty, Glen Campbell, Marie Osmond and many more voices rang out in song at the same theatre as theirs now did. It was an honor to be listed among these great talents.

In keeping with their famous stage predecessors, these three young people, whose career began in New York City, brought an amazing show to the country town of Branson. In what other show will you find such a variety of music—jazz, rhythm and blues, gospel, soul, pop and patriotic—the songs delivered as though each genre was their specialty. The raw talent, the honed skill, the uncompromised commitment to excellence, the enthusiasm of these youthful performers and the grace of God have worked together to create a fun, fast-paced, don't-want-it-to-end show. The Voices of Glory were nominated for Best Show in Branson and Best New Show in Branson for 2013. Nadia was awarded Young Female Entertainer of the year for 2013 (ages 11-17) awarded by Branson Show Awards.

The Hughes Brothers had asked them to choose a name for their show. The kids tossed around many ideas, running them past their parents, their manager Uncle Gerard and the Hughes Brothers. Finally, their dad suggested "Ayo". It was an apt choice from a song co-written by the trio and being used in their show. It would be a great representation of the lively performance by these three young artists as the word "Ayo" means *"joy"* in the Nigerian dialect of Yoruba.

From the "Ayo" song Voices of Glory humbly express…"if we hold onto hope…rise up and leave our troubles behind… when we set our hearts on what is true…it's a brand new day… let's give it a try…Let's go…Ayo…Ayo…Ayo."

Ayo speaks to the heart of this family. It speaks to the heart of these courageous kids who stood in faith when one disappointment after the other confronted their young lives, to the courage of Mike who stood strong when all seemed lost, to the courage of Felicia who fought her way back to life, and to the dedication of their Uncle Gerard.

So just as the words of the song say—just as the show "Ayo" testifies ... They truly did hold on to hope... they all rose up and left their troubles behind!

"May the God of **hope** fill you with all **joy** and **peace,** as you **trust** in Him, so that you may overflow by the power of the Holy Spirit." (Romans 15:13, NIV)

After Thoughts

※

VOICES OF GLORY HOPE **their story of triumph has blessed you and encouraged you to see God as your personal, wonderful heavenly Father whose heart is toward His children. He is a Father that is always present, ready and willing to help in any situation. He is loving and powerful, merciful and forgiving. Receive Jesus as your Savior and begin living the life God has always intended for you. Allow Him to touch your life as He has the Cole family as you trust in Him.**

God Bless You.

If you desire to have a relationship with Jesus, pray this prayer with confidence that He hears you, and that He is pleased with you for trusting in Him and making Jesus Lord of your life.

Prayer of Salvation

Dear God in Heaven, I believe with all of my heart that Jesus died on the cross for me. I repent now for my sins and ask for your forgiveness. I believe Jesus was raised from the dead and sits at the right hand of the Father. I ask You, Jesus, to come into my heart and be the Lord of my life. I believe I receive my salvation. I believe I am clean from sin, washed in the precious blood of Jesus and in God's Word. Please fill me with Your Holy Spirit, in Jesus' name. Amen."

If you prayed with no doubt in your heart, then you will spend eternity with Father God. (Luke 5:10, NCV) tells us, "In the same way, there is joy in the presence of the angels of God when one sinner changes his heart and life." The angels in heaven are celebrating your decision—your salvation.

Now choose to walk in the authority that God gave mankind at creation. Find a Bible teaching church, be baptized and start living a fulfilling God-led life.

About Felicia

THE COLE FAMILY IS happy to report that everyday Felicia's health continues to improve. She takes no medication. She is now walking with assistance. Her hands no longer shake. She is able to bathe, dress and feed herself. Even though she still uses a wheelchair to move around, she helps with household chores and meal preparation. If she has your telephone number, you have probably received a text from her, as her fingers are nimble, able to manipulate her keypad as though she was never injured. Her wit and humor will keep you on your toes. She walks on the treadmill and goes miles on the exercise bike at the gym. You can't keep a good woman down is her theme. She attends every performance with Voices of Glory, worshipping and praising God for her life and celebrating the remarkable success of her children.

Felicia is the same woman of faith she was before the accident. Her faith is what has brought her through and it is what will carry her on to her first independent steps. She is a woman who draws her strength from the Lord Jesus. She is the same ambitious, resolute, go-getter she always was. She has astounded the medical community with her recovery.

If you ask how she did it, she will raise one hand, her forefinger pointing up and sweetly reply, "To God be the Glory."

Butterfly

FOLLOWING IS A POEM written by James Cole about Warrie Cole—brother and sister of Mike Cole, Sr. at the time of Warrie's accidental death. James has not shared this poem with many, even some family members have not read it. However, James wanted their sister honored by including this poem in their family chronicle.

Butterfly
(An Ode To My Sister)

Struggling to break free,
Plagued by much doubt,
Against improbable odds,
We both inched our way out.

I a bit older
A marginal degree,

One pupa,
One larva,
Both fighting to be.
We were left by our mother
And father for chance,
Alone,
All alone ,
On a wooden tree branch.

So caring
So loving ,
This sister of mine,
A joyous distraction,
Had come just in time,
The very same instance
My wings became mine.
A nuisance at times
Crawling all over me,
But there was no doubt
Together was where
We most wanted to be

Though it wasn't apparent
Who kept us from harm,
Together we weathered
Or clinged through a storm

Then without warning
My yearn for the sky
My wings kept demanding
"You're destined to fly!"

I thought she'd be happy
She started to cry.

With suspecting,
Dejected,
Weary, watery, eyes,
"You picked a fine time.
To say your good byes"

No words could console her
My best, this reply,
"Don't worry!"
"I promise!"
''I won't soar too high."

With her most feared upon her
Declaring its day,
Nature came to carry
Her one thing away.

Scared of the changes
Beginning to show,
All unsuspecting
All knowing forgo.

She started to panic
Sink deep in her shell
"Help me!"
"Please help me!"
She started to yell.

Captured by darkness
No means to escape,
Cocooned,
Torn apart,
Being forcefully draped.
"Where's my dear brother?"
I heard her faint cry,
"I need my big brother,"
Now echoed the sky

I did not,
I could not,
Promptly reply,
It wasn't so easy
Maneuvering to fly;
Avoiding the fowls,
Swooping to rip me
Clean out of the sky.

Though I tried
And I tried
To respond to her cry,
Directionless
Fluttered
Unskilled how to fly.

Caught in a whirlwind
Each landing a chance
The more that I struggled
I couldn't get home
To that wooden tree branch.

In spite of my efforts
Now both on our own
She went through her changes,
Metamorphosed alone.

Though battered, unbeaten
From her inner most struggles,
She came out of her shell
Mushrooming her troubles:
Broke from the bondage
Life molded and bubbled,
Flaking off vestiges
Spiraling, Spiraling
Piling on rubble.

As she stretched out her wings
Admiring her dye,
While approaching my landing
She started to fly.

So beautiful
Her beauty
Despite the onslaught
In spite of her struggles
Pure beauty was wrought.

Celebrating flight day,
Admiring each other
When the afternoon fell
"Farewell", waved the other.

"I'll love always
My sister'"
"I'll love always my brother",
Were the very last words
We said to each other.

Though now in HIS safety
I've yet to recover,
Except when reminded
"I'll love always my brother."

Written by: James Cole

From The Author

I HOPE YOU ENJOYED reading the true story of this typical American family. Their story is but one of millions. Everyone born on this earth has a story to tell. Everyone's life has disappointments and sadness and everyone's life has highlights.

Share your thoughts with us. If this book has touched you, if you have learned from it, or if you just enjoyed it as a good read, we would appreciate your feedback and comments.

Go to www.higherthanme.com to see
book reviews and reader comments.

My author website is www.readtheirstory.com

My author email is Claudia@readtheirstory.com

I would love to get your feedback on <u>Higher Than Me</u> plus you can see the other available books, <u>I Thought You Had a Bigger Dream</u>, <u>Melton Snow A Happy Heart Christmas,</u> and soon coming <u>She's a Lady</u>.

Follow Voices of Glory on Facebook.

To purchase Voices of Glory products go to
Voices of Glory website: www.thevoicesofglory.com

Contact Information for Voices of Glory management:

Attn: The Voices of Glory
3000 Green Mountain Drive
Suite 107-352
Branson, Missouri 65616

Photo Album

Mike Cole with teacher and other students from Susquehanna Valley Home 1971

Michael Cole

Mike Cole Senior High School picture 1976

340

Cybald Luke Cole born in Sierra Leone Africa circa 1926 (Father of Michael Cole Sr.)

Mike Cole playing guitar at Saturday night prison ministry.

Felicia Cole at annual dance performance – age 13

Felicia Cole after college 1989

Felicia Cole June 2005

Mike and Felicia Cole's Wedding Day April 6, 1991

Mikey Cole and mom Felicia 1994

Mikey Cole and dad Mike 1994

Nadia, Felicia, Sadie Stanley (Felicia's mother)

Nadia getting kisses from Daddy 1999

*Avery and dad
Mike 2001*

*Nadia playing
dress up with
mom Felicia*

Michael Cole II, Nadia Cole, Avery Cole 2002

Michael Cole II 2003

Avery Cole school
picture-age 13

Nadia school
picture 1st grade

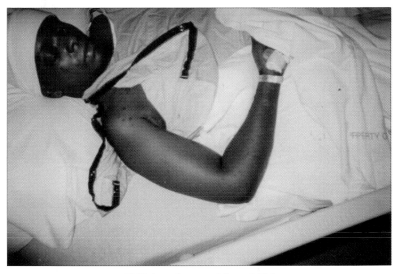

Felicia after accident 2005

Felicia (Fortunate) Joyful

The thief does not come except to steal, and to kill, and to destroy. I have come that they may have life and that they may have it more abundantly

John 10:10

" NOTE – Here we see the desired will of the Lord for every believer, that we experience abundant life. According to this verse He came for this very purpose. We also see clearly that it is not God who afflicts us. The word here for life is the Greek word "zoe." One highly respected commentator describes the true meaning of the word in this verse as: "life being the highest and best of which Christ is." In light of that meaning, you can easily see the wonderful gift of life the Lord wants for each of us. Sickness and disease are truly not in His plan for us, simply because He has none to give.

Healing Verses-"Joy" posted by Felicia's bedside

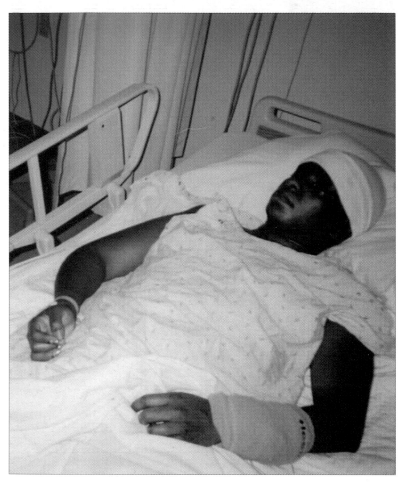

Felicia still comatose 2005

Mike and Felicia Cole 2009

*Michael II, Nadia and Avery on America's Got Talent
after singing God Bless America-2009*

*Performing at Icon Theatre in Branson—
Celebration of first VOG CD release*

Michael Cole II

*Avery
Cole*

Nadia Cole

VOG performance of "The Greatest Love at Hughes Brothers Theatre, Branson

Voices of Glory performing one of their favorites "Summertime"

Voices of Glory performing " Rhythms Gonna Get You"
at their AYO show in Branson

Voices of Glory is honored to take the stage at the Hughes Bros. Theatre where many famous stars have performed.

The Cole family July 2013